P9-CCK-325

SECRETS OF THE INNER MIND

JOURNEY THROUGH THE MIND AND BODY

Other Publications:
WEIGHT WATCHERS® SMART CHOICE RECIPE COLLECTION
TRUE CRIME
THE AMERICAN INDIANS
THE ART OF WOODWORKING
LOST CIVILIZATIONS
ECHOES OF GLORY
THE NEW FACE OF WAR
HOW THINGS WORK
WINGS OF WAR
CREATIVE EVERYDAY COOKING
COLLECTOR'S LIBRARY OF THE UNKNOWN
CLASSICS OF WORLD WAR II
TIME-LIFE LIBRARY OF CURIOUS AND UNUSUAL FACTS
AMERICAN COUNTRY
VOYAGE THROUGH THE UNIVERSE
THE THIRD REICH
THE TIME-LIFE GARDENER'S GUIDE
MYSTERIES OF THE UNKNOWN
TIME FRAME
FIX IT YOURSELF
FITNESS, HEALTH & NUTRITION
SUCCESSFUL PARENTING
HEALTHY HOME COOKING
UNDERSTANDING COMPUTERS
LIBRARY OF NATIONS
THE ENCHANTED WORLD
THE KODAK LIBRARY OF CREATIVE PHOTOGRAPHY
GREAT MEALS IN MINUTES
THE CIVIL WAR
PLANET EARTH
COLLECTOR'S LIBRARY OF THE CIVIL WAR
THE EPIC OF FLIGHT
THE GOOD COOK
WORLD WAR II
HOME REPAIR AND IMPROVEMENT
THE OLD WEST

For information on and a full description of any of the Time-Life Books series listed above, please call 1-800-621-7026 or write:
Reader Information
Time-Life Customer Service
P.O. Box C-32068
Richmond, Virginia 23261-2068

SECRETS OF THE INNER MIND

JOURNEY THROUGH THE MIND AND BODY

BY THE EDITORS OF TIME-LIFE BOOKS
ALEXANDRIA, VIRGINIA

CONSULTANTS:

GHAAZI ASAAD is a clinical associate professor at New York Medical College. He is a diplomate of the American Board of Psychiatry and Neurology. Asaad has written extensively on the subject of hallucinations.

J. D. COWAN is a professor of applied mathematics and theoretical biology at the University of Chicago, where he is also affiliated with the Brain Research Institute.

BRENDA DUNNE manages the Princeton Engineering Anomalies Research Laboratory at Princeton University in New Jersey.

KLAUS D. HOPPE is a clinical professor of psychiatry at the University of California at Los Angeles School of Medicine and director of research and continuing medical education at the Hacker Clinic in Los Angeles.

JOHN R. MOFFETT teaches at Georgetown University, where he does research on neurotransmitters in the visual system.

RUDOLPH T. PIVIK is a professor at the University of Ottawa School of Medicine, where he teaches in the departments of psychiatry, psychology, and physiology. He has published extensively in the field of sleep research.

KARL PRIBRAM is director of the Center for Brain Research and Informational Sciences at Radford University in Virginia.

ROBERT L. VAN DE CASTLE is a professor emeritus of behavioral medicine and psychiatry at the University of Virginia Medical School, where he was also director of the Sleep and Dream Laboratory for many years. He has authored numerous books and articles about sleep and dreams.

JONATHAN WINSON is a professor emeritus of neuroscience at Rockefeller University in New York. His work has been in the field of memory, especially memory processing during waking and sleeping states.

JOURNEY THROUGH THE MIND AND BODY

Library of Congress Cataloging-in-Publication Data

Secrets of the inner mind / by the editors of Time-Life Books.
p. cm. — (Journey through the mind and body)
Includes bibliographical references and index.
ISBN 0-7835-1036-5 (trade)
ISBN 0-7835-1037-3 (library)
1. Dreams. 2. Creative ability. 3. Extrasensory perception. 4. Mind and body. I. Time-Life Books. II. Series.
BF1091.S36 1993
154—dc20 93-31415

First printing. Printed in U.S.A.
Published simultaneously in Canada.
School and library distribution by Time-Life Education, P.O. Box 85026, Richmond, Virginia 23285-5026

This volume is one of a series that explores the fascinating inner universe of the human mind and body.

CONTENTS

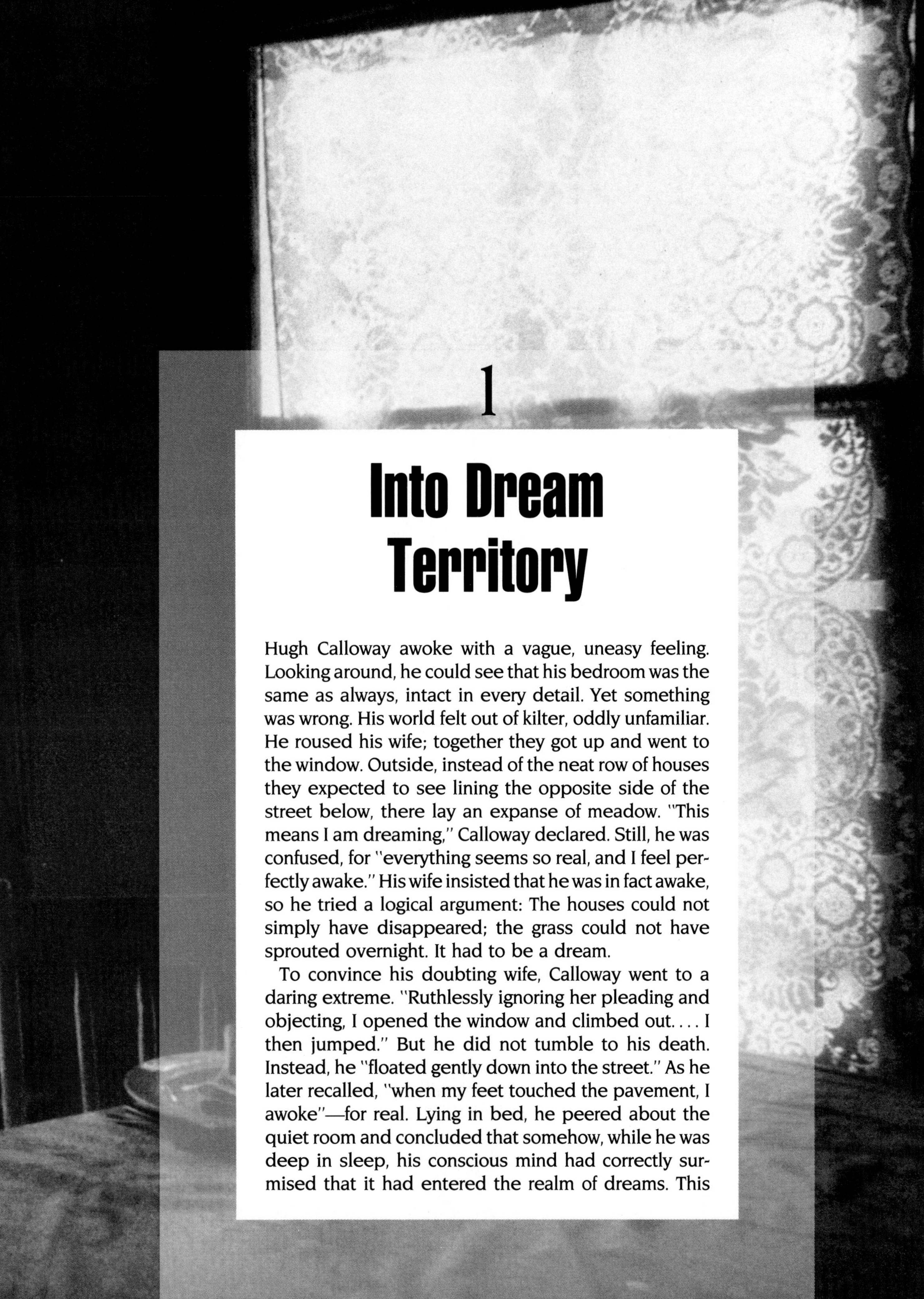

1

Into Dream Territory

Hugh Calloway awoke with a vague, uneasy feeling. Looking around, he could see that his bedroom was the same as always, intact in every detail. Yet something was wrong. His world felt out of kilter, oddly unfamiliar. He roused his wife; together they got up and went to the window. Outside, instead of the neat row of houses they expected to see lining the opposite side of the street below, there lay an expanse of meadow. "This means I am dreaming," Calloway declared. Still, he was confused, for "everything seems so real, and I feel perfectly awake." His wife insisted that he was in fact awake, so he tried a logical argument: The houses could not simply have disappeared; the grass could not have sprouted overnight. It had to be a dream.

To convince his doubting wife, Calloway went to a daring extreme. "Ruthlessly ignoring her pleading and objecting, I opened the window and climbed out. . . . I then jumped." But he did not tumble to his death. Instead, he "floated gently down into the street." As he later recalled, "when my feet touched the pavement, I awoke"—for real. Lying in bed, he peered about the quiet room and concluded that somehow, while he was deep in sleep, his conscious mind had correctly surmised that it had entered the realm of dreams. This account appears in a journal that Calloway published under his pseudonym, Oliver Fox. An English amateur psychologist around the turn of the 20th century, Calloway had a keen interest in dreams and the occult. Although he would not have used the term, scientists today would call his bizarre bedroom drama a lucid dream—one in which the dreamer is completely absorbed in a phantom reality yet at the same time aware that the events unfolding before him are the products of his own mind. Although most people rarely have such dreams, a few have learned to stimulate them, and some—impossible as it may sound—can deliberately steer or alter the action in the dream while remaining asleep.

Such control and the sense of power that comes with it can be exhilarating for the dreamer. For scientists, the implications go beyond mere entertainment. The idea that the "knowing" self can influence events in dreams challenges traditional assumptions about the gulf between the conscious and unconscious minds. Indeed, today's scientist-explorers have extended their search past the wakeful self deep into that complex and largely uncharted universe we might call the inner mind, peering beyond the layers of brain tissue and cells toward the mysterious region that houses the human essence.

Whatever its nature or source—be it impulses racing through the brain or a cognizant mist floating independent of time and space—the inner mind is both wellspring and engine of our loftiest endeavors. Some hope the quest will lead to the headwaters of creativity, the remote reaches that somehow give rise to symphonies, novels, paintings, even simple solutions to everyday problems. Other scientists, taking advantage of windows opened by drugs and meditation, are attempting to document the extraordinary abilities that arise from so-called altered states, realms lying just beyond the ordinary waking mind. Still others, approaching their subject from the dual perspectives of Western science and Eastern mysticism, hope to capture what may be the most elusive of all intellectual quarries: consciousness itself.

Of all these pursuits, perhaps none is more tantalizing than the ephemeral worlds conjured by the sleeping brain. Dreams, and the shadowy characters who inhabit them, often exhibit a spontaneity that can be quite different from—and often distinctly at odds with—perceptions of the waking mind. For one thing, when we are awake, the brain is continuously bombarded by information from outside the body that is relayed by the eyes, ears, nose, and skin—signals that convey the shape of the world as governed by the laws of physics. The conscious mind ignores this physical reality, and related norms of social behavior, only at great peril. When we fall asleep, however, the sensory input comes to a halt; as the real world fades away, the mind stirs to a world of internal sensations—to a form of awareness, unencumbered by reality, called the dream state.

Such liberation can bring unparalleled euphoria, but our experiences in the dream state can also be quite unsettling. Familiar faces and events can become blurred or recast, acquiring new significance or characteristics that range from the terrifying to the preposterous. Events in dreams may seem disjointed, and the ordinary logic of cause and effect may dissolve. Dream characters may flout the laws of physics or behave in ways that seem wildly out of character. Indeed, when the mind is freed of its normal shackles, dreamers can radically reshape themselves and everything around them.

Fantastical as the dreamscape may seem, however, it is not unfamiliar territory. The inner theater of dreams —where adults are thought to spend six to eight percent of their lives— has fascinated people of all cultures from the earliest times. About 5,000 years ago, in what is now Iraq, high priests of the Mesopotamian civilization of Sumer considered dreams to be direct instructions from heaven to the kings. The Egyptians, a thousand years later, regarded dreams as a source of supernatural wisdom and kept inventories, which have since been recovered by archaeologists, of the most important types of dreams and what they might predict. As told in the Old Testament's Book of Genesis, Joseph interpreted the Egyptian pharaoh's dreams as visions of a coming famine. Tibetan Buddhist lamas even today believe that dreams can reveal the shape of life to come after reincarnation.

For the most part, people seeking to understand the dream world no longer look to the supernatural for answers. Over the past century researchers have focused instead on two earthly sources of information: analysis of the human self, or sense of identity (psychology), and physical probing of the body and brain (physiology). A great deal of modern research falls in the second category and rests on data from experiments conducted on laboratory animals. But although these scientific explorations have shed valuable light on what physically happens to the brain when it enters the dream state, they have not solved the essential mystery of why we dream. In many ways, they have only deepened it.

The first comprehensive examination of the reason for dreams was put forth nearly 100 years ago by psychoanalyst Sigmund Freud in his revolutionary book *The Interpretation of Dreams*, published in 1900 and still considered the most influential treatise on the subject. Freud called dreams the "royal road" to the unconscious, which he regarded as a primitive region of the mind, dominated by inarticulate emotions. By tracking dreams back to their origins, he said, one could uncover clues about a person's deepest memories and feelings.

Freud's view of dreams reflected his medical training and his experience as a clinician. He had studied neurology at the University of Vienna, and then, having found that a researcher's salary could not support his growing family, he launched a medical practice. Many of his patients suffered nervous disorders that took the form of hysteria, depression, and various forms of anxiety. Steeped in the neurology of his day, Freud tried to explain their behavior as a type of electrical overload in the nervous system. Although modern scientists know that the nervous system controls muscles of the body with electrochemical signals that both inhibit and activate movement, Freud assumed, as did others, that the brain sent only activating impulses.

Basing his dream theory on this activation-only model, Freud reasoned that urges arising from primitive desires in the brain must somehow find release. If not acted upon, or "resolved," as he put it, these urges would have to find another route of escape. The impulses that most concerned him were the drives that human beings share with other animals—appetites for sex, food, and dominance. Freud believed that a higher part of the mind, which he called the ego, acts as a censor, keeping these urges not only under control but often under wraps. Though stifled, they continue to knock at the mind's door, especially during sleep.

According to Freudian theory, the brain has developed a clever ruse to prevent this internal clatter from disrupting the body's rest. It dresses the sexual and violent urges in acceptable attire, sneaks them past the censor, and permits them to appear as images that parade through the mind in the form of dreams. But because

Making Use of Lucid Dreaming

"If you are usually a timid and shy person, in lucid dreams you can practice being open and assertive," says Stephen LaBerge, leading exponent of the strange phenomenon in which the conscious mind is said to observe and influence the dreaming mind. "If you like the results, you will find it easier to do the same while awake." Building self-confidence is just one of the powers claimed for lucid dreams. Examples of others include a 12-year-old who in one night of lucid dreaming developed a tennis serve good enough to win the big tournament, a chemistry student who dreams solutions to molecular equations, and a surgeon who rehearses in dreams every cut and suture to be made the next day.

LaBerge says that lucid dreams can be purposefully induced by either of two broad approaches. The most frequently successful strategy is for a sleeper to wait until a dream is under way and then make it lucid. The result is called a dream-initiated lucid dream, or DILD. At home, lucid dreamers usually achieve such dreams by autosuggestion, telling themselves before sleeping that they will wake up inside a dream and control it. In the sleep lab, where instruments alert researchers to the onset of the rapid eye movements (REM) that usually indicate dreaming, subjects sometimes are notified in their sleep by signals from an audiotape, a vibrating bed, or a trademarked LaBerge invention, the DreamLight—sci-fi-like

goggles that flash red lights over the sleeper's eyelids.

An alternative approach to a dream-initiated lucid dream is a wake-initiated lucid dream, or WILD. WILDs begin with a very brief awakening—perhaps lasting only a few seconds—from REM sleep, something that can occur spontaneously several times in a night. When this happens, the dreamer must attempt to keep the conscious mind active despite a strong inclination to fall right back to sleep. In the most common technique, the subject concentrates on the hypnagogic mental images that tend to precede sleep. As sleep takes hold, these flashes of light and parades of geometric shapes gradually become full-blown dreams, but the dreamer maintains a lucid overview. Lucidity can also be maintained by performing other mental tasks, such as counting.

Practiced lucid dreamers claim to possess several tricks for controlling their dreams and keeping them going. If a lucid dream starts to fade or disintegrate, for instance, a dreamer may restore its intensity by rapidly spinning in place in the dream. Some say they use spinning to change the surroundings or subject matter of a dream, while others prefer consciously "changing the TV channel" for that purpose. Flying like the fictional character Superman is another common way of changing settings, although many lucid dreamers apparently fly just for the sheer pleasure of the experience.

dreams represent, in effect, forbidden material, the dreamer has difficulty recalling them in the morning.

The renegade images captured in dreams are valuable for psychoanalysis, Freud believed, because they embody the dreamer's unspoken fears and desires. To be understood properly, however, they must be exposed for what they really are. Much of Freud's work was thus aimed at helping patients strip disguises from their dreams. If polite society found these revelations shocking, he said, it was because dreams, at their core, are primitive urges that were suppressed in childhood.

Freud's technique was to ask patients to "free-associate," or jump rapidly during a discussion from one image or thought to another. He often began by asking his client to recall a dream, with the goal being to follow the links of association back to a deeply anchored emotional problem. The process was long and often painful, but when the patient began to talk about sexual conflicts or childhood memories, Freud believed he had penetrated the person's emotional center. At that point, he would challenge the patient to resolve the uprooted trouble and lay it to rest.

With its internal logic and powerful appeal, Freud's thesis dominated dream analysis for half a century—but divisions appeared in the ranks early. By 1913 even Freud's most famous student, Carl Jung, who collaborated with Freud for several years, differed with some of the master's pronouncements. Ultimately, Jung broke with his mentor largely over their differing views regarding the nature of dreams.

The younger psychiatrist did not accept Freud's heavy emphasis on sex and aggression, arguing that many dreams are only what they appear to be—echoes of mundane human life. Jung did agree, however, that dreams are messages from the unconscious, mental stage plays in which each character represents a facet of the dreamer's own personality. To that end, Jung saw dreams not as twisted images of undesirable thoughts, but often as positive expressions of wisdom, drawing not only on the individual's personal unconscious, but also on a set of universal patterns and experiences he called the collective unconscious.

Psychologists who followed in the footsteps of Freud and Jung continued to rely on the two pioneers' fundamental explanation of dreams as signals from the unconscious mind. In the 1920s, for example, Austrian psychoanalyst Alfred Adler put forth his view that dreams represent a person's will, both conscious and unconscious, and that they help to illuminate the person's goals for the future. A few decades later, Berlin-born Frederick (Fritz) Perls brought his Gestalt therapy to the Esalen Institute in Big Sur, California; during the late 1960s and early 1970s, Perls taught thousands of people to resolve their inner conflicts by reenacting their dreams. Yet even as these practitioners operated within Freud's basic psychoanalytic approach to dreams and their meaning, a remarkable discovery in dream studies sprang from an entirely different source—the physical side of medicine.

Like a fresh breeze, a new way of thinking about dreams swept through the scientific world in the early 1950s as scientists in their laboratories began to focus on sleep's long-ignored physiological aspects. The work reestablished links with observers dating back to the Roman poet Lucretius of the first century BC, who watched a hunting dog twitch as it lay napping by the fire and concluded that the animal was chasing phantom prey in its mind. But while Lucretius had only his natural powers of observation, modern researchers could use sophisticated electrical sensors to record sleep behavior in great detail.

At the University of Chicago in 1951, a young graduate student by the name of Eugene Aserinsky was conducting lab studies on wakefulness and sleep under the direction of physiology professor Nathaniel Kleitman. While studying sleeping infants, Aserinsky noticed that periodic body shifts were frequently accompanied by jerky motions of the eyes under closed lids. He decided to measure movements of the infants' eye muscles using a polygraph, generating a printout called an electrooculogram (EOG). To get a more complete picture of physiological changes that were taking place, he also attached electrodes to his subjects' scalps and hooked these sensors up to an electroencephalograph (EEG), which measures the tiny electric currents rippling across the brain.

Aserinsky noticed right away that when his young subjects took afternoon naps, the eye-muscle sensors showed periodic bursts of movement. Instead of shifting to lower and lower states of activity during sleep, as one might expect, the infants' eyes eventually began twitching rapidly from side to side. Intrigued, Aserinsky and Kleitman (working now as partners) conducted similar tests on adults and determined that people of all ages exhibit the same behavior. The major difference, it later became clear, is that children reach this agitated sleep state faster than adults and remain in it longer, a fact that may have helped bring it to Aserinsky's attention.

As is often the case with major discoveries, this one—after its announcement in the journal *Science* in 1953—suddenly seemed glaringly obvious. Many people had observed the restless eye movements of sleepers, but no one had recognized the regularity of the twitches or had tried to puzzle out their significance. Once the news was out, however, other researchers quickly confirmed the phenomenon, and it was formally dubbed rapid eye movement, or REM, sleep. The next step was to figure out what purpose REM served.

Wires from sensors taped to the forehead, near the eyes, and under the chin of this participant in a sleep experiment lead to a triple-purpose monitoring system outside the bedroom of a sleep lab. By recording brain waves, eye movements, and the degree of muscle relaxation, the equipment produces a continuous report of the subject's sleep cycle. Typically, one night's sleep generates a paper chart a thousand feet long.

From the beginning, Aserinsky and Kleitman guessed that the eye movements might be linked to dreaming, so they decided to put their hunch to the test in their sleep-research laboratory. Volunteers agreed to sleep in the lab and allow researchers to wake them randomly. Sure enough, as the scientists discovered, sleepers awakened during REM sleep were more likely to recall a dream—and to give a longer narrative of what they had experienced—than those awakened during non-REM sleep. With the corroborating work of another of Kleitman's students, William Dement, the connection between rapid eye movement and dreaming seemed clear. For several years after the REM discovery, Dement and his copioneers explored and described this remarkable pattern of behavior.

Soon one laboratory after another began to report similar results, using sensors to track eye movements and electroencephalographs to monitor brain activity during sleep. Studying the peaks and valleys inked on rolls of graph paper by the machines' mechanical pens, researchers determined that brain waves fall into several general groups. They also noticed that the brain descends through four stages of non-REM sleep, each characterized by a different wave or combination of waves (*pages* 20-21).

When a person falls asleep for the first time at night, his or her eyes remain fairly relaxed for about 45 minutes as the brain moves deeper and deeper, through all the stages of sleep. Then the process reverses itself, and the sleeping brain moves back up through the levels. But then, instead of ascending from stage 2 into stage 1, the brain shifts into a different phase: Pens recording eye movements jerk across the page—and the mysterious REM period begins.

As researchers had noticed, REM sleep usually comes after a sudden body shift in bed. The subject's eyes immediately start to dart back and forth, while the brain emits waves that resemble those in the alert, wakeful state. But the sleeper's muscles—monitored by yet another group of sensors—become still. Only the tips of the fingers and toes move. Snoring stops. Because of this contrast between the quiet muscles and the active brain, the REM state has been called paradoxical sleep. The limbs are motionless, as though they were tied down to prevent them from acting out the scenes flashing through the sleeping mind.

One of Dement's most important contributions was to establish just how long people linger in the REM state, thereby providing an estimate of the duration of dreams. Most adults, he determined, spend 20 to 25 percent of the night in REM sleep, a figure that drops to about 17 percent in the elderly. Children, on the other hand, sleep longer than adults and spend more of that time in REM. Premature babies spend about 80 percent of the night in REM sleep, infants about 50 percent.

No one had ever tried timing a dream before, but many people had long subscribed to the opinion of French psychologist Alfred Maury, who postulated in 1861 that dreams were infinitesimally brief. Maury based his view, in part, on personal experience. Maury once dreamed that he had been executed by guillotine, only to awake and find that a bedrail had fallen on his head. Maury later reasoned that the long and complex scenario leading up to his dream beheading must have occurred in the instant between the falling of the rail and his awakening.

Now researchers laid Maury's theory to rest, as it were, when they discovered how long the REM periods lasted. In one group of experiments, Dement and Kleitman, working as a team, awakened volunteers during a REM sequence and asked how much time they thought had passed while they were dreaming. The subjects' guesses were remarkably close to

Signatures of the Brain at Work and at Rest

The brain is alive with pulses of electricity zipping along nerve cells in a bustle of activity, creating brain waves that can be detected, as German scientist Hans Berger discovered in 1929, by sensors attached to the scalp. Sent by wires to a machine developed by Berger and called an electroencephalograph (EEG), the bursts of electricity are first amplified and filtered of extraneous signals, then used to pen a squiggly record of the brain's electrical murmurings.

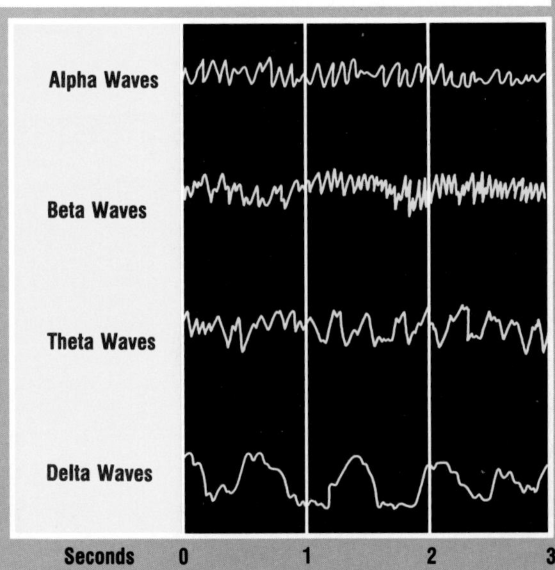

Brain waves come in four major varieties, differing from one another in frequency (how often bursts occur) and amplitude (how strong they are). Waves from the brain of a fully alert person are called beta waves. As shown below in the second trace from the top, beta waves vary considerably in frequency—between 13 and 30 cycles per second, or hertz—and in amplitude over the three seconds or so recorded in the chart. Alpha waves of about eight to 13 hertz appear in someone who is sitting or lying relaxed with eyes closed. During descent into sleep, brain waves shift from the alpha state into the lower frequencies of theta waves (four to eight hertz) and delta waves, below four hertz.

the actual time spent in REM sleep.

As intriguing as it was, none of this early research explained why our bodies go through this strange routine every night. The first clues began to emerge in the late 1950s, when Dement—now a psychiatrist at Mount Sinai Hospital in New York—conducted experiments in which he intentionally deprived volunteers of REM sleep for a week. He woke them each night whenever their eyes began moving rapidly. As the days passed, the subjects became harder and harder to rouse, apparently becoming ever more determined to enter REM sleep, and they showed signs of increasing apathy, uneasiness, anxiety—even panic. One of the volunteers reportedly began to have hallucinations.

When the experiment was finished and the volunteers were allowed to sleep normally, they lingered a much longer time in the REM stage, as if trying to catch up on dream time. After Dement identified the same pattern in cats subjected to REM-deprivation tests, he concluded that these strange eye oscillations must perform some important, perhaps even essential, biological function—though what that function might be was anybody's guess.

On the other side of the Atlantic, Michel Jouvet and his colleague François Michel, at the University of Lyon in France, learned of Dement's work in 1958. The French researchers, who had been studying the behavior of cats for an investigation into the nature of attentiveness, immediately recognized the importance of the REM sleep period. In experiments of their own on cats, the French scientists located the area that inhibits muscle activity during REM sleep: a segment of the brainstem at the base of the skull called the pons (Latin for "bridge").

By making small incisions and applying an electrical pulse just below the pons, Jouvet and Michel were able to induce muscle relaxation and REM-like eye movements in cats. Stimulation above the pons did not produce these effects, indicating that this structure and not the higher brain controls REM behavior. In one set of experiments, Jouvet produced quite convincing evidence that animals do in fact dream. Working again with cats, the scientist electrically destroyed the area within the pons that paralyzes body muscles during REM. The animals fell asleep normally, and when they entered REM sleep their eyes began to twitch, just as expected. But instead of lying still, the cats suddenly began to move. Some, though their eyes were tightly closed, lifted their heads as if to look around them. Others stood up and attacked invisible enemies or chased unseen prey.

In 1962 Jouvet published findings suggesting that the pons is the master control zone for REM sleep, but he left unresolved the larger question of why REM sleep and dreaming exist at all. Almost immediately, scientists began offering their own theories, many of which seemed to speak to Dement's conclusion that REM sleep serves a vital function. One group speculated that dreams make the mind alert and able to sense possible danger while the body is resting. According to this view, REM serves as a kind of sentinel, keeping the nervous system tuned up and ready to respond to external threats.

Other scientists thought that REM activity might be a vestigial behavior, perhaps inherited from an earlier stage of evolution, no longer of specific use for human beings. In the mid-1960s, a psychiatrist named Howard Roffwarg, at Columbia University in New York, suggested that nervous activity during REM sleep helps to stimulate the developing brain in very young children, thus promoting the growth of neural connections necessary for learning. In adults, according to Roffwarg, REM serves, like physical exercise, to maintain tone in the central nervous system.

The notion that REM could be a cru-

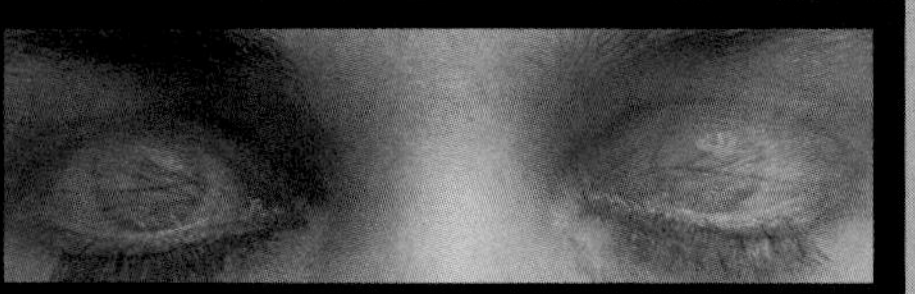
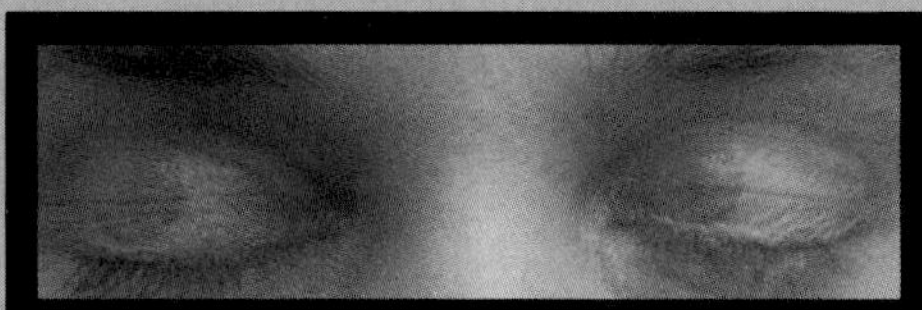
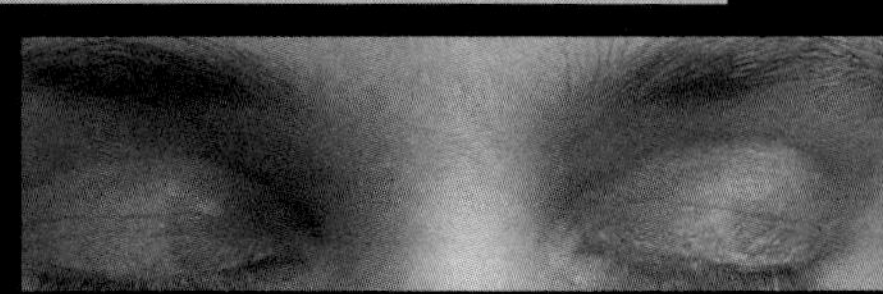

Seeking a Physical Explanation for Dreams

To understand dreams, researchers must study sleep, the time when dreams occur. Sleep scientists recognize two types of sleep, the more curious of which is called rapid eye movement, or REM, sleep. REM sleep, examined on the following pages, is unique. "I consider it a third state of earthly existence," said sleep investigator Frederick Snyder, "at least as different from sleeping and waking as each is from the other."

Our most powerful nighttime visions occur in REM sleep, explaining why dream researchers have focused most of their attention on it. Indeed, after discovering the phenomenon in 1951, scientists came to equate it with dreaming, because most people who were awakened during REM sleep reported a dream in progress. Since then, however, researchers have found that dreams also occur during the other kind of sleep—NREM, or non-rapid eye movement, sleep. Dreams launched during any of NREM sleep's four distinct stages tend to be shorter and more mundane than the often vivid and bizarre REM dreams, but not always. "There are many exceptions," notes Canadian sleep researcher Terry Pivik. "There are times when you can have full-blown dreams—using nearly any definition—in NREM sleep."

To explain these seeming anomalies, dream researchers have begun looking even more closely at REM sleep. Their hope is to identify some as yet unnoticed physiological "dream marker" that will also show up in NREM sleep—and unlock the mystery of dreaming.

A Sleeper's Roller-Coaster Night

Although sleep patterns vary from person to person, this graph charts a typical night for a young adult sleeping from 11:00 p.m. to 7:00 a.m. During the first hour, the subject experiences only NREM sleep *(yellow)*, descending rapidly through stages 1 and 2, slowing in stage 3, and lingering the longest in stage 4. Next the sleeper quickly climbs back to stage 2 and then enters the night's first REM period *(red)*, which lasts only a few minutes. Continuing the cycle, the subject reenters REM sleep about every 90 minutes. As the hours pass, slow-wave NREM stages 3 and 4 stop recurring and REM periods gradually increase in length. Altogether, the sleeper spends most of the night in stage 2 sleep.

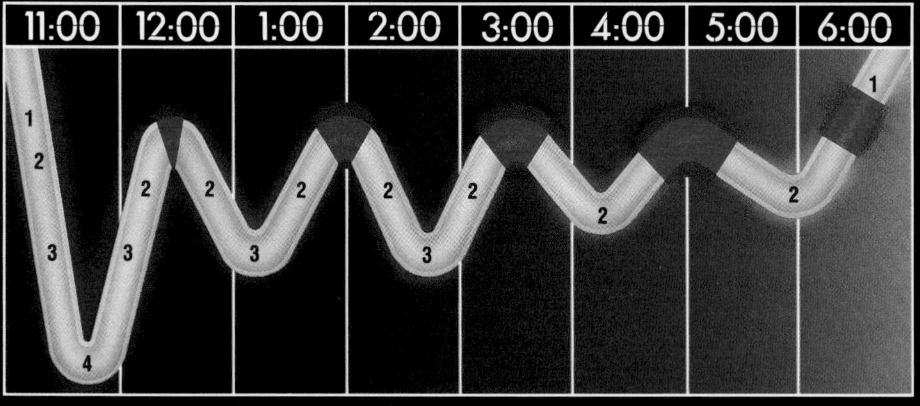

THE BRAIN DURING REM. The illustration at right highlights brain activity that takes place when most dreams occur. Green arrows rising from the midbrain (4)—which along with the medulla (2) and pons (3) regulates life functions such as breathing and heartbeat—represent signals to the cerebral cortex (13), which contains the brain's centers for thought and other high-level mental activity. Absent from the cortex during NREM sleep, midbrain pulses contribute to the brain-wave similarities between REM sleep and wakefulness. A single green arrow pointing at the eyes shows the route of signals from the pons that elicit coordinated eye movement in REM sleep. The white arrow symbolizes messages that the pons and medulla send down the spinal cord (1) to inhibit muscle activity, explaining the body's near inability to move during REM sleep.

GRAPHIC COMPARISONS. At right, electrical traces of brain waves, the movements of both eyes, and muscle tone show not only the similarities between REM sleep and wakefulness, but how greatly both states differ from the four stages of NREM sleep.

Brain waves: The short, closely spaced brain-wave squiggles of REM sleep resemble those of wakefulness. (The big spike in all the wakefulness graphs is a muscle twitch.) Between stages 1 and 4 in NREM sleep, peaks in the brain-wave trace become taller and occur less frequently.

Eye movement: Mirror-image peaks and valleys in the eye-movement graphs for both REM sleep and wakefulness indicate that the eyes move in unison. In NREM sleep these lines reflect brain activity rather than eye movement, which is rare after stage 1.

Muscle tone: The trace here differs noticeably between REM sleep—where it is hardly more than a line—and wakefulness. Lack of muscle tone explains why people in REM sleep are temporarily paralyzed—a quirk that does not occur in NREM sleep, when muscle tone is present.

	REM Sleep	Awake
Brain Activity		
Eye Movement		
Muscle Tone		

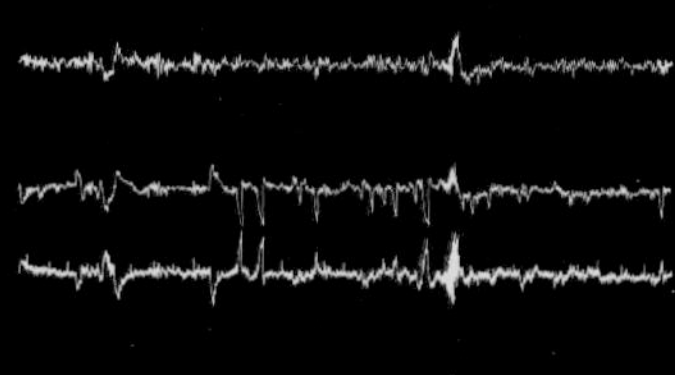

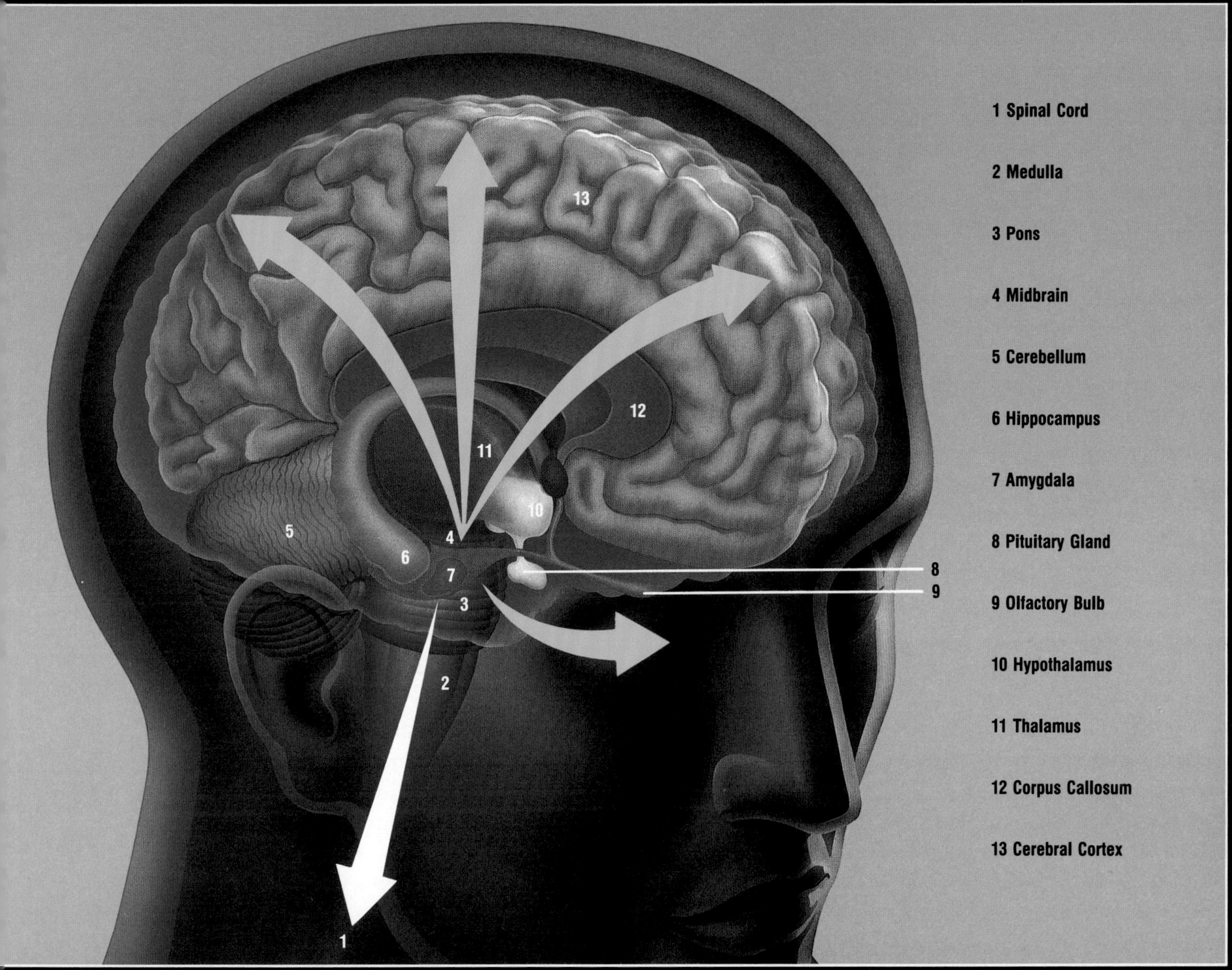

1 Spinal Cord
2 Medulla
3 Pons
4 Midbrain
5 Cerebellum
6 Hippocampus
7 Amygdala
8 Pituitary Gland
9 Olfactory Bulb
10 Hypothalamus
11 Thalamus
12 Corpus Callosum
13 Cerebral Cortex

Stage 1
Stage 2
Stage 3
Stage 4

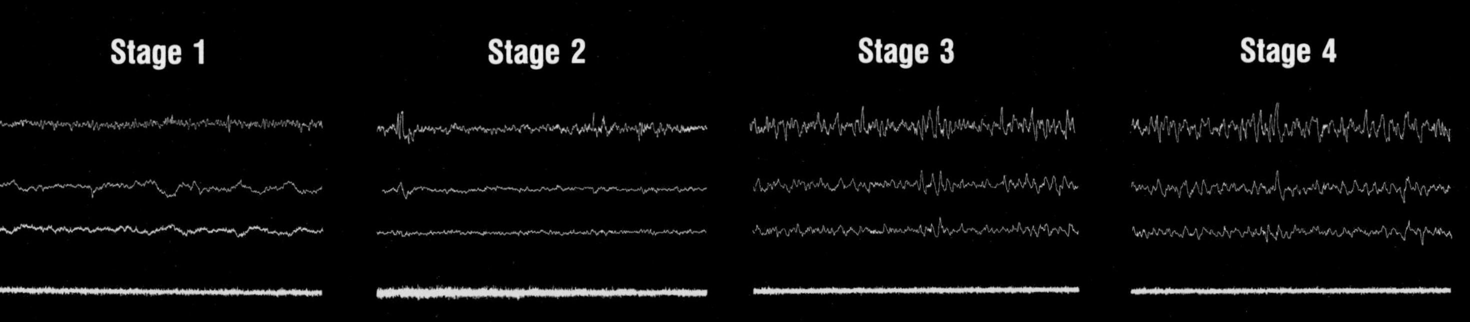

cial ingredient in the learning process gained momentum during the 1970s following the work of Boston psychiatrists Ramon Greenberg and Chester Pearlman. In the laboratory, Greenberg and Pearlman deprived rats and mice of REM sleep while training the animals to run through a variety of mazes. The researchers discovered that while REM loss caused test rodents to perform only slightly worse on simple routines that they had already mastered, it had a markedly adverse impact on the animals' ability to carry out more complex tasks or to learn new ones, of whatever degree of complexity.

Greenberg and Pearlman noted that the same pattern appeared to be true with people. Human volunteers who went without REM sleep could perform routine activities without much trouble but had much greater difficulty tackling complicated word-memorizing tasks. This finding led the psychiatrists to conclude that the mind is doing serious work when it dreams—specifically, it is incorporating newly learned information into a long-term memory bank. According to this theory, REM may thus be critical in stimulating the development of associative thought in infants and young children. The theory would also explain why humans, who must constantly adapt to meet new challenges, exhibit so much REM activity.

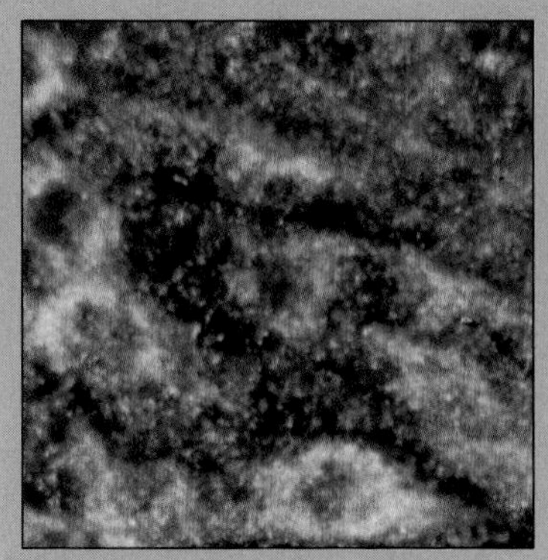

The Brain Chemistry of Sleep and Dreaming

The brain is never entirely idle. Even in sleep, the chemical transmission of electrical impulses among nerve cells continues, as is evident in the brainstem (*page* 21), where many of the body's automatic functions—heartbeat and breathing, for example—are regulated.

Substances called neurotransmitters play a crucial role in this process—some by carrying impulses across the narrow gap between one nerve cell and another, some by preventing their passage. Of the 50 or so neurotransmitters identified, three have been studied extensively for their significant roles in sleep and dreaming.

In the photograph above, brainstem nerve cells producing the neurotransmitter norepinephrine appear as fluorescent green spots. The release of this impulse-blocking neurotransmitter and another called serotonin wanes in most stages of sleep, as does the production of acetylcholine, which signals muscle activity. During REM sleep, however, production of norepinephrine and serotonin stops altogether, while the presence of acetylcholine increases—hence the telltale eye movements of REM sleep.

The idea that the mind is doing meaningful labor while asleep was not altogether original, of course; Freud himself had coined the term "dreamwork" to describe some aspects of the image-forming process that takes place in sleep. But now the idea that dreams had meaning or served a biological function suddenly came under attack.

Leading the assault were two psychiatrists working at the Harvard Medical School in Boston, J. Allan Hobson and Robert W. McCarley. In 1977 the duo published a study in the *American Journal of Psychiatry* supporting their claim that dreams are not disguised messages from deep in the unconscious but simply random—and perhaps meaningless—by-products of the nervous system.

Hobson and McCarley based their theory on experiments they had performed in their Boston laboratory. Using tiny electrodes to stimulate the brains of cats, they identified two specific clusters of cells in the pons that seemed to function essentially as "on" and "off" switches for REM sleep. Cells in one region of the brain produce the neurochemical acetylcholine, which triggers the rapid eye movements, while cells in the locus ceruleus supply norepinephrine, which brings REM to an end.

Hobson and McCarley showed that by injecting a drug similar to acetylcholine into the pons, they could cause rapid eye movements to begin, and by injecting a form of norepinephrine, they could end them. The researchers also showed that nerve signals originating in the pons radiate up into the cerebral cortex, where memories and input from the senses come together.

The clear implication, according to Hobson and McCarley at least, was that the pons is the true source of the dream state and the Freudian unconscious plays no role in dream production. After the pons shuts down body movement during REM sleep, it continues to generate nerve impulses, which in turn scatter away and excite other nerve networks within the brain. In Hobson and McCarley's view, the cortex processes these signals as though they were the sensory input that arrives during consciousness, then assembles them into semicoherent packages known as dreams. "In other words," wrote Hobson and McCarley, the more sophisticated thought-producing area of the brain "may be making the best of a bad job in producing even partially coherent dream imagery from the relatively noisy signals sent up to it from the brain stem."

This activation-synthesis process, as the Boston pair called it, left no room for the notion that dreams arise from deep emotional conflicts or that, as Freud would have it, the mind is busily censoring sexual urges and dressing them up in disguises. Hobson and McCarley also argued that people fail to remember dreams not because the mind actively represses them as forbidden material but because a special nighttime amnesia simply blocks the recording of dream events in memory. And, finally, the dreams we do recall seem so bizarre and disjointed because that is exactly what they are.

Publication of the Hobson-McCarley paper rocked the world of psychiatric medicine. According to the *American Journal of Psychiatry*, never before had a single article provoked such a heated response. Psychoanalysts were irate—not so much because Freud's ideas had been belittled, but because the Hobson-McCarley thesis threatened to rob dreams of all meaning. One sleep specialist later characterized the Hobson-McCarley thesis as an "overreaction" at the time to new scientific findings about the nervous system.

While granting that random signals may trigger REM activity, those who disagreed with Hobson and McCarley insisted that dreams themselves are not necessarily random. Regardless of

Tiny lights glow red inside experimental goggles—worn by their designer, dream researcher Stephen LaBerge—to signal the onset of REM sleep, when most dreams occur. Set off by rapid eye movements, the blinking lights alert the dreamer to an opportunity to influence the course of the dream, a technique LaBerge calls lucid dreaming.

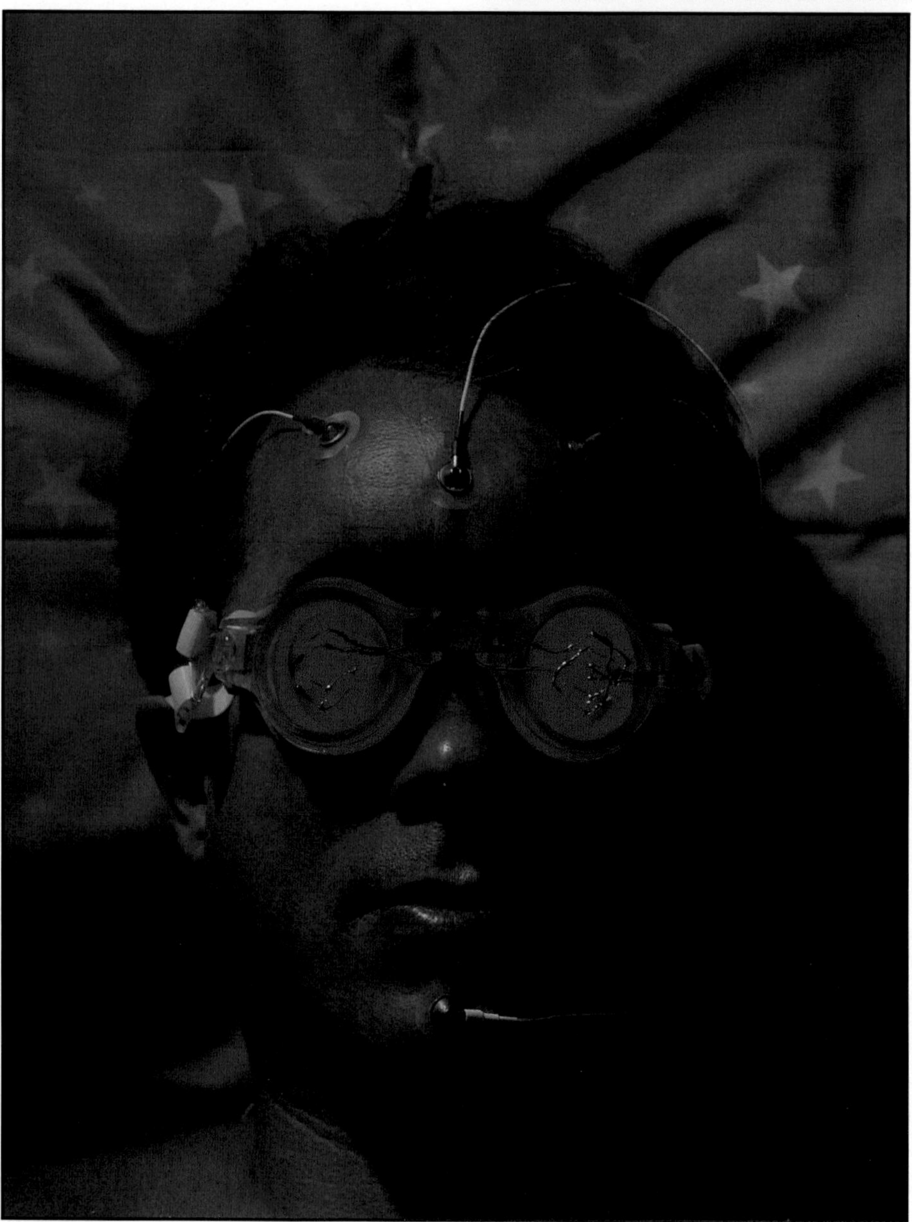

what their physical origins might be, the critics pointed out, dreams do reflect differences in personalities and individual lives. Some dreams, in fact, have remarkably long and cohesive plots—hardly what one would expect of static.

Faced with this cross fire, Hobson in the mid-1980s modified his interpretation of his earlier experiments on cats. It is possible, he conceded, that random nerve activity in the pons could stimulate coherent mental processes in the cortex. The mind "does its best to attribute meaning to the internally generated signals" that shoot up from the pons, Hobson wrote, and "it is this synthetic effort that gives our dreams their impressive thematic coherence." In effect, he said, the mind must do some elaborate storytelling to weave together the random nerve signals. And the stories that unfold "are likely to reveal specific cognitive styles, specific aspects of an individual's projective view of the world, and specific historical experiences."

Finally, in 1989, Hobson retracted much of his original theory, concluding that random nerve activity in the pons served merely as a switch from one dream to the next. And although he continued to reject the Freudian idea that dreams are disguised conflicts emerging from the unconscious, he acknowledged that the mind, even when asleep, is "fundamentally artistic," creating dreams that act as what Hobson called "a remarkable mirror of our inner selves." For all the effort to replace the unobservable unconscious with hard physiological data, modern science was thus obliged to leave room for the workings of an inner mind—some form of consciousness that seemed to be very busy at its dreamwork.

Even as Hobson was fencing with his colleagues over both the mechanism and the meaning of dreams, a West Coast researcher named Stephen LaBerge was gathering evidence of lucid dreaming, the peculiar kind of sleeping awareness experienced by Hugh Calloway earlier in the century. The phenomenon—in which the mind of the dreamer appears to be simultaneously in both the dream state and the waking state—had a long if somewhat spotty history. Aristotle described it in ancient times, as did Dutch psychiatrist F. W. van Eeden in his day (he actually coined the term in 1913) and British parapsychologist Celia Green in the 1960s. LaBerge would bring the topic to a wider audience with the publication of his book *Lucid Dreaming* in 1985.

LaBerge first came to the subject in the early 1970s when, after studying chemistry at Stanford, he grew interested in hallucinations and altered states of consciousness. One night, after a lecture by a Tibetan monk who spoke of a way to remain conscious while dreaming, LaBerge rediscovered a skill that he had developed as a child and since forgotten. As he described the experience later, he found himself climbing up through a high mountain snowdrift in Nepal. "I noticed I was wearing a T-shirt," he wrote. "I instantly recognized that I was dreaming." Then, just as he had during his childhood dreams, he took charge of events: He deliberately leaped off the mountain and flew through the air.

As a student and later a staff member in the Stanford sleep laboratory, LaBerge became increasingly fascinated with lucid dreaming and began searching for a way to verify the phenomenon. Knowing that most muscles in the body—except those of the eyes—are immobilized during REM sleep, he hit on the idea of using rapid eye movements themselves to send a message from within a dream to the outside world.

In January 1978, LaBerge bedded down at the Stanford sleep lab with electrodes taped to his head and around his eyes. His nights of practice at home paid off: Asleep in the lab, LaBerge was able to recognize when he was having a dream and, without waking, to move his eyes rapidly in two complete left-to-right sweeps, thus signaling the onset of lucidity. When LaBerge and his colleague Lynn Nagel later studied the sensor readings, they could see the unmistakable back-and-forth eye movements embedded in an otherwise normal stretch of REM tracings.

LaBerge tried to publish his findings in 1980, but he had trouble winning acceptance in the scientific community. Lucid dreaming had often been described in nonscientific publications by people with an interest in the occult, thereby weakening the subject's credibility among most academicians. But the Stanford team was now taking lucid dreaming out of the realm of mystics by offering hard physical evidence. In 1981 LaBerge had the opportunity to present his work at a sleep-research conference and was able to publish the results in the psychology journal *Perceptual and Motor Skills.* (Afterward LaBerge learned that British parapsychologist Keith Hearne had reported a similar eye-signaling technique a year earlier in a lesser-known scientific publication.) As other researchers began

Glimpses of Reality in the Realm of Dreams

One night during her fourth month of pregnancy, a woman named Robyn dreamed that she was swimming in a warm ocean, fighting a strong undertow to reach a house just a few yards away. She could see the house clearly, in every detail, right down to the nailheads in the shingles. At one of the windows was her mother, waving to her and smiling. Robyn knew even as she struggled that she would eventually make it to the house. Then, looking around, she noticed all sorts of turtles in the water, swimming alongside her. At that point she awoke.

Despite its otherworldly quality, Robyn's dream in many ways reflected the realities—both physical and psychological—of her waking life. Indeed, dreams often bear the imprint not only of our state of mind but also of our physiological circumstances. Sleep researchers have identified an assortment of physical conditions, from various degrees of sickness to such disabilities as blindness and deafness, that give rise to certain patterns of dreaming. For example, a 1987 study of heart-disease patients revealed that the more serious their illness, the more frequently the patients dreamed of death or of being separated from their loved ones. But even more intriguing evidence of the relationship between particular physical states and dream content has emerged from investigations of the vivid inner nightlife of pregnant women such as Robyn.

Oceans, Animals, and Architecture

That pregnant women's dreams might hold some special significance was first recognized as long as 4,000 years ago. According to ancient Mesopotamian texts, the Hittites performed cleansing ceremonies on women considered to have been "contaminated" by dreams they had before giving birth. Modern analysis of pregnant women's dreams has increased since the 1960s, with researchers collecting dream reports from hundreds of women in various stages of pregnancy.

Descriptions similar to Robyn's are remarkably common. Most pregnant women conjure visions of water, which psychologists say may represent the amniotic fluid. The fetus itself often appears in the guise of a baby animal such as a puppy or a kitten or, as in Robyn's case, an amphibious creature such as a turtle. Overall, pregnant women dream about animals significantly more often than do women who are not expecting. Architectural imagery is also typical, apparently emblematic of an increased focus on the body and its changing dimensions. And as she herself grows larger, a woman may go from dreaming about single rooms or small houses to multiple-story edifices, or even skyscrapers.

Several studies indicate that the sweet dreams of early pregnancy may become troubled later on, perhaps reflecting a growing anxiety about childbirth. Soothing respites in warm, tranquil waters become harrowing journeys down narrow, roiling channels. The small animals of early dreams grow larger and more threatening: Kittens, for example, may turn into tigers. And the house by the sea may now teeter on the edge of a cliff or be threatened by storms or fire.

Some researchers speculate that these common threads ultimately trace to the physiological changes that all pregnant women experience, such as variations in the amounts of certain hormones in their systems. Higher levels of estrogen and progesterone, for example, which are known to intensify a pregnant woman's emotions during her waking life, may also account for the vividness of her dreams and their evocative quality. Of course, individual personality and attitude stand as the prime

influences on how a dream unfolds: Robyn's feeling in her dream that she would overcome the undertow may have stemmed from an inner confidence that all would turn out well despite her fears.

Dreams of the Blind and the Deaf

Although the specific content varies to a greater degree, the dreams of both blind and deaf people also seem specially attuned to their condition. How blind people dream depends primarily on when they lost their sight. Those born blind have no visual dreams at all but instead have more vivid auditory dream experiences than sighted people. A subject in one study reported a dream in which she was carrying on several conversations at once while at the same time hearing a hair dryer, a washing machine, and somebody "scrambling with the dishes." Children who lose their vision between the ages of five and seven may dream in pictures later, but as they grow older, other sensory elements including touch, taste, and smell take center stage. Most people blinded after the age of seven continue to dream visually and in some cases create images in their mind's eye of people they have met after losing their sight.

The dreams of deaf people similarly reflect the circumstances of their disability. In one study, the congenitally deaf and those who had lost their hearing before the age of five reported dreams with more vivid colors and more three-dimensional detail than individuals afflicted later in life—almost as if the dreaming mind had done a better job of compensating for the missing sense when the dreamer had no real-life experience or little memory of it. As for communicating, even deaf people who could remember hearing tended to use sign language in their dreams.

testing the procedure with similar results, lucid dreaming gained wider acceptance as a valid phenomenon.

At Stanford, meanwhile, LaBerge and Nagel recruited a group of volunteers—natural lucid dreamers eager to hone their skills—who were willing to take part in experiments. One of the most adept subjects was Beverly Kedzierski, then a student computer scientist. As a child, she had had a recurrent nightmare of witches chasing her around the yard. Kedzierski eventually learned to turn this terrifying experience into a lucid dream, telling the witches, "You can have me in tomorrow night's dream, but just let me go free now." After several nights, she confronted the fiends. "What do you want?" she asked—and they vanished.

LaBerge, Kedzierski, and other volunteers called themselves the "oneironauts"—a Greek-derived term meaning dream explorers. They mastered the technique of raising their level of awareness during sleep and swiveling their eyes to indicate the beginning or end of a dream sequence. They further substantiated Dement and Kleitman's findings that dreams take place in real time, and that a lucid dreamer can estimate with fair accuracy how rapidly time is passing during a dream. The oneironauts also established that lucidity can occur deep in REM sleep, not just during brief moments of awakening.

On the question of whether or not dreams have meaning, LaBerge sided with Hobson and McCarley's critics. In his view, the fact that dreams are often, as he put it, "superbly coherent and entertaining stories" indicated that the thought-producing areas of the brain must have "at least an occasional or partial degree of control during dreaming." The flaw in Hobson and McCarley's original theory, he believed, was that it described a process in which signals travel only from the pons to the cortex. In reality, LaBerge argued, messages can travel both ways, with higher cortical functions actually stimulating dream production deeper in the brain.

According to LaBerge's theory of dream function, when impulses trickling up from the pons activate nerve networks in the cortex, they trigger well-established image patterns based on past experiences and emotions. The mind processes these stored images as though they were fresh sensory messages from the outside world, then interprets them in ways characteristic of the individual. A fearful person might see monsters and villains, for example, while another interprets the same stimulus as friendly. Dreamers respond to these internally generated images with emotions ranging from terror to ecstasy. If one could train the cortex to steer dreams in a desired direction, then, lucid dreaming would clearly be of therapeutic value.

At about the time that LaBerge published his book on lucid dreaming, a researcher by the name of Jonathan Winson, a neuroscientist at Rockefeller University in New York City, also weighed in on the side of those who agreed, with Freud, that dreams are a window into the personality of the dreamer. At the time, this position was widely dismissed as esoteric and unscientific. In *Brain and Psyche*, published in 1985, Winson pulled together two bodies of evidence from neurobiology to support two of Freud's basic tenets—first, that the unconscious exists, and second, that dreams give us access to that hidden realm. Winson did not, however, agree with Freud's belief that dreams are the disguised expressions of repressed concerns that had been buried in the unconscious.

The first part of Winson's theory hinged on the brain anatomy and sleep patterns of a small, burrowing Australian animal called the echidna, or spiny anteater (*opposite*). By studying the creature's peculiar makeup, Winson suggested, scientists might

The echidna, or spiny anteater—the only known land mammal that does not experience REM sleep—belongs to a group of primitive mammals called nontherians, which includes just one other species, the platypus. Although these unusual creatures are warm-blooded and nurse their young, they lay eggs and seem in other ways to resemble reptiles.

learn how and why dreaming evolved.

For one thing, the echidna has the largest prefrontal cortex relative to brain size of all mammals, including human beings. This region of the brain, located just behind the forehead, is where short-term, minute-to-minute decisions are made and, in mammals at least, seems to function as a kind of strategy-planning center. The echidna also is the only known mammal, besides dolphins and other cetaceans, that does not experience REM sleep. If, as other researchers had noted, the pervasiveness of REM sleep implies that it serves some vital function, how does the echidna survive without it—and what can this fact tell us about our own brains and mental processes?

The connection between REM sleep and the prefrontal cortex has to do with the transfer of newly learned behavior and other information needed for survival from short-term to long-term memory. In mammals, long-term memory storage areas lie elsewhere in the cortex, and the crucial transfer, as indicated by various studies of REM deprivation, seems to occur during REM sleep.

Long-term storage is particularly important to mammals—and especially to humans—Winson argued, because we need to consult with experience in order to respond to a myriad of current challenges. Adult humans therefore spend as much as a quarter of their sleep time in REM, integrating the constant influx of new information and shifting it to longer-term memory. By contrast, birds, whose behavior is so reflexive that they have little need to store memories long term, spend only one to five percent of their time in REM sleep. And reptiles, even more primitive and genetically programmed creatures, have no REM sleep at all.

To explain the echidna, then, Winson hypothesized that the creature has an enlarged prefrontal cortex and needs no REM sleep because, although its behaviors are relatively complex by reptilian standards, its outsize prefrontal cortex is capable of performing two tasks at once. That is, even as the animal is reacting to present events, its prefrontal cortex is updating the record of experience to allow the creature to respond appropriately in the future.

Obviously, this solution would not work for a species with more complicated memory requirements, and indeed, evolution along the echidna's lines came to a halt. Winson pointed out that if all mammals had followed the echidna down this road, humans would have to carry their prefrontal cortices around in a wheelbarrow.

The next part of Winson's theory drew on research into the role of the hippocampi—sea horse-shaped structures in the brain that act as a kind of switching device in the transfer of information into long-term memory. People whose hippocampi are damaged are able to remember events from their distant past but are incapable of retaining anything new for more than a few moments—be it what they had for breakfast or the fact that someone reentering the room had been there just 10 minutes earlier. The hippocampi are also part of the limbic system, a complex of brain components that are involved in emotions as well as in the rhythms of reproduction and hunger.

To the work of researchers who had studied the link between REM sleep and learning Winson now added his own and others' studies of certain brain-wave rhythms generated by the hippocampi of lower animals. The waves in question, theta rhythms, are produced when animals carry out certain behaviors while awake, behaviors that vary by species but are always significant for that species' survival—exploratory behavior in rats, for example, or predatory behavior in cats.

The only other time theta rhythms occur in these animals is during REM sleep, and Winson argued that movements during that period represent nothing less than activities that the animal's brain is integrating into its neural pathways. That the echidna's hippocampi generated theta rhythms when the animal was burrowing but not during sleep (since it has no REM sleep), Winson wrote, implied that the creature's large prefrontal cortex was processing information "as it was acquired (in computer terms, the processing is on-line, rather than off-line in REM sleep)."

All of these bits of evidence, Winson contended, buttressed his theory that REM sleep is "a fundamental part of the functioning of the mammalian brain." As he put it, "From this one can understand the origins of dreaming in man and what dreams represent." The dreams associated with REM sleep must offer a view into the way our brains organize psychological strategies for survival and transfer them into memory. (With humans, of course, the information to be stored away has expanded to include virtually all experience and not just certain categories of experience as in other animals.) These signals are not meant for conscious consumption, however; it is only a "matter of chance," Winson wrote, that we are able to catch glimpses of this process in dreams from time to time.

Nevertheless, the oftentimes fragmentary nature of dreams does not imply a lack of meaning, Winson argued; on the contrary, dreams contain all kinds of experiences of undoubted value to the individual. Dream content seems fragmentary and confusing only because the larger pieces of experience have been condensed, in effect, for long-term storage. And because the hippocampi are involved, the dreaming process mixes in associated emotions and thoughts before storing everything away. As a result, dreams are concoctions that, in Winson's words, reflect the individual's "wishes, hopes, and fears."

The idea that the material in dreams is being condensed for long-term storage borrowed directly from computer technology, a burgeoning field at the time Winson published his book. In fact, Winson and a number of other researchers regarded the computer as a useful analogy for the ethereal machinations of dreams. Stanley R. Palombo, for example, was among the first to notice the parallel. A psychoanalyst in Washington, D.C., Palombo pointed out in 1976 that both the human mind and large computers exploit two kinds of information handling, a daytime and a nighttime variety.

By day, human and machine operate in what is known in the computer world as real time—performing tasks involving incessant transactions with the outside world. The transactions go to a temporary holding area before being transferred to more permanent storage, a process that takes place off-line, at night. Just as the computer blocks communication with its myriad terminals in order to carry out internal processing of its files for storage, the human mind cuts off all motor activity during REM sleep to carry out its internal chores, sorting and storing new experiences in lasting memory. Just as Winson would argue nine years later, Palombo suggested that dream images seem odd only because they have been processed in a different way from real-time images.

As plausible as the computer comparison might be, many researchers of the cognitive school of psychology find the model far too mechanistic to reflect the subtlety of the human mind. For these psychologists, the ultimate goal is to gain insight into humankind's most distinctive attribute: the ability to sustain thought. Among the early leaders in this pursuit was David Foulkes, who in the late 1960s began looking for clues to human consciousness in the world of dreams, an area that most of his peers had neglected.

Foulkes and his co-workers at the University of Wyoming in Laramie quickly determined that the most widely disseminated sleep studies in the 1950s had painted too simple a picture of the nighttime brain. Dreaming, he found, was far subtler and more complex than any EEG meter could reveal. Furthermore, the correlation between dreams and REM was not as neat as many had claimed.

In particular, Foulkes took issue with REM researchers who jumped to the conclusion that infants or—more preposterously, in his view—animals dream. He once quipped, for example, that there is no more reason to believe that birds dream than to believe that they are pondering the state of the world from their perches on telephone lines.

The problem with early REM studies, according to Foulkes, was that researchers were so excited to discover that dreaming took place during REM sleep that they assumed the two were inseparable. As a consequence, these studies overlooked what was happening in the brain during the other stages of sleep. Foulkes, in fact, claimed to have found plenty of evidence that people dream both before and after entering periods of rapid eye movement.

Foulkes came to this conclusion while he was working in a sleep laboratory and trying to discover at what point after the onset of REM dreams actually begin. He kept waking volunteers earlier and earlier but never found a time when they were not dreaming. Poring through a body of less well known dream research, he noticed the same pattern. In one 1959 study, for instance, more than half of the volunteers recalled dreams after being awakened from non-REM sleep. To Foulkes, this meant that dreams are not strictly linked to the eye-twitching state.

Foulkes found more proof in his own research with children at the University of Wyoming during the late 1960s and early 1970s, and then at the Georgia Mental Health Institute in the 1980s. He and several collaborators recruited youngsters of various ages to sleep in the lab. The volunteers were awakened every so often and asked to describe their dreams. Foulkes, who published his findings in the 1982 book *Children's Dreams*, discovered that as the age of his subjects increased, so did the frequency of their dreams—even though they were spending increasingly less time in REM sleep.

Perhaps more intriguing, Foulkes also noted that dream patterns closely tracked the development of self-awareness. For example, children under five reported very few dreams, if any. Those between five and eight described simple dreams that resembled snapshots. After the age of eight, children began to have dreams like those of adults, with animated scenes and long narratives.

Since the dreaming mind appeared to follow the same developmental track as the conscious mind, Foulkes concluded that dreams deserve to be studied in a similar fashion. Dreams are not eruptions of animal urges, he insisted, nor are they mere flickers of brain static or off-line computer printouts. Rather, dreams are nighttime echoes of the same complex thought processes that take place during the day. Indeed, says Foulkes, "when the waking mind relaxes and lets down its controls, we have the same fanciful, imaginative thinking that we have in dreams."

For cognitive psychologists such as Foulkes, dreams cannot adequately be explained by neurochemical activity, no matter how sophisticated the electrical or chemical sensors used. Although technicians have documented in detail the physical changes that take place, moment by moment, as the body and mind slip from wakefulness into sleep, scientists have traveled only inches toward a goal that still lies miles ahead. They have hinted at what may produce the strange sensations, the feeling of entering another world, the elation and the fears that often engulf us during the night. But after decades of intense study, the dream state remains every bit as mysterious as it must have seemed to Lucretius.

The intense emotional coloring of these nighttime illusions is, for many people, the most intriguing aspect of the dream state. Certainly the emotional content of dreams is what attracted Sigmund Freud to the subject a century ago. Yet this emotional dimension, like the whole of dream research, today remains a territory in dispute, a realm in which psychoanalysis and the creative arts are tools just as valid as those of "hard" laboratory science. Perhaps, in the end, the dream world will yield its deepest secrets not to those who probe it with the most advanced scientific instruments, but to those who explore it with the most imagination.

THE STUFF OF DREAMS

In the second century, a Greek named Artemidorus Daldianus compiled five volumes listing and attempting to interpret hundreds of events and items that appear in dreams. Recognizing how the dreamer's life would impinge on any interpretation, he well understood the difficulty of his task. Some 1,800 years later, researchers are still trying to catalog and analyze dreams—and the job has become no easier.

Studies depend on what dreamers report when awake. They may forget or purposely not mention some dream experiences. And the test itself may affect results. Subjects awakened repeatedly in a sleep lab may relate mundane dreams, but after a night of uninterrupted sleep at home may recall only dramatic dreams, presumably having forgotten the dull ones.

Still, scientists continue to dissect dreams in sometimes excruciating detail. Researchers surveying 1,000 dreams of American college students, for example, counted no fewer than 1,170 different objects and places, learning, not surprisingly, that the subjects as a group dreamed of home 118 times and dorms 46 times, but orchids only twice. Such studies suggest insights, like the one explored on the following pages: that dreams tend to change as people age.

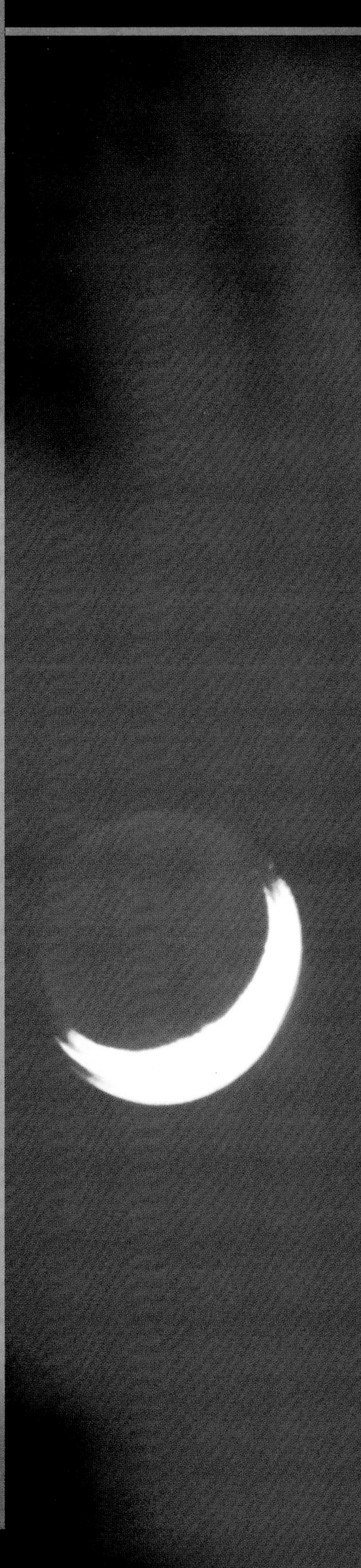

THE SWEET AND SCARY DREAMS OF CHILDREN

Children report dreams that are shorter and simpler than those of adults, and the more so the younger the child. But simplicity is double-sided: Studies of American children, for example, suggest that they dream more often than grownups about pleasurable objects such as toys, but they also have a greater number of frightening dreams involving aggression and weapons. Many authorities believe the fearful dreams reflect the precarious aspects of being smaller and less powerful than almost everyone else in an oversize world.

Perhaps the most dramatic difference is that dream images of animals—including ferocious beasts—appear much more frequently to children than to adults. But youngsters also seem to dream more often about people they know and less about strangers than do grownups.

Some studies indicate that girls have more pleasant dreams than boys—at least they experience less physical aggression in their dreams. Childhood dreams also differ from culture to culture, sometimes for no readily apparent reason. For example, one study of middle-class children in India found that they tend to dream about food more often than do children in the United States, even though the Indian youngsters in the sample were as well fed.

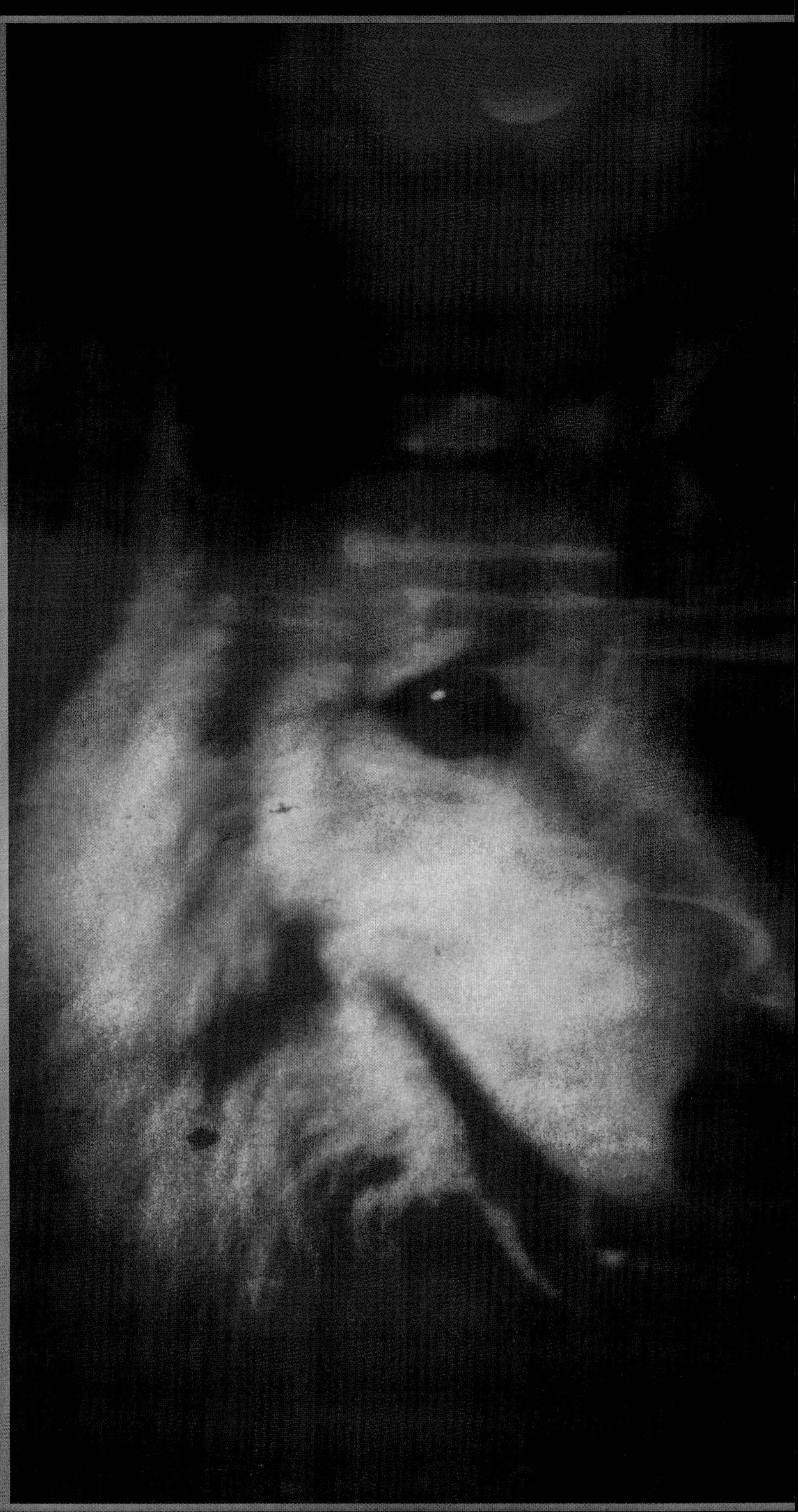

Animals—some threatening and some, like this dog, friendly—appear in about 39 percent of young children's dreams, a rate that falls to roughly 14 percent for teenagers and only 7.5 percent for college-age students, according to one study. Children in the sample found scary wild creatures, such as wolves, tigers, and alligators, in their dreams about as often as they did domestic animals.

Nightmares involving terrifying images like the one above are more common for children than for adults. Another phenomenon, called a night terror, makes some youngsters wake up screaming. The nature of the event is unclear, but it tends to happen during slow-wave non-REM sleep in the first two hours of the night. The terrors usually cease as a child ages.

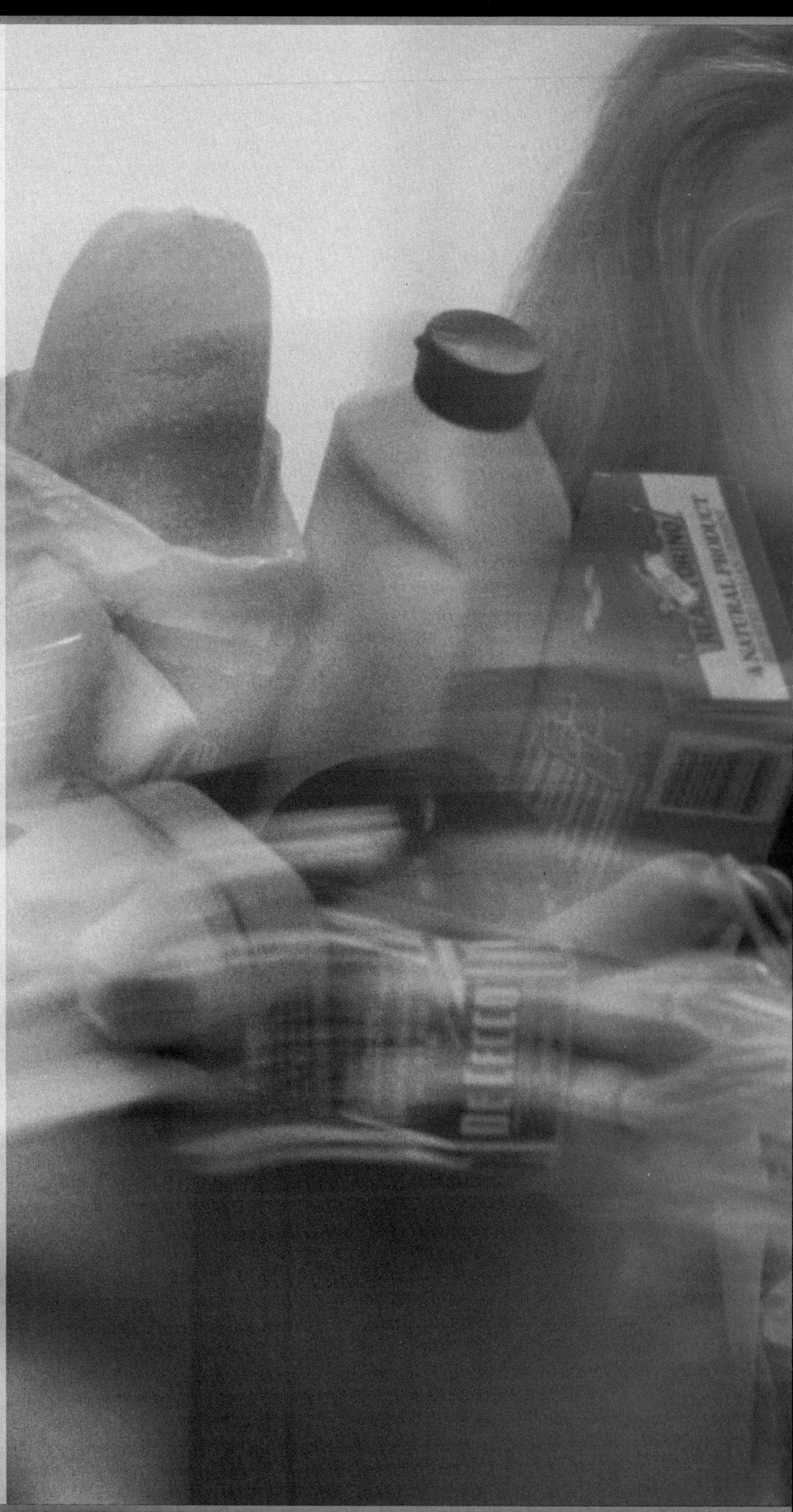

REALITY IN THE ADULT DREAM WORLD

Although people tend to remember bizarre or fantastical dream scenarios, the large number of ordinary dream situations described by sleep-lab subjects suggests these are the norm—perhaps reflecting concerns rooted in the real world. As reflections, such dreams are likely to vary with the dreamer's waking life.

For example, aggressive dreams are common in the United States. But Panama's Cuna Indians, who show virtually no aggression among themselves, never dream about attacking one another. A 1940s survey found that U.S. men dreamed of themselves as active and outdoors, while women dreamed of themselves as passive and usually indoors. Recent studies suggest, however, that such gender differences may be disappearing, perhaps in response to corresponding changes in society.

Some authorities on the subject believe that dreams are sleepers' attempts to work out emotional problems as well as practical ones (*pages* 38-39). Elias Howe, for instance, is said to have struggled for years to build a sewing machine before a dream gave him the solution—putting the needle's eye at its tip. But like waking inspiration, dreams can disappoint: Poets William Morris and John Squire both dreamed verse so bad it could not be published.

Everyday events, such as the juggling act this woman performs as she rushes to answer the phone with her arms full of groceries, are common dream material. People frequently dream that they are talking on the phone—evidence that dreams change to reflect changing life, since before the telephone's invention no one could dream about it. Like waking life, most dreams are in color.

As in the symbolic representation above of a scientist's dream about molecular structures, problem solving can continue during sleep. Nobel Prize-winning chemist Albert Szent-Györgyi said he personally believed this to be true "because I wake up, sometimes in the middle of the night, with answers to questions that have been puzzling me."

In the dream depicted at right, the young man will "wake up" totally unprepared for an exam about to begin. This typical panic dream has many forms. Musicians, for example, may dream they are not ready for an audition. But the exam dream is so common that, even decades after college, some people still dream about not having studied for the big test.

Dreaming of being chased by menacing pursuers, a victim like the woman above may feel she cannot move at all, or that her limbs function so sluggishly that she is bound to be caught. Some researchers think this aspect of dreams may be linked to the muscular paralysis the body experiences during REM sleep. The chase dream can turn into a nightmare that awakens the dreamer.

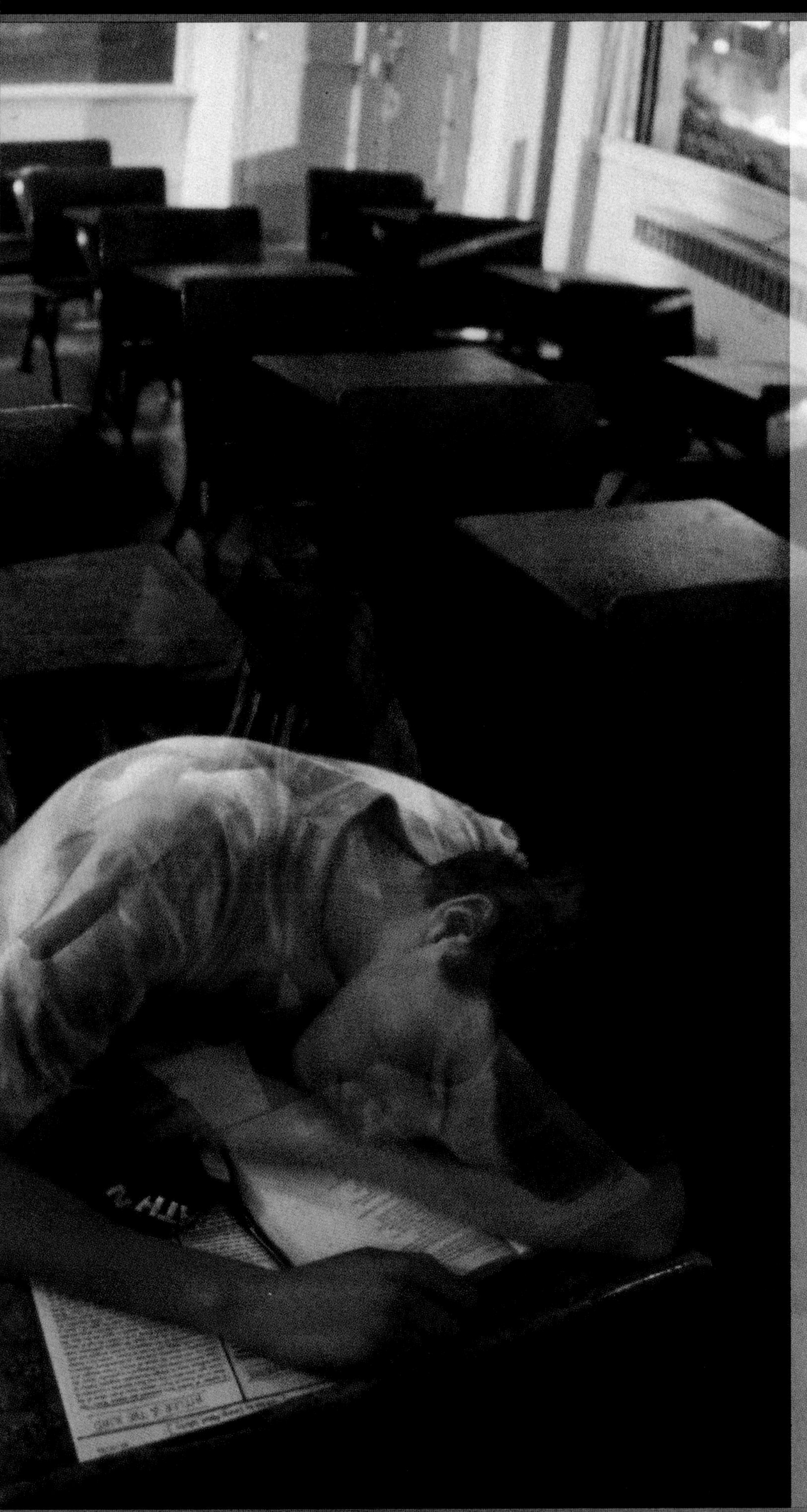

Despite their ordinary settings, adult dreams are often disturbing, albeit not as frightening as those of childhood. Surveys show that negative dream emotions—fear, anxiety, anger—outnumber positive feelings by two to one. Some researchers think this is because sleeping people are trying to resolve issues that are important in their waking life, and the problems that require the most dream processing are emotionally charged.

The distress that is experienced in dreams, however, may ultimately be beneficial to the dreamer. As psychologist Rosalind Cartwright has put it, "In dreaming, you update the program of who you are every night." A person involved in a crisis such as divorce, for instance, must dramatically change his or her self-image, and the difficulty of the task can be reflected in dreams until the dreamer works through the crisis.

People not in life crises may also have disturbing dreams, some so common that psychologists count them among those labeled "typical." Such dreams include appearing unclothed in public, being chased, being unprepared for an exam, falling, and the death of a loved one.

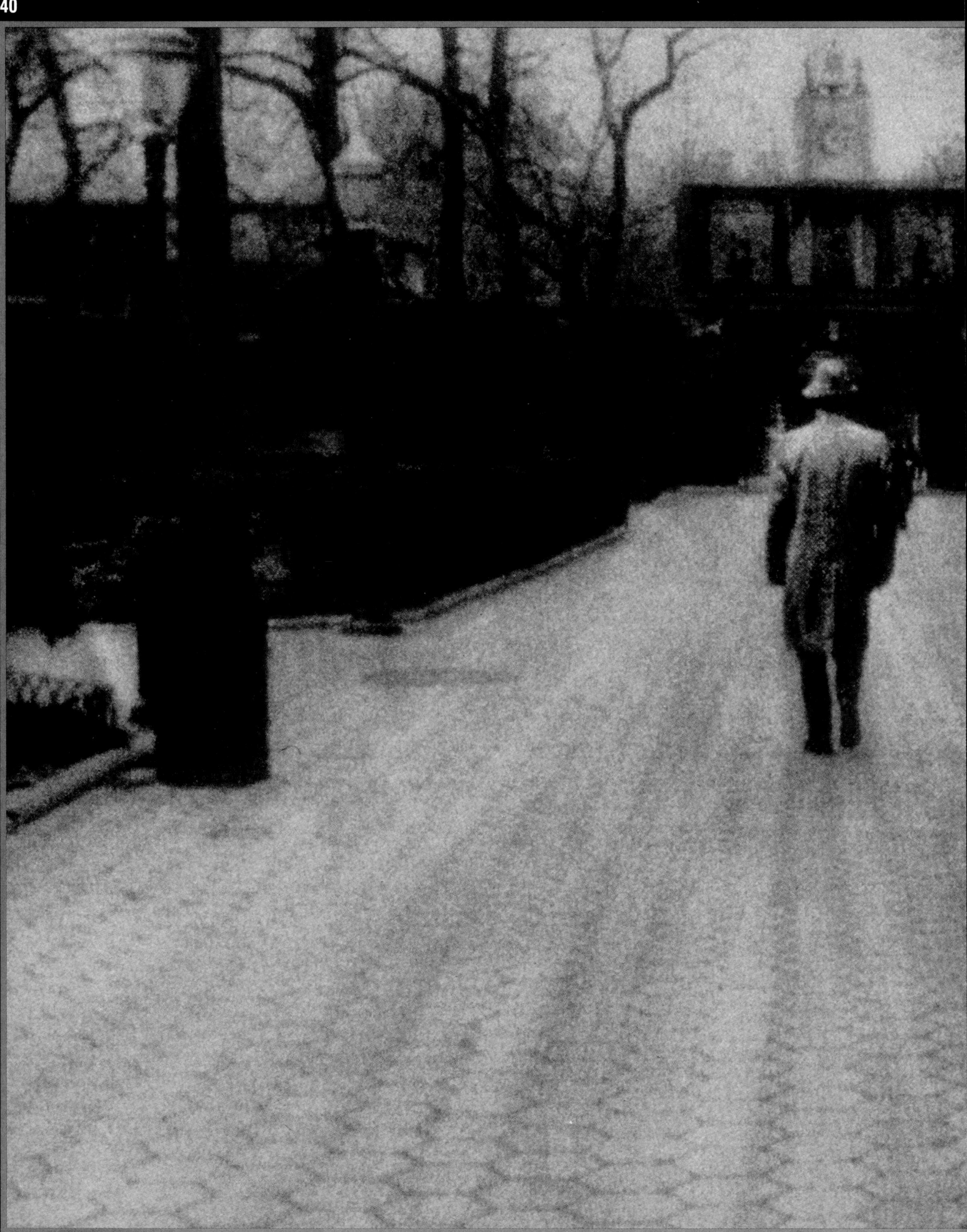

VISIONS IN THE TWILIGHT YEARS

Studies of the elderly suggest that as people age their dreams continue to change in ways that reflect their changing lives and circumstances. Sufferers of chronic brain syndrome, or senility, for example, have simple and repetitive dreams, almost child-like—possibly because, like small children, they feel powerless. Similarly, the elderly often dream of losing all their resources—money, property, the ability to take care of themselves—or of getting lost and not knowing how to get back home, fears mirroring real-life anxieties.

One fairly common characteristic is that in dreams as in their waking lives the aged behave less aggressively than younger persons and are more inclined toward passivity and introspection. These traits are not universally evident, however. Older women, who can be more assertive than older men in waking life, may also behave less passively in dreams.

2

The Creative Spark

The sun streaming through his bedroom window set the 16-year-old Albert Einstein thinking as he dressed for school one morning in 1895. He knew that the light, radiating through space at the incredible rate of 186,000 miles per second, transmitted information about the world to observers who were either at rest or moving at a vastly slower pace relative to light itself. But, young Einstein wondered, what if he, too, could somehow travel at the speed of light? What effect would his own motion have on the speed of light or on the information it conveyed to his senses?

These and related questions—which certainly exceeded the scope of Einstein's physics courses—were of vital interest to scientists of the day. They were mystified by recent experiments involving the speed of light, the results of which seemed to be at odds with classic Newtonian physics. Einstein found no immediate answers, but over the next several years he continued to play with his thought experiment, as he called such mental exercises.

Then, nearly a decade after he first posed the question, Einstein awoke one morning and sat bolt upright in bed, the pieces of the puzzle suddenly fitting together so naturally that he never questioned his solu-

Some Telltale Signs of a Creative Mind

Creative people are characterized by rampant streaks of individualism. Even so, psychologists agree that inventive minds share certain habits of thinking. And the crucial ability to come up with original ideas is merely a first step in the process. Most creators have in common an exceptional perseverance that carries them beyond the first spark of an idea's conception through to its fruition.

Throughout, their motivation springs from an inner drive rather than a desire to meet the expectations of others. In fact, while not unaware of the world around them, creative people especially in literature and the visual arts are in some ways unaffected by it. They often manage to avoid the socializing forces that can stifle the imagination; instead, they retain an openness to new experiences, feelings, and fantasies. Whereas some people shun ambiguity, preferring to see the world in black-and-white terms, imaginative individuals accept and even thrive on complexity and paradox. They also tend to have a keen sense of humor, another trait that involves suspending rules and looking at life in new ways.

Some studies have linked frequent nightmares with creativity. Additional research indicates that creative people are more readily hypnotized than others, perhaps because their minds can easily conjure vivid images. But psychologists have found that creativity is not necessarily tied to exceptional intelligence. Nor are creative people uniformly either self-confident or lacking in self-esteem. Indeed, while researchers can point to many traits that seem to correlate with creativity, this uniquely human impulse remains enigmatic.

tion. Others would, however, for his breakthrough was to discard the common-sense notion of how time and space work.

Einstein spent a few weeks refining his theory before submitting it to *The Annals of Physics* as a paper entitled "On the Electrodynamics of Moving Bodies." Within a year of its publication in 1905 his hypothesis—that the speed of light is absolute (independent of the motion of the observer) and that therefore space and time are relative—was the subject of hot debate among physicists the world over.

On the one hand, relativity theory, as it came to be known, seemed to explain, among other things, a discrepancy in the orbit of Mercury—but the theory required too great a leap for some scientists. The immutability of time and space had been proclaimed by Isaac Newton himself, in formulas that had explained the working of the universe for more than two centuries. Many were reluctant to give up this familiar perspective for one that seemed to run counter to everyday experience.

But Einstein had already sensed the consequences of relativity in his own mind, and he felt that anyone open to new ways of looking at the physical world could quickly grasp the theory's elegance and applicability. This unflappable conviction would later prove well founded.

In 1907 Einstein began making extensions to his theory. One elaboration showed him that objects moving at nearly light speed undergo an increase in mass proportional to their kinetic energy. This correspondence between mass and energy led him to the conclusion that the two are interchangeable, their linkage described by history's most famous algebraic equation: $E=mc^2$. When an independent experiment failed to detect relativistic mass changes in high-energy particles, Einstein was unperturbed. The theory was simply too right to be wrong; it must be the experimenter who was in error. As it turned out, of course, subsequent work by other researchers showed that to be the case, and Einstein's principle of special relativity soon became part of the scientific canon.

Einstein's breakthrough was a creative triumph, a powerful blend of intuition and rationality that transformed physics and ushered in the atomic age. For all its extraordinary consequences, though, his brilliant contribution was not a singular event in the history of humankind. Such creativity has characterized the human race since its earliest members struck stone against stone to forge simple tools for felling trees, butchering meat, and sparking fires. Indeed, the ability to blend old knowledge and new perspectives to produce something original appears to be a trait distinctive to the species. *Homo sapiens*, or "man the wise," might well have been dubbed *Homo faber*, or "man the maker," to describe the unremitting desire not just to build but to innovate. It lies behind every artifact of civilization or lofty idea of the mind, from mousetrap to megalopolis, from the simplest axiom to the most profoundly complex philosophy.

Although many thinkers have tried over the centuries to discover how the brain reaps its harvest of inventive thoughts, they have until recently met with only modest success. Even those for whom creativity is a way of life, whose livelihoods depend on their intuitive abilities, find the creative moment—the unconscious workings responsible for a newfound comprehension or innovative idea—shrouded in mystery.

However, this much is clear: A signal event in the creative process is a burst of illumination that generally strikes independently of conscious control. "When I am, as it were, completely myself, entirely alone, and of good cheer," wrote the 18th-century Austrian composer Wolfgang Amadeus Mozart, "it is on such occasions that my ideas flow best and most abundantly. Whence and how they come, I know not; nor can I force them."

Unfazed by the sketchiness of such bulletins from the front, modern scientists in the latter half of the 20th century have tried to identify concrete aspects of the creative faculty and to measure people's creative abilities. They have also looked to the inner workings of the brain, hoping to find the anatomical and biochemical roots of imagination and insight. In so doing, they have carried out exhaustive studies of patients who have undergone certain sorts of brain surgery. They have even attempted to determine whether creativity is tied to genetic factors and can be passed down from parents to children. Around the world, psychologists and cognitive scientists have studied writers and inventors, musicians and engineers, hoping to discern patterns of thought and behavior that these innovators customarily engage in before, during, and after composing or designing new works.

In the process, many investigators have abandoned the long-held view that creativity is the gift of a select few and have embraced instead the notion that the quality can be cultivated and encouraged in all persons. Far from being confined to the rarefied venues of art and science, creativity is also at work when, for example, a secretary devises a more efficient way of keeping an inventory of supplies or a househusband invents his own version of chili con carne. Today, scientifically tailored programs aim to instill creative thinking in elementary school children, and workshops teach college students and adults how to "brainstorm" by suspending self-criticism and letting their imaginations run free.

Researchers have also come to recognize that the study of the creative process must involve multiple disciplines—not only aesthetics and semantics but also psychology and neuroscience—for this uniquely human talent occupies a kind of fertile border zone; some aspects can be examined empirically, while others can only be inferred. The quest for the sources of creativity also occurs outside the university and clinic, among a wide range of people who have turned for guidance to everything from biofeedback and hypnosis to Zen Buddhist techniques designed to harness the "wild" mind—the free-associating, uninhibited unconscious. From these studies have emerged tantalizing glimpses of the internal gears and springs of inventiveness, the psychic machinery that enables humans to shape their world.

Creativity's part in stimulating change and progress has led artists at least from the time of the ancient Greeks to pay it homage in speech and song; philosophers have long probed its mysterious workings. Aristotle and Plato, for example, considered the impulse behind creativity to be divine, and Greek myth is rife with plaints directed toward Mount Olympus, as mortals in need of inspiration invoked the aid of the gods. Roman orators, writers, and performers seeking help also called upon the Muses, the immortal ones who specialized in such varied fields as poetry, history, music, and astronomy.

Following the classical lead, Western thinkers from the Renaissance onward identified creativity as a spontaneous spark—perhaps deriving from on high, or from the very essence of the human soul. By the 18th century, the relationship between imagination and rationality was a critical element in a monumental project, taken on by philosophers such as England's John Locke, to comprehend all of human thought.

Locke and his fellow rationalists, as they came to be known, saw creativity as an act of assemblage. In their view, the mind made original things, be they objects or ideas, in much the same way that a cook bakes a cake, from a welter of raw ingredients. Thus, in *The Pleasures of Imagination*, published in 1744, English physician Mark Akenside described an artist in the midst of the creative moment: "Anon ten thousand shapes, like spectres trooping to the wizard's call, flit swift before him. From the womb of earth, from ocean's bed they come: the eternal heavens disclose their splendors, and the dark abyss pours out her births unknown." Receiving these unbidden gifts, the artist then exerts his own powers. "With fixed gaze he marks the rising phantoms," Akenside wrote. "Now compares their different forms; now blends them, now divides, enlarges and extenuates by turns; opposes, ranges in fantastic bands, and infinitely varies."

To the romantics, who took the European stage in the latter half of the 18th century, such analysis diminished the creative act. The German poet Goethe, for one, proclaimed that "the artist alone sees spirits," while England's William Wordsworth believed that the artist tapped into the vast creative force that informed the universe. Wherever possible, the romantics fought to establish imagination at the pinnacle of human achievement, infused with the breath of the Divine. Special insight and innovation were deemed gifts given only to certain remarkable individuals, geniuses thought to be tinged more often than not with insanity.

This view held sway, off and on, for many decades. In 1864, Cesare Lombroso, an Italian psychiatrist, declared that dozens of historical figures, from Napoleon to Newton to Beethoven, suffered from mental illness. Lombroso was adept at winning attention for his ideas (another was that a person's criminality could be read from bodily features such as a long lower jaw or an asymmetrical skull), and

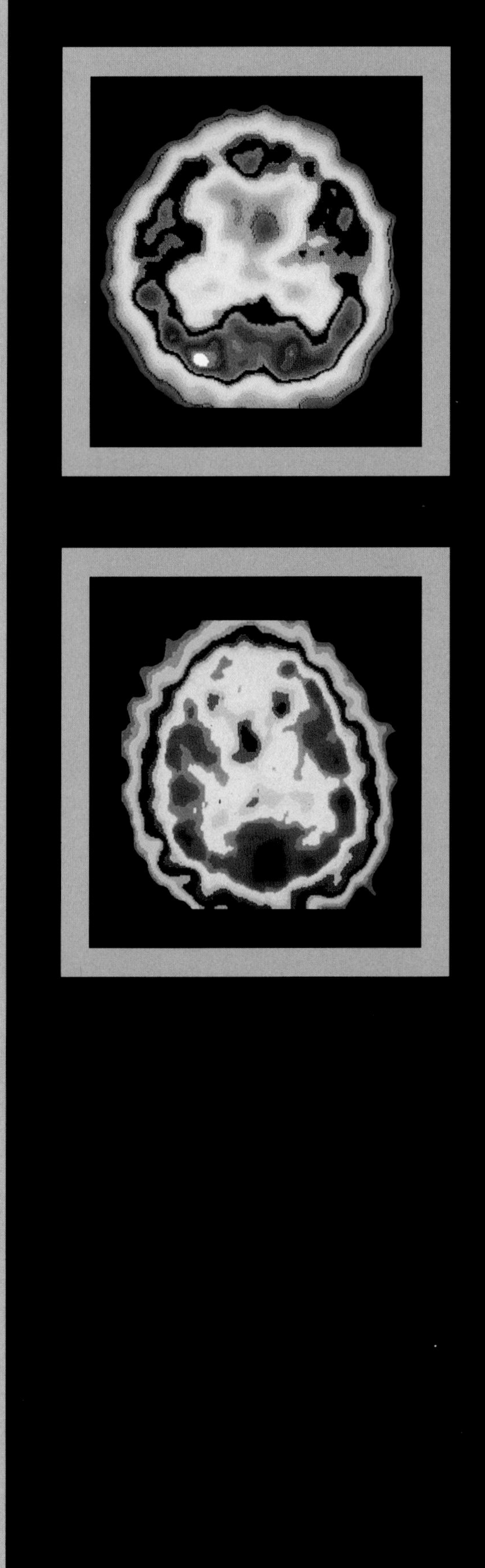

Madness and Art

As recently as a hundred years ago, it was commonly believed that genius, the gift of extraordinary artistic or scientific creativity, was an aberration—if not, in fact, a form of insanity. The 19th-century Italian psychiatrist Cesare Lombroso, for one, pronounced genius to be a "degenerative psychosis of the epileptic group." Although the stereotype of the "mad genius" lingers to this day, it has become clear that bolts of imagination can strike on either side of the asylum wall. With this recognition has come greater insight into the capabilities of the mentally ill and, indeed, the nature of creativity itself.

In 1922 German psychiatrist Hans Prinzhorn published *Artistry of the Mentally Ill*, a collection of drawings and other artwork by patients in mental hospitals. Among those inspired by the book was French painter Jean Dubuffet, who saw true artistic merit in these works. Dubuffet went on to champion what he termed *l'art brut*, or outsider art—renderings by mental patients and others, such as criminals, traditionally disregarded by society and the art establishment.

Much of the outsider art produced by the mentally ill has come from people with schizophrenia, a group of severe mental disorders having a neurological basis: In the PET scans at left, a healthy brain (*top*) shows more activity (*red*) in the forward-lying cognitive centers than does the brain of a schizophrenia patient (*bottom*). Yet researchers have found that schizophrenics, though often unable to function outside of an institution, share characteristics with creative people who are of sound mind. In controlled tests, for example, subjects rated highly creative and patients with a certain type of schizophrenia were likely to consider a wider range of options in forming responses than were subjects deemed less creative. Schizophrenic and creative subjects also tended to make unusual associations and to generate floods of ideas. However, compared with the creative subjects, the schizophrenics proved less able to harness their thoughts and, therefore, to solve problems efficiently. Thus most scientists today, while perhaps conceding similarities between innovation and madness, dismiss the notion that the one must spring from the other.

Of the five artists represented by the gallery shown here, three have been diagnosed with a mental illness, while the other two have not. The painters are (clockwise from lower left): Jean Dubuffet (1901-1985), who promoted the work of art outsiders though he was not one himself; Scottie Wilson (1888-1972), a British-born shopkeeper who went on to win international acclaim as an outsider artist; Adolf Wölfli (1864-1930), a Swiss laborer who spent more than 30 years in an institution writing and illustrating dozens of self-bound volumes about travels to other countries and planets; August Walla (1936-), an Austrian committed to a clinic for the first time at 16, who intertwines letters, symbols, and images of mythical beings; and Aloïse Corbaz (1886-1964), a Swiss governess institutionalized at the age of 32, who drew secretly at first but, like Wölfli, eventually earned acclaim as a "schizophrenic master."

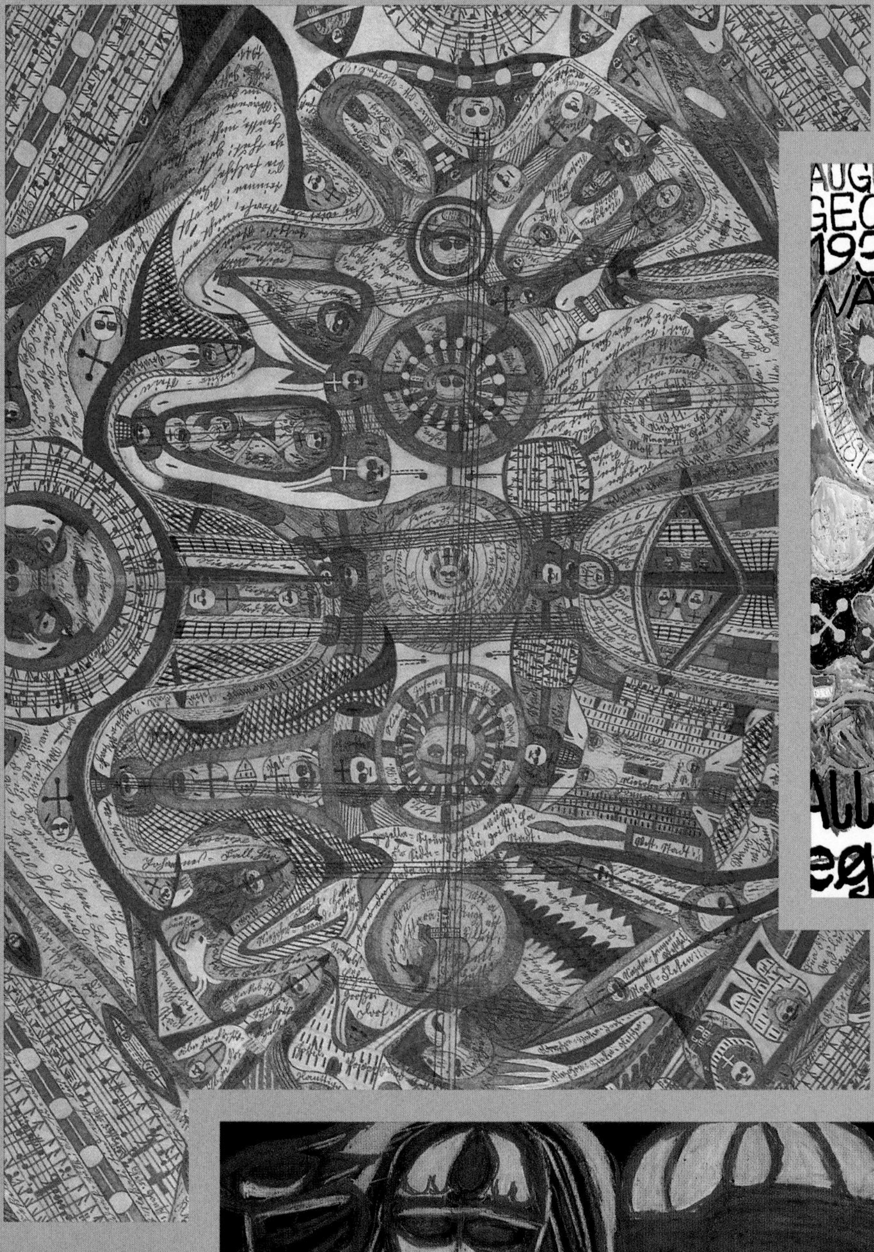

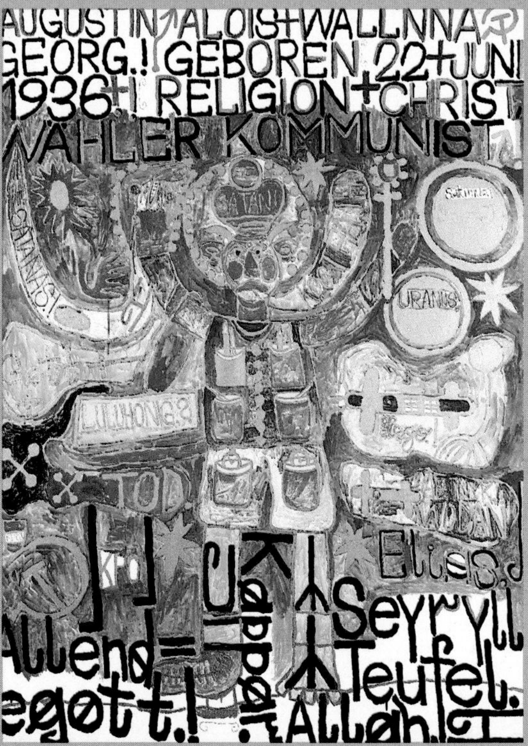

although other researchers subsequently found fault with his analysis, genius and insanity remained strongly connected in the popular consciousness until well into the 20th century.

However, even as Lombroso was propounding his theories, scientific opinion began to shift. In 1870 Britain's Francis Galton, cousin to Charles Darwin and a multifaceted scientist who was the intellectual force behind the development of IQ testing, suggested that genius constituted a highly refined version of an inborn "general intelligence." As such, Galton maintained, genius could be bred, through selective mating of talented people. Galton's new "science," called eugenics, enjoyed some popularity in Europe and in the United States—but lost most of its credibility when it provided the intellectual underpinnings for Nazi Germany's invidious attempts to create an Aryan superrace in the 1930s and 1940s.

Well before then, with the advent of Freudian psychoanalysis at the turn of the century, the hunt for the origins of creativity plunged into the previously unexplored realm of the unconscious. Freud saw similarities between the riddle of how original thoughts emerge seemingly from nothing and the way dreams arise from the sleeping mind. He suggested that creativity, like dreams, resulted from the operation of psychological defense mechanisms. In his scheme, artists, plagued by forbidden instinctive impulses, act to relieve themselves by sublimation, veiling their inner conflicts in fantasy.

Because artists rely so heavily on sublimation, said Freud, they lie closer on the psychological spectrum to neurosis than to health. Indeed, Freud went so far as to imply that in a hypothetical world in which all people had overcome their primitive defenses and attained psychological wholeness, art would cease to exist—or even to be necessary.

But Freud's disciple, Carl Jung, disagreed. Jung held that the psyche ran on the energetic life force he called libido, which flowed, like an electrical current, between the opposing psychological poles of the conscious and the unconscious. Any prevailing movement toward the conscious Jung designated progression; toward the unconscious, regression. Progression furthered the basic maintenance of the body, helping people to adapt to and exploit their environs, while regression served the unconscious, carrying them back into a disorganized realm of hazy images. And just as dreams drew on what Jung called the collective unconscious, the underlying repository of memories accumulated by the human species over the course of millennia, so too did this precious inheritance give rise to dances, drama, and magical ceremonies—in short, the entire panoply of individual and cultural attainments.

In counterpoint to these grand theoreticians, psychologists in the 1950s occupied themselves with more limited investigations of the mental and emotional skills involved in creativity. They began surveying wide cross sections of society—rich and poor, young and old—hunting for personality traits that might endow people with the ability to express novel thoughts.

During the course of these studies, researchers found that a primary mark of a productive intelligence was, as American novelist F. Scott Fitzgerald put it, the ability "to hold two opposed ideas in the mind at the same time, and still retain the ability to function." In the 1950s, for example, American psychologist Erich Fromm compiled a list of mental attributes that he believed enabled individuals to engage in what he called self-transcendence—creativity by another name. Fromm believed that inspired people—those who, in his view, tap into and harness a kind of universal force—had the capacity to maintain an objective view of themselves combined with a willingness to abandon the status quo. Creative people, he suggested, could accept the many tensions and contradictions of life, without losing the ability to concentrate and to be surprised and intrigued by the mystery of it all.

At about the same time, Carl Rogers, a clinical psychologist then at the University of Chicago working toward a comprehensive theory of creativity, identified three character attributes that he deemed essential. Creative people, Rogers said, seemed to rely on openness to experience, memory, and desire, acquiring somehow an acute sensitivity to every facet of their lives. In addition, these people displayed an intellectual flexibility that enabled them to mix and match disparate elements—ideas, shapes, and relationships, for example—with a spontaneity that has much in common with childlike play. And finally, Rogers observed, artists possess self-generated standards for weighing the worth of their creations. Their motivation is not a desire for praise from others, but rather a deeply felt need to express a part of themselves, their pain or ecstasy.

In the 1960s researchers Phillip Jackson and Samuel Messick proposed a more detailed model of creativity, breaking it down into basic components. They described four broad categories and several subcategories of mental tendencies and behaviors that they found essential to creativity. Again, key characteristics were the ability to tolerate a degree of uncertainty and to press on despite emotional or intellectual ambiguity. Creative people were also open-minded and flexible in the face of unusual experiences. Another skill the researchers identified was the capacity for engaging in both intuitive and analytic thinking, rather than relying heavily on one or the other. Jackson and Messick also said that creators typically alternated between taking the time to mull things over and moving quickly to act on sudden intuitions.

Studies like these helped produce a general picture of the creative mind at work: fiddling with ideas and images, recombining them at will, contemplating opposites, with a generous admixture of daydreaming and fantasy. But these activities alone are not sufficient. Consistently creative people, it seems, go through a whole series of discrete mental processes in the course of producing their work.

Researchers have come up with many descriptions of these phases, but one that has long been widely accepted was proposed in 1926 by British political scientist Graham Wallas, a founder of the London School of Economics, who was interested in

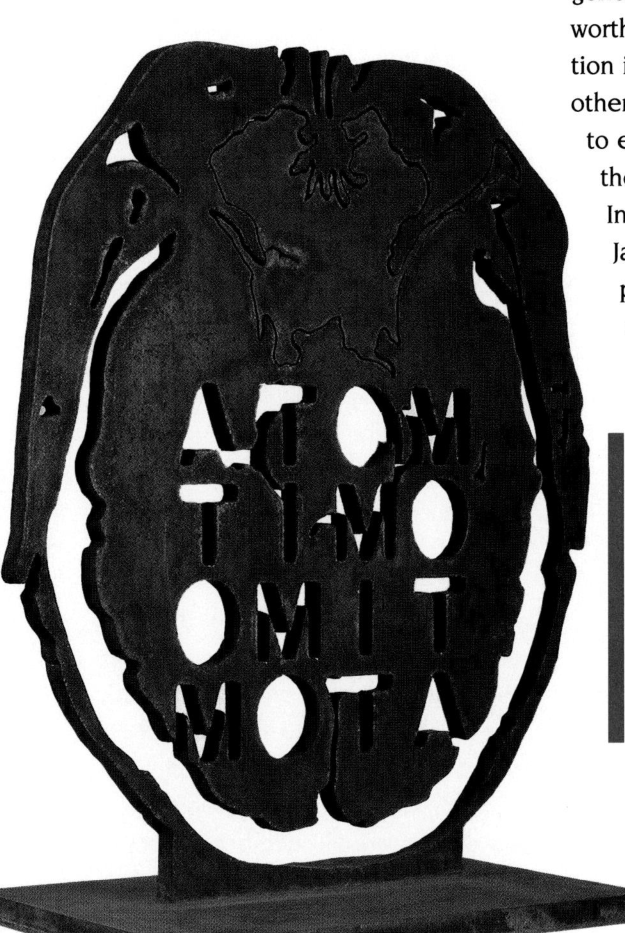

Purely for art's sake, German artist Sabine Schiebler has her brain scanned and produces paintings and sculptures based on the resulting magnetic resonance images. In this steel sculpture, she has included letters that challenge viewers to reflect on both images and words—"atom" and "omit."

understanding what motivated people. As illustrated on pages 65-73, Wallas identified four phases of creation: preparation, incubation, illumination, and verification.

Preparation might entail a lifetime of learning, or merely an afternoon. During this period, a person acquires knowledge and skills that lay the foundation for accomplishment. The next step, incubation, may also take a lot of time or a little—as knowledge and information percolate into memory and become fodder for manipulation by the unconscious. The French mathematician Jules-Henri Poincaré, whose musings on his own creativity helped inspire Wallas, noted that he arrived at "sudden inspirations" only after a period of concerted and frustratingly unproductive mental labor. Such insights, Poincaré wrote, "never happen except after some days of voluntary effort which has appeared absolutely fruitless and whence nothing good seems to have come, where the way taken seems totally astray."

Wallas designated the sudden arrival of enlightenment as illumination, and while some creators have described it as striking like lightning, others have recalled that it wafts in on the wings of a drug, or over the course of hours during which they are plunged into a trancelike state and are oblivious to the passage of time. Among the most famous tales of illumination is that told by romantic poet Samuel Taylor Coleridge concerning his *Kubla Khan*. Although scholars have questioned the veracity of his statements, Coleridge claimed that the exotic images of the poem came unbidden during an opium dream, rising up "as things, with a parallel production of the correspondent expressions, without any sensation or consciousness of effort"—whereupon he took up his pen to write the poem down. Partway through his reverie, Coleridge says, he was interrupted and upon returning to his desk found that the vision had evaporated.

Verification, the final phase identified by Wallas, figures as perhaps the most critical. During this stage, insights are perfected, and leads are pursued and organized. Without the labors undertaken during this period, nothing will be created.

In the United States, this empirical approach to creativity was significantly boosted by the 1957 launch by the Soviet Union of *Sputnik* 1, the first artificial satellite to orbit Earth. Fearing that the country was falling behind in the space race, the federal government initiated a campaign aimed at developing young scientists. Social psychologists and other researchers involved in measuring cognitive skills such as IQ began to focus upon creativity, seeking tools for gauging it.

Students were subjected to a variety of creativity surveys, many modeled after the Unusual Uses Test developed around this time by American psychologist J. P. Guilford. A typical question was "Think of as many unusual uses of a brick as you can." The students who wrote out the longest lists in a given time period were considered to have the most creative responses. The uses did not have to meet any standard of correctness; one student won credit for proposing a "bug hider"—"Put the brick on the ground for a week, then pick it up and look at the bugs hiding under it."

At the University of Minnesota in the 1960s, psychologist E. P. Torrance developed a set of creativity tests, many based on Guilford's model. One, called the Incomplete Figures Task, presented the subject with 10 unfinished drawings, such as parallel lines or two semicircles. Each student was asked to sketch in a design "that no one else in the class will think of," and to write down the name of what they had drawn. A complicated scoring protocol awarded points for the number of drawings completed, the number of different categories of objects drawn, the number of important details in each drawing, and the

A Prodigy's Enchanted Brush

At the age of two-and-a-half, Wang Yani scribbled across an oil painting that her father, a well-known Chinese artist, had just completed. As well as a scolding, he gave the eager toddler her own paper and brushes. Yani raced through the developmental stages of learning to draw that normal children take years to master. Within a few months her pictures showed signs of prodigy. Her first exhibition was held in Shanghai when she was four. By age six Yani had completed 4,000 pictures. And at 14 she became the youngest artist ever to have a one-person show at the Smithsonian Institution in Washington, D.C.

Yani was born in 1975 in Gongcheng. She paints in a style called *xieyi*, or "idea-writing," using brushes of varying widths, a mixture of water and pigment, and sheets of absorbent rice paper, some larger than she is. Yani's spontaneous method of composition flies in the face of more structured explanations of creativity. She does not make preliminary sketches, and may not even decide what to paint until her brush is poised above the paper. Then, working in bold strokes, she improvises, often incorporating spills or drips into the picture.

Even among child prodigies, Yani stands out for her tendency to create wholly original compositions. She also shows remarkable maturity in the way she arranges figures to create visual tension. Yani began painting monkeys after a trip to the zoo when she was three. As she has grown up, she has expanded her subjects to other animals, people, and landscapes.

Most three-year-olds draw only simple lines or circular forms *(above)*. Yani captured a cat's stealthy pacing *(left)*.

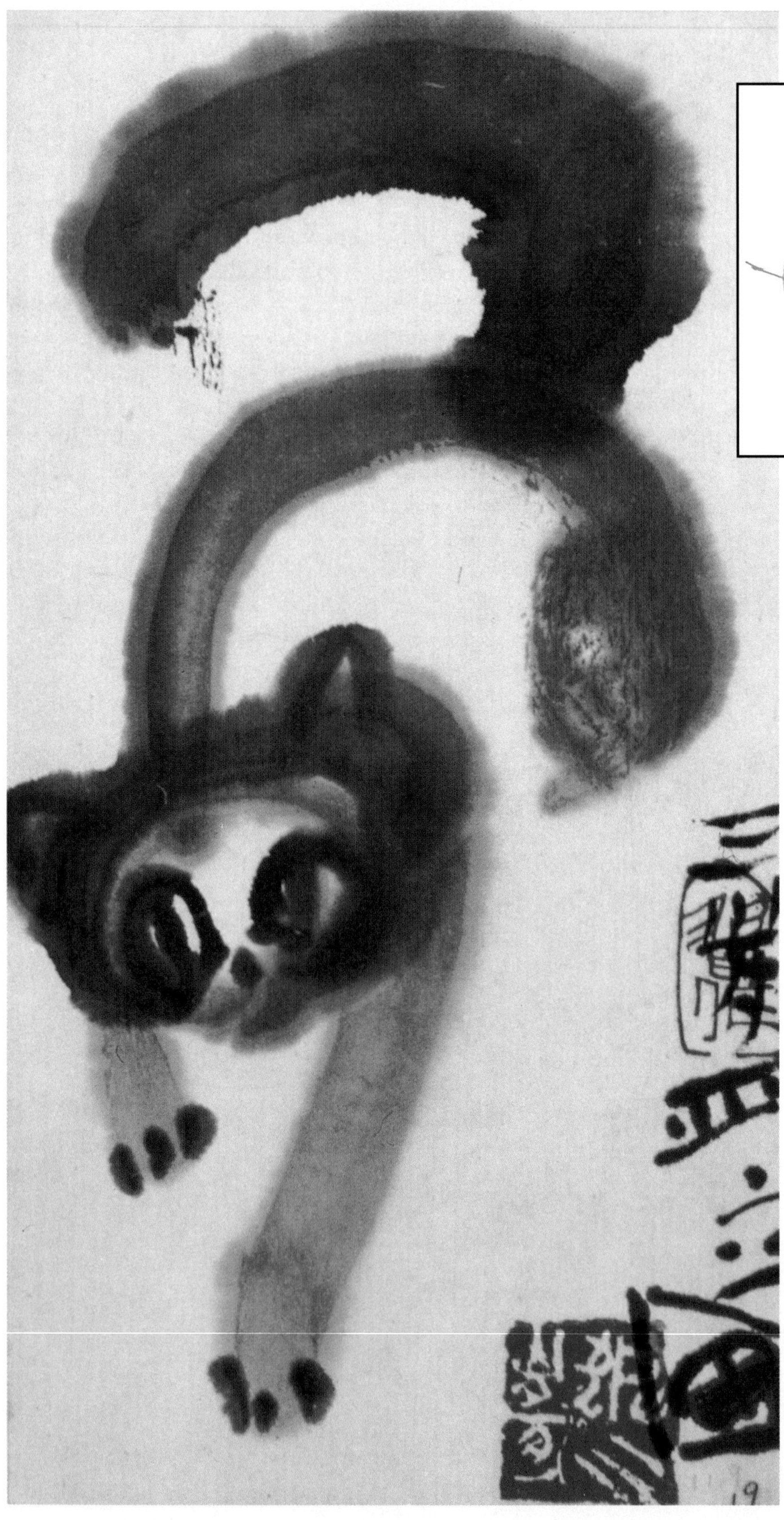

A six-year-old who was considered gifted drew the horse at left. When Yani was five she depicted these baby monkeys grasping fruit *(above)*.

At age eight, Yani used formal elements of design to create a stylized herd of horses *(below)*.

originality of each drawing compared to those of a sample group.

The Minnesota tests also included exercises designed to detect children's ability to explain unusual sounds or topics—"the dog that doesn't bark," for example—and the combined results were considered to provide a reading of students' relative levels of originality. By performing complicated statistical operations on the test data, investigators developed generalized pictures of the sorts of responses that signified creativity, and refined their tests accordingly.

Building his case on this kind of evidence, Guilford concluded that the act of creation was largely a matter of problem solving. Innovators attacked intellectual puzzles by two main means: divergent thinking, in which the mind ranged over a whole host of sometimes contradictory options, and convergent thinking, which assumes that for each question there is only one answer. Guilford proposed that the first style of thought enabled a person with ample memory to generate fresh ideas, while the second provided the means for culling only the best of those to elaborate upon.

Further study along such lines has served to undermine the old notion that intelligence and creativity go hand in hand. While an artist may well score above her peers by orthodox measures of intellect, this is not a prerequisite for her to accomplish notable things in the world of art. It is also true that a high measured IQ does not automatically identify a mind as fertile ground for novel enterprises. More consequential than IQ, as psychologists have repeatedly determined, is an ability to persist in creative endeavors even when confronted by discouragement, and to formulate independent judgments of the value of one's work.

These attributes probably factor into the choices creative people make in their lives, whether in personal attire, relationships, or financial matters, and may therefore be responsible for the reputation they have as being oddballs and iconoclasts. Nonetheless, when it comes to mental matters, innovative people, while tolerating disorder better than the average person, also exhibit a far greater than normal desire to discover amid the chaos some type of order. According to one researcher, for example, creative people taking a Rorschach test "insist to a most uncommon degree" on interpreting the inkblot as a single, comprehensive image, accounting for all the details.

Although the outlines of creative problem solving and insight appear to have been clarified through intensive research, their actual dynamics remain murky. In recent years psychiatrists and neurologists have begun to advance numerous theories, sometimes overlapping or contradictory. They have identified broad types of thinking, proposed new categories of mental activity, and hazarded guesses about what goes on in the unconscious during the period of incubation before the moment of illumination.

Psychiatrist Albert Rothenberg of Harvard Medical School has centered his discussions on a concept he has termed Janusian thinking, after Janus, the Roman god of entryways who was always depicted with two faces, one looking forward, the other backward. A citizen of ancient Rome would have understood Janus's gaze to be fixed on past and future events, but Rothenberg employs the symbol to refer to the union of opposites. In an article published in 1971, he echoed F. Scott Fitzgerald in describing Janusian thinking as the ability to consider "contradictory ideas, concepts, or images simultaneously." According to this theory, bringing conflicting elements into the conscious mind provides opportunities for new combinations and outcomes.

Rothenberg's views also resemble those of novelist Arthur Koestler, who proposed in 1964 that insight is produced mainly by a mechanism he

Everyday Inventiveness

The creative impulse inspires not only highbrow art, literature, and music, but also the craftsmanship of everyday objects. A Ghanaian carpenter named Kane Kwei, for example, has turned ordinary coffins into fanciful vehicles for the deceased's journey to the next world. And more than a century ago, Samuel and Sarah McFadden, a Kansas couple, devised an ingenious butter churn that was operated by their dog.

Kane Kwei built his first coffin at the request of a dying uncle, a fisherman, who asked for a special coffin and got one modeled after his boat. It created a sensation. Kane Kwei now runs a workshop that produces two dozen designs. The cost of such a coffin, painted with enamel and lined with satin, equals the annual per capita income in Ghana.

Symbolizing an important local agricultural product, an onion-shaped coffin like this one might be commissioned by a wealthy farmer.

Kane Kwei's coffins make reference to the life of the deceased. This likeness of a mother hen and her chicks would serve for a woman with a large family.

Sarah McFadden shows off the dog-powered butter churn that she and her husband constructed and used in Peabody, Kansas, in the 1880s.

called bisociation. That is, imagination is the act of juxtaposing items that normally reside in different unconscious realms, each subject to its own rules—a remembered melody linked to an abstract concept such as one, for example, or a logical axiom combined with a dash of strong feeling. Like the encounters of people from diverse cultures, this contact affords the opportunity for bold insights.

If creativity indeed derives from substantially different modes of mental activity, then it may be built into the very structure of the brain. Edward de Bono, director of Cambridge University's Cognitive Research Trust and a leading authority on teaching creative thinking, has suggested just such an organic basis for creativity. In *The Mechanism of Mind*, published in 1969, de Bono notes that the brain, unlike most information-storing systems such as a card catalog or a computer, requires no external entity to impose organization upon the data it gathers. Instead, the brain's own cells and nerve networks appear to have inherent sorting properties that somehow produce conceptual frameworks for information.

Moreover, these inherent properties provide the brain with two ways to gain access to stored information, which de Bono called vertical and lateral. According to his hypothesis, vertical thinking proceeds along linear paths, moving in a somewhat plodding fashion from one piece of data to the next. Vertical thinking weighs pieces of information and retains or eliminates them depending on their suitability to the task at hand.

Lateral thinking, by contrast, is a mental strategy that aims at stepping outside of existing models and preconceptions. Its foremost characteristic is a kind of random hopscotching from item to item, sometimes along several unrelated pathways. In this fashion, lateral thinking allows for the consideration of multiple bits of data, whether suited to the problem or not. If vertical thinking is concerned with what is, lateral thinking considers what might be. Though vertical thinking is almost guaranteed to arrive at a correct answer, however slowly, lateral thinking, says de Bono, delivers the striking, unusual insights that are an essential precondition of invention.

As psychologists have drawn an ever more detailed picture of the creative process, an increasing number of researchers have begun to focus on its neural origins. In the 1960s and 1970s, the work of Caltech neurophysiologist Roger Sperry on whether there are functional differences between the brain's left and right hemispheres spurred other investigators to probe the relationship between creativity and hemispheric specialization.

Sperry's pioneering studies involved people who had undergone surgery to alleviate the symptoms of severe epilepsy. All suffered a form of the ailment that did not respond to drugs or other treatments, and had agreed to an innovative procedure in which neurosurgeons severed the corpus callosum, a bundle of some 600 million nerve fibers connecting the brain's two cerebral hemispheres.

The surgery did in fact relieve many patients of debilitating seizures, but it did not leave them unscathed. Although they were capable of normal behavior in ordinary life, tests in the laboratory revealed significant changes in certain brain functions. The patients appeared to exhibit two separate and sometimes conflicting personalities, with dual sets of desires and perceptions.

That the two hemispheres could function independently was not a complete surprise. Several years earlier, Sperry and University of Chicago's Ronald Myers had carried out split-brain experiments with cats and discovered that when a cat had mastered a routine with one hemisphere it had to learn it all over from the beginning with the other hemisphere. In human split-brain patients, moreover,

These PET scans show in red the brain activity sparked by musical tones. A subject *(top)* untrained in music shows more activity in the right half of his brain, linked to emotions. A musically knowledgeable subject *(bottom)* listened analytically, using the brain's left hemisphere—which also processes speech.

Sperry and his colleagues found that the two brain hemispheres often did not share the same skills. Spatial and symbolic abilities, for instance, seemed to occur mostly in the right brain; verbal and computational skills, largely in the left.

As split-brain investigations continued to point to hemispheric specialization, a husband-and-wife team at the University of Southern California in Los Angeles, Joseph and Glenda Bogen, considered whether eliminating traffic through the corpus callosum significantly reduces a person's capacity for original thought. Split-brain patients in the Bogens' own studies in the 1970s, for example, reported that their dream life had diminished or become more realistic and mundane, less bizarre. In many instances, these patients' speech lost its liveliness as well; they used few adjectives, and their sentences became more passive and indirect.

By severing the link between the hemispheres, the Bogens suggested, surgeons may have inadvertently lessened a certain mental fluidity in their patients. One could expect, the Bogens concluded, that "artistic creativity in general benefits from interhemispheric collaboration." Indeed, according to neurologist Joseph Bogen, "each of us has two minds," which manifest themselves in many ways. He disagrees with the notion that people possess one set of views. Not only are the two cerebral hemispheres capable of generating separate minds, he argues, but with training the two can work independently—perceiving, considering, and acting on their own to generate two types of thought, which Bogen calls propositional and appositional.

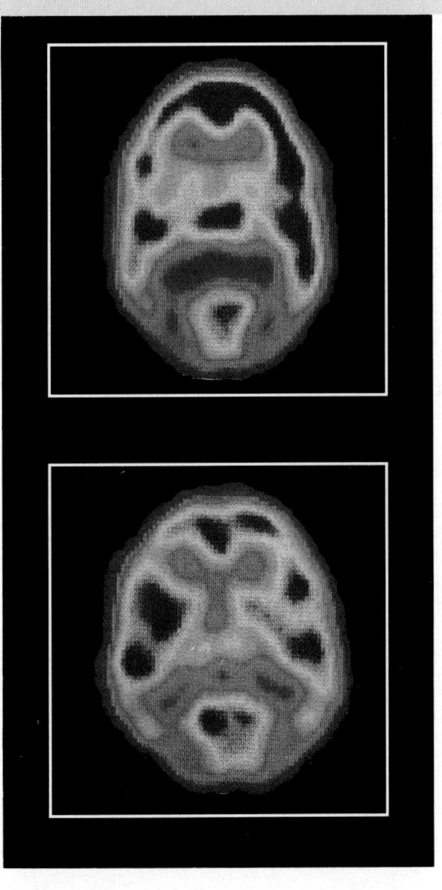

Propositional thought, most evident in the left brain, is verbally oriented and follows logical rules. Appositional thought, which Bogen ascribes largely to the right brain, includes comparisons of an assortment of perceptions, ideas, and memories. Creativity thus arises from two distinct information processes, which manipulate data in markedly different ways and then share the results.

Researchers then began to wonder whether right and left brainedness might explain the sudden "jolt" of inspiration. If ideas are incubated in the more symbolic, nonverbal right brain, the theory went, then the analytic, language-endowed left brain would not be able to express the ideas until they were sent over through the corpus callosum—at which point they would seem to be coming out of nowhere.

Subsequent investigations carried out in the 1970s and 1980s seemed to lend support to this thesis. University of Maine psychologist Colin Martindale, for example, found in 1977 that when people who had been identified as creative by a number of methods were hooked to EEGs and given such tasks as the Unusual Uses Test, swarms of electrical signals flooded

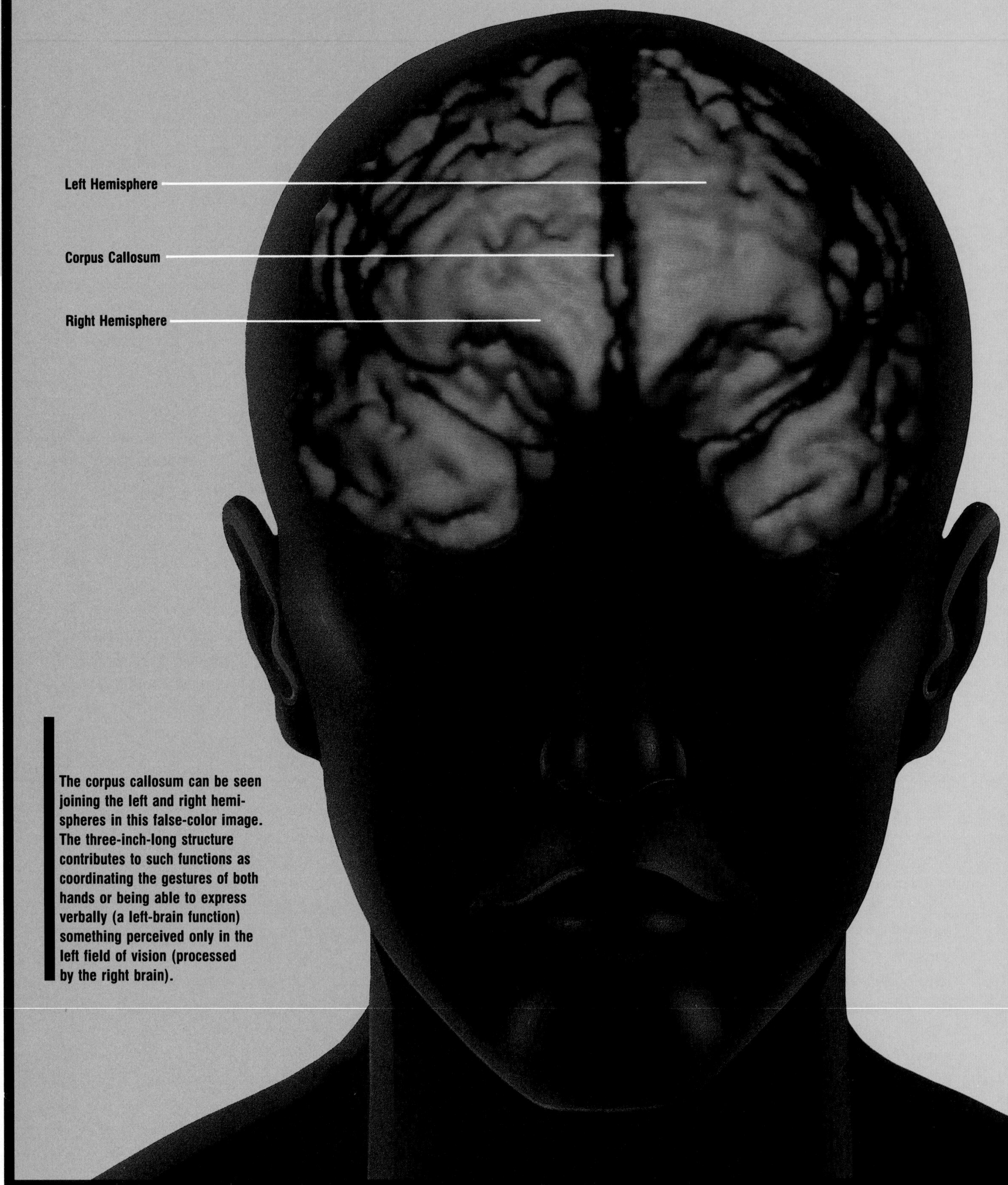

The corpus callosum can be seen joining the left and right hemispheres in this false-color image. The three-inch-long structure contributes to such functions as coordinating the gestures of both hands or being able to express verbally (a left-brain function) something perceived only in the left field of vision (processed by the right brain).

Bridging the Brain's Two Minds

According to a theory expounded by Klaus D. Hoppe of UCLA, the corpus callosum—the main neural communications link between the left and right hemispheres of the brain—plays a greater or lesser role in creativity at different stages of the creative process. During the information-gathering, preparation stage of creativity, and later during verification, goes the theory, the analytic powers of the left hemisphere make it the major player; because the right hemisphere makes a small contribution, the need for communication across the corpus callosum is less. Similarly, if incubation of an idea relies more on the symbolic powers that seem to dwell in the right hemisphere, the corpus callosum would again play a minor role. But at the moment of illumination, Hoppe hypothesizes, the symbols created in the right hemisphere cross over the corpus callosum, where they are transformed and verbalized in the left hemisphere. Hoppe calls this act of creative synthesis symbollexia.

In this view, the brain's two halves are separate entities whose contributions are inextricably entwined. Thus, only rare individuals show evidence of the independent workings of the two hemispheres. One such case is Jennifer, an accomplished amateur artist whose corpus callosum malfunctions in a way that reveals the separate nature of each side of her brain. She paints equally well with either hand, yet Jennifer's left-handed pictures bear little resemblance to her right-handed ones (*below*). Dominated by the logical left side of the brain, the right-handed paintings are more realistic than her left-handed efforts. The artist herself prefers the results of her left hand: "I have complete freedom with my left hand," she says, "whereas my right hand is censoring me."

These paintings show competing styles harbored in Jennifer's brain. She painted the nearer, more impressionistic picture with her left hand; the other, a portrait of an elderly model, is a right-handed work.

their right hemispheres while their left hemispheres showed lower levels of excitation. In less-creative subjects, right-hemisphere activity was markedly lower during the same tasks.

Further clues about the role of the hemispheres in creativity emerged when researchers examined individuals suffering from a rare disorder known as alexithymia, from Greek origins meaning "no words for emotion." Although their brain hemispheres are anatomically connected, alexithymics have difficulty verbalizing fantasy and expressing feelings in words; even the most intelligent among them also appear to think only in the most plodding fashion. Only dimly comprehending of ideas presented symbolically, they subsist in a world that is, in effect, the opposite of creativity.

In a series of experiments led by Warren TenHouten, Klaus Hoppe, and colleagues at the University of California at Los Angeles in the late 1980s, alexithymics were shown a short movie that symbolically depicted the death of a baby and a little boy through images (an empty crib, an abandoned swing set) and evocative music signifying loss and mourning. The subjects were consistently unable to grasp the thematic content of the film. Hooked to EEG machines, the alexithymics showed diminished hemispheric interaction, and their descriptions of the movie lacked appropriate emotional expression.

Oddly, an experiment by Dr. D. W. Zaidel seems to muddy the waters regarding hemispheric function in the creative process. In the late 1980s, Zaidel, then an associate of Roger Sperry's at Caltech, carried out studies in which, through special visual techniques, the right and left hemispheres of normal subjects were exposed to a series of realistic and surrealistic paintings. She found, contrary to expectation, that the allegedly more spatially perceptive right brain was able to remember only the realistic images while the supposedly more analytic left remembered both real and surreal. More recently Zaidel has noted that if creativity is defined as the ability to transcend traditional norms or tolerate the atypical, then the left brain is a key player. As she has acknowledged, however, creativity must rely ultimately on interhemispheric communication.

As others have pointed out, the halves of the healthy brain work like two people in a happy partnership. Each side tends to perform its own set of tasks most of the time, but each is able to assume, either partly or in full, the tasks of the other when necessary—due, for example, to damage to one side of the brain. (Some types of creativity, such as composing music, probably rely heavily on both hemispheres and may be severely curtailed if either side is impaired by injury or disease.)

Maine's Colin Martindale, for example, found that although people who are identified as creative tend to show higher activity readings in the right hemisphere than in the left when performing creative tasks, the whole brain is almost always involved in problem solving. When creative individuals took standardized creativity tests, they produced uniformly stronger readings of alpha waves—which indicate relaxation in the cortex, the portion of the brain involved in higher mental functions—than did noncreative subjects.

Martindale, noting that cortical arousal is linked to the ability to focus attention, concluded that the creative subjects diffused their attention when expected to perform creative tasks. They seemed able to lapse, perhaps at will, into a zone in which the mind is less like a laser beam than a diffused low-wattage light bulb. Strangely, this unfocusing process, rather than dampening mental acuity, actually enhances it.

Although most creativity research, like Martindale's, works from the assumption that creative people operate within the limits of normal physiology and psychology, creativity's long-presumed links with insanity are part of the popular culture. The Italian painter Polidoro da Caravaggio's violent rampages, for instance, Dutch artist Vincent van Gogh's self-mutilation, and the suicides of the postwar American poets Sylvia Plath, John Berryman, and Anne Sexton have become emblematic of the psychic cost that creativity imposes. The romantic poet George Gordon, Lord Byron wrote of his struggles as he penned his epic *Childe Harold's Pilgrimage*: "I was half mad during the time of its composition, between metaphysics, mountains, lakes, love unextinguishable, thoughts unutterable, and the nightmare of my own delinquencies." The torture was so profound, Byron wrote, that "I should, many a good day, have blown my brains out, but for the recollection that it would have given pleasure to my mother-in-law."

As late as the 1980s, some researchers argued that emotional disarray almost invariably accompanies creativity. In one study, two sets of college art students—one group considered more creative than the other—were given various psychological tests. The investigator found that the more creative students were racked by profound and painful emotional conflicts typical of classic neurosis. However, among these youth, a telling character trait was, as the researcher put it, "a willingness first to face, then to shape, to mold, to work the painful material within rather than to merely moan."

Statistical surveys of artists reveal that writers in particular seem especially prone to bipolar disorder, in which they swing unpredictably from mania—frenzied periods of elation and productivity—to depression, in which they succumb to bleak moods and sometimes total psychic paralysis. In surveying 47 living British poets, playwrights, novelists, biographers, and artists in 1989 (the subjects' identities were not disclosed), psychiatrist Kay Jamison of the Johns Hopkins University School of Medicine in Baltimore found that 38 percent—mostly male poets—had taken medications, sought psychotherapy, or been institutionalized for depression or bipolar illness. By contrast, the rate of unipolar depression in the general population is only five percent, and that of bipolar disorder just one percent.

Virtually all subjects revealed that they had also undergone periods of manic activity, during which they slept less than usual, worked longer hours, and felt a certain exhilaration and greater self-confidence than usual. Jamison concluded that such mood swings, if not too severe, were not necessarily destructive, but instead played a key role in the production of her subjects' works.

However, other studies have countered the notion that a touch of madness is essential to being a creative individual. Examining the lives of 32 renowned British poets through the ages, scholar Harold Nicholson found only two who were stricken by what could be considered full-blown mental illness. One was the 18th-century lyric poet William Cowper, who suffered a nervous breakdown as a young lawyer, attempted suicide, and lived with a caretaker most of his adult life. Cowper became so immobilized by depression at times that he could not write. On several occasions, to encourage him to write, his caretaker assigned him subjects, and two of his most famous poems were produced in this manner. Nicholson's other debilitated poet was Jonathan Swift, the Irish satirist and curate who suffered from an inner ear disorder that gave him vertigo, and in the final years of his noisy, politically boisterous life fell into senility, which robbed him of his wickedly brilliant intellect before his death in 1745.

Today, psychologists and psychiatrists generally agree that mental illness does not generate creativity, but that some mentally disturbed individuals are able, despite emotional difficulties, to carry out creative endeavors. The vast majority of those who have achieved success in artistic or scientific ventures in fact exhibit such hallmarks of sanity as rational thought and the abilities to conceive and execute plans, to gauge reality, to identify and overcome obstacles, and (no small matter) to persevere until reaching a goal.

Although no necessary link exists between insanity and creativity, many people have reported altered states of consciousness while working out new ideas or objects. On such occasions they lose all sense of time and place and are carried forward by a kind of river of energy. Psychiatrists have only recently begun to take such accounts seriously and to recognize their similarity to stories told by mystics and others about experiencing a state in which only the present exists. Athletes, too, talk of "being in the zone," when vision sharpens, time unrolls in slow motion, and alertness and physical skill peak. Scientists have dubbed this phenomenon "flow" and are beginning to explore its possible biochemical causes.

The answer may lie in the brain's opiate receptors—special docking sites on brain cells for certain neurochemicals. One type of these chemicals, known as endorphins, by binding to opiate receptors, has been found to dampen pain, and also to produce the elation—nicknamed the "runner's high"—that some people feel after prolonged exercise. Neuroscientist Candace Pert suggests that opiate receptors may also play a role in creativity, by "filtering reality" in a way that is conducive to an altered state of consciousness.

In addition, research has shown that opiate receptors are 30 times more common in the frontal portion of the brain than in the rear, a finding that has led some scientists to posit a new theory on creativity and the brain. Because the frontal lobes seem to be heavily involved in so-called higher thought processes, the theory goes, the salient division may be front-to-back rather than left-to-right.

This line of reasoning leads naturally to the hope that synthetic drugs could stimulate creativity or that techniques akin to biofeedback might enhance people's ability to affect the chain of neurochemical events in which endorphins are released, thus facilitating the sort of cognitive processes that lead to innovation.

Beyond biochemistry and the boundaries of science lies metaphysics. For many students of creativity who view the rigors of experiment and theoretical surmise as only part of the picture, answers lie in this realm. For them, the physical brain is powered by that ineffable, nonmaterial entity, the mind. Creativity may arise not in the neurons or larger structures of the brain but in a place beyond the reach of present-day scientific tools to explore.

Candace Pert, for one, believes that mind and brain are separate. "The mind is in a different realm than the molecules of the brain," Pert contends. "The brain is a receiver, not a source." British psychologist and writer Anthony Storr would tend to agree. Storr views creativity as "motivated by a 'divine discontent' which is part of man's biological endowment. Mystery and disorder spur man to discovery, to the creation of new hypotheses that bring order and pattern to the maze of phenomena." If these researchers are correct, then the most promising terrain for further explorations of creativity may prove to lie beyond the normal purview of science in areas customarily falling to theologians, philosophers—and, indeed, artists themselves.

CREATIVITY BY DESIGN: A GALLERY OF ART

Chinese-born architect I. M. Pei, acclaimed worldwide for his spectacular art museums, is creativity personified. Perhaps his most innovative shrine to art is the East Building of the National Gallery of Art in Washington, D.C., designed in the 1930s by architect John Russell Pope. As explained on the following pages, the four widely accepted stages of creativity—preparation, incubation, illumination, and verification—are easily seen in Pei's labors between 1968, when he was granted the commission, and the opening of the East Building 10 years later. Preparation began for Pei—as it does for most mature talents—decades earlier, as the young student from Shanghai continued his education in architecture at Harvard University in 1942. Under the tutelage of Walter Gropius and Marcel Breuer, two of the day's most influential architects, Pei designed an art museum for the city of Shanghai. Though nothing more than a school exercise, the project launched I. M. Pei into an orbit that would eventually bring him to the creative challenge of a lifetime.

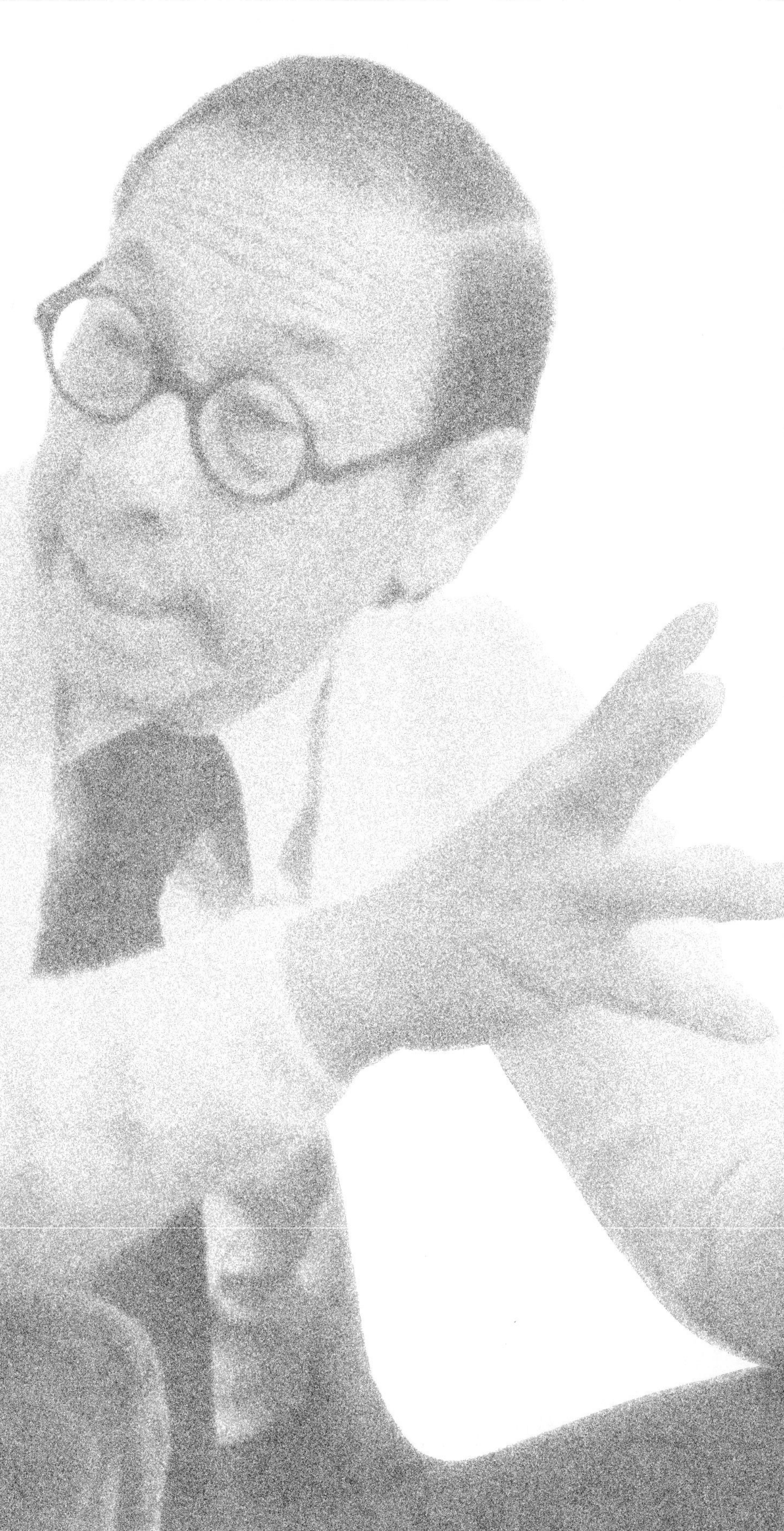

GRASPING THE ISSUES

To begin the preparation stage of creating the East Building, Pei had to address the constraints on any work of architecture—site and function. A structure's exterior should take account of its surroundings, which are typically populated with other structures. The interior must serve the purpose envisioned for the building.

The site, said Pei, was "the most difficult piece of land I've ever worked with." Roughly triangular in outline, the plot virtually ruled out a rectangular building, which would have wasted much of the land.

Whatever its form, the exterior of the East Building would have to complement the other monuments and museums located nearby and establish a connection to the National Gallery's Pope Building across the street, of which Pei's creation was to be an extension. Municipal regulations governing height and setback from the street would further limit the design.

Inside, the museum would need spaces large enough to display enormous works of art, as well as more modest galleries for viewing smaller paintings and sculpture in an appropriately intimate setting. The design would have to allow for interior traffic patterns to handle thousands of visitors a day, and part of the space had to accommodate museum offices and an art study center.

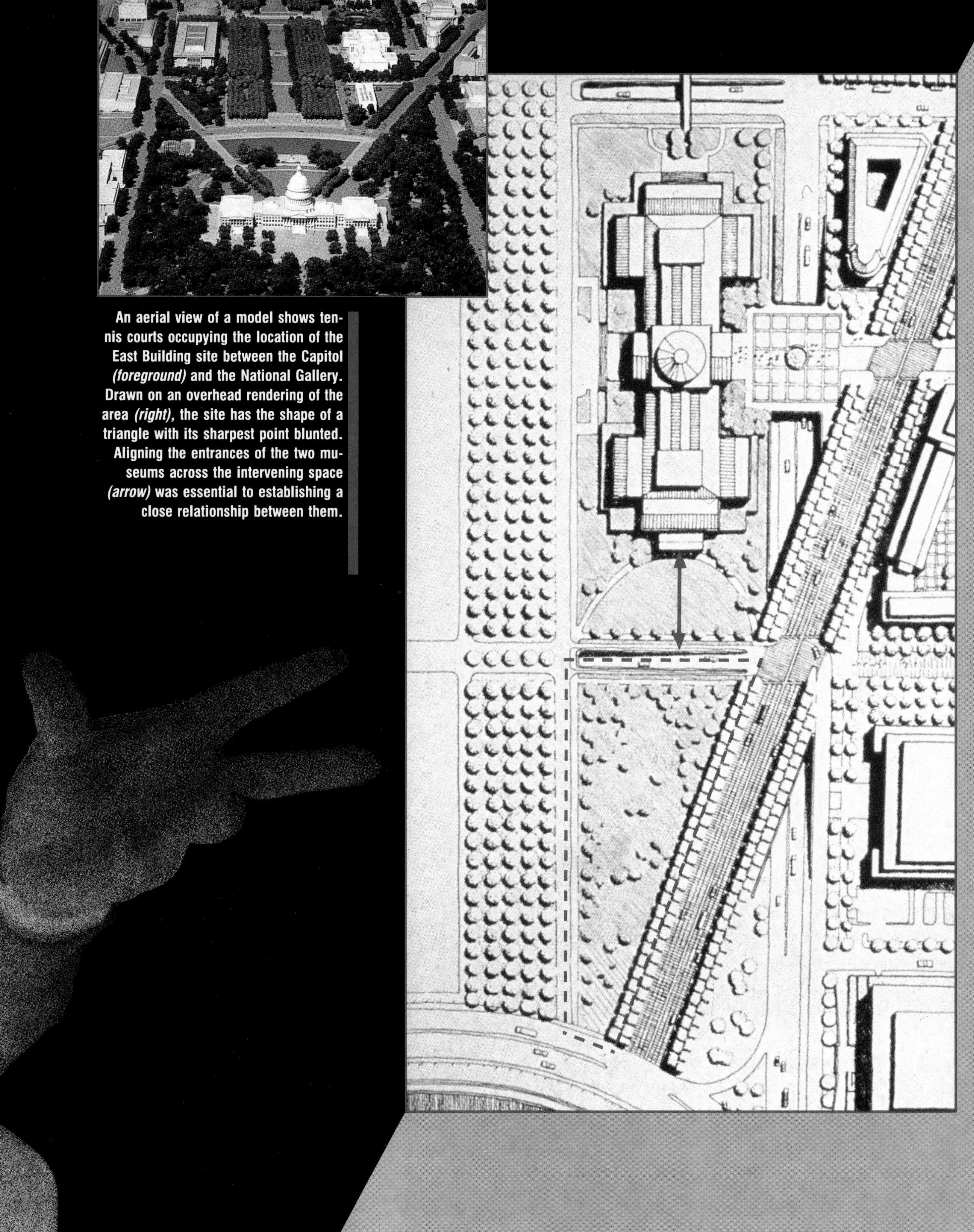

An aerial view of a model shows tennis courts occupying the location of the East Building site between the Capitol *(foreground)* and the National Gallery. Drawn on an overhead rendering of the area *(right)*, the site has the shape of a triangle with its sharpest point blunted. Aligning the entrances of the two museums across the intervening space *(arrow)* was essential to establishing a close relationship between them.

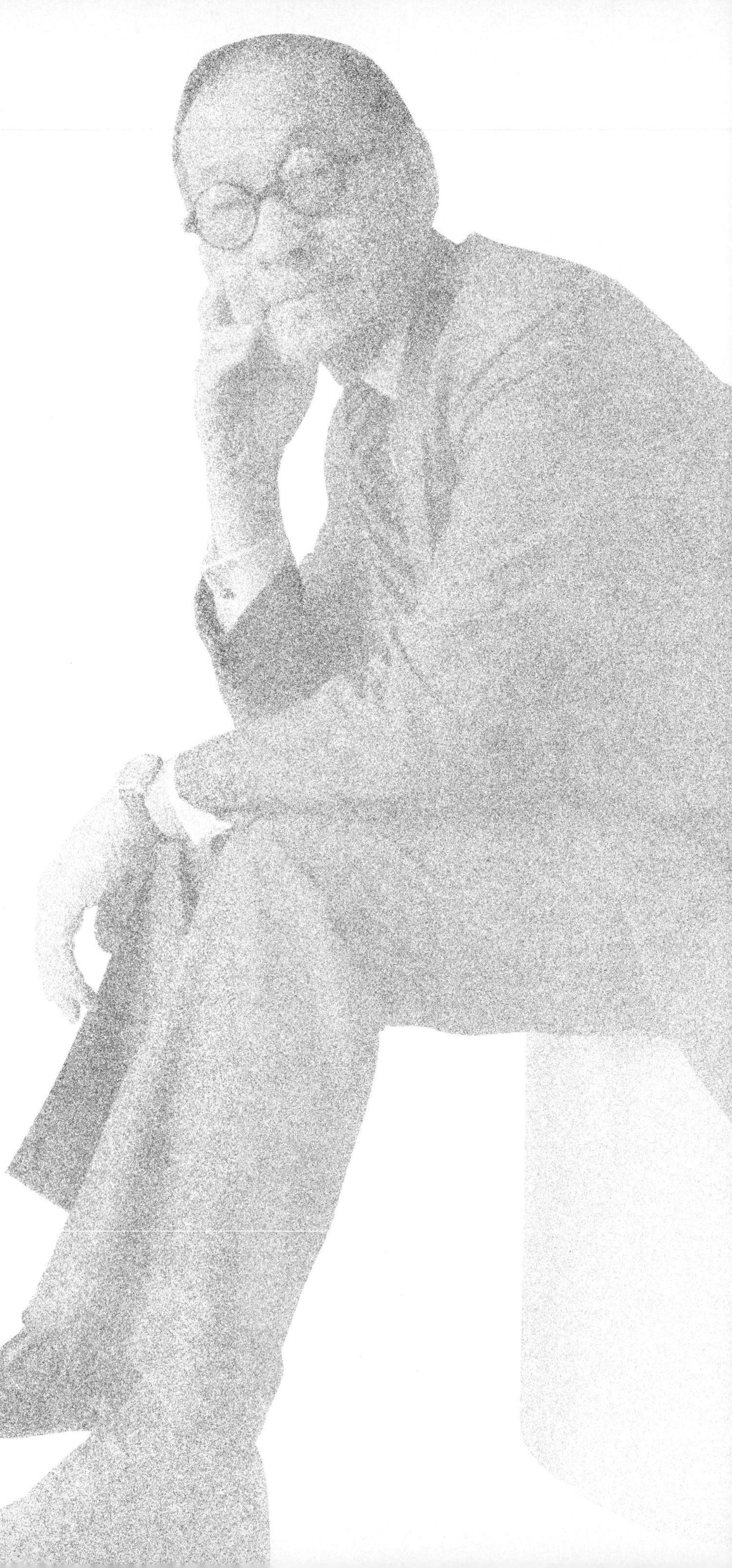

THE MUSES AT WORK

A fuzzy boundary separates the preparation and incubation stages of creativity. Incubation, the largely subconscious process of problem solving, can begin almost simultaneously with preparation, as trial solutions spring into awareness. Or the incubation process may not begin until preparation is virtually complete.

In Pei's case, incubation might be said to have gotten under way shortly after he won the commission to design the East Building, when he and National Gallery director Carter Brown departed for a three-week tour of museums in Europe.

During this preparatory jaunt, the two men came to recognize the importance of daylight in art museums and that a big museum presented itself best as a collection of smaller ones, ideas that would find their way into the design of the East Building.

But the insight, the flash of illumination that crystallized the design for the museum, came weeks later, as Pei flew to New York one afternoon in 1968 after a planning session in Washington. Picking up a red ballpoint pen, the architect quickly sketched a building composed of two triangles. The larger—a symmetrical triangle with its centerline on the axis of the Pope Building—would be gallery space. The smaller triangle would house the study center and offices.

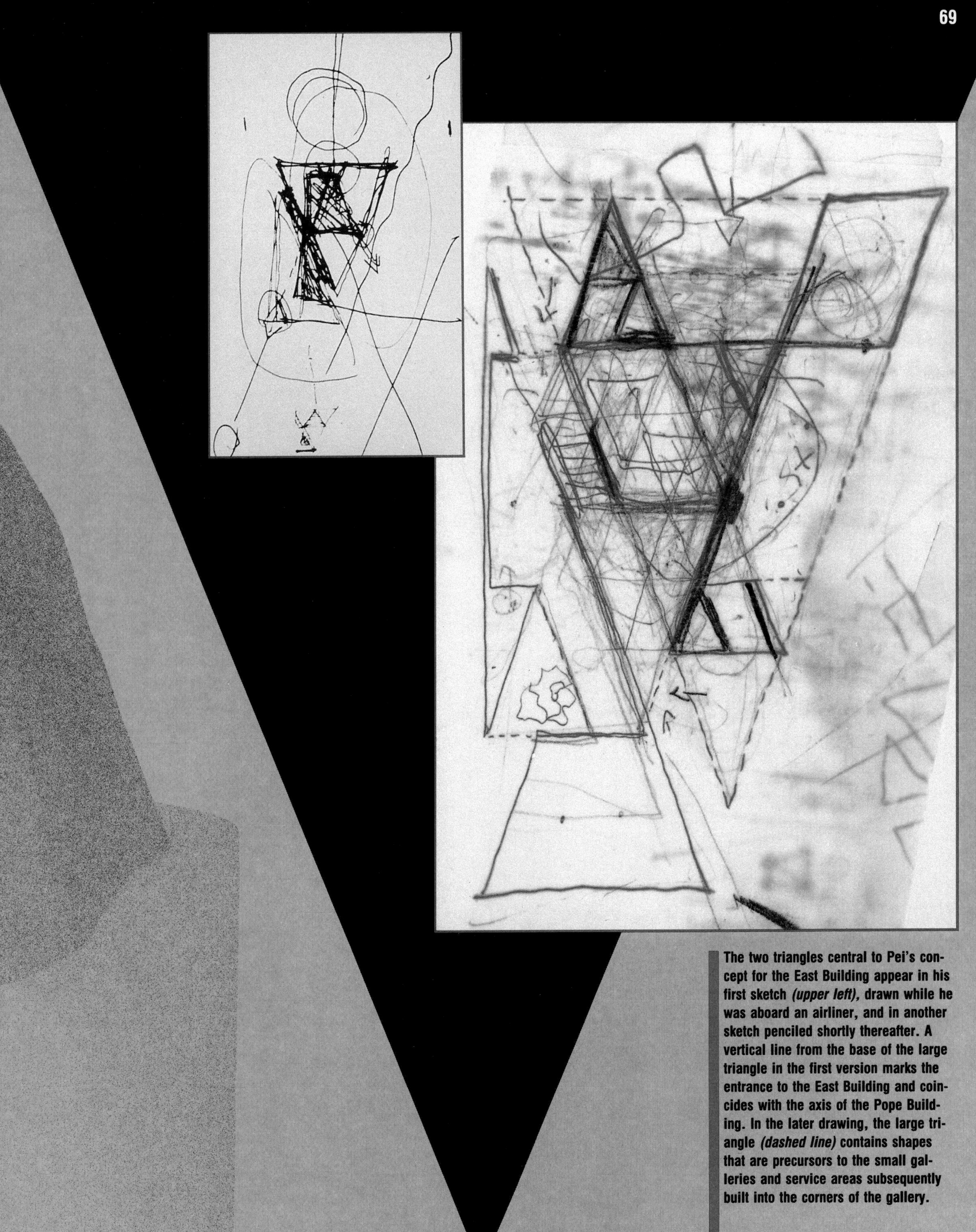

The two triangles central to Pei's concept for the East Building appear in his first sketch *(upper left)*, drawn while he was aboard an airliner, and in another sketch penciled shortly thereafter. A vertical line from the base of the large triangle in the first version marks the entrance to the East Building and coincides with the axis of the Pope Building. In the later drawing, the large triangle *(dashed line)* contains shapes that are precursors to the small galleries and service areas subsequently built into the corners of the gallery.

SWEATING THE DETAILS

After inspiration comes the perspiration of getting the details right for the blueprints. Among the particulars Pei and his colleagues sorted out during this verification stage (which some psychologists expand to include construction) were the shapes of the intimate exhibition spaces in the corners of the triangle. Art hung in these narrow angles would be almost impossible to see, so Pei walled off the sharp corners, creating rooms with wider angles—the best viewing space for paintings. Behind the walls he put stairs, elevators, power cables, and other utilities.

The architect stipulated that marble for the facade come from an idle quarry in Tennessee that had supplied the stone for the National Gallery in the late 1930s. As in the earlier structure, darker tones of the marble would fill lower courses; upper courses would be lighter in hue—so that the building would seem substantial, yet airy. To achieve this goal, Pei had the quarry reopened and coaxed from retirement the 72-year-old marble expert who had been in charge of such details some four decades earlier.

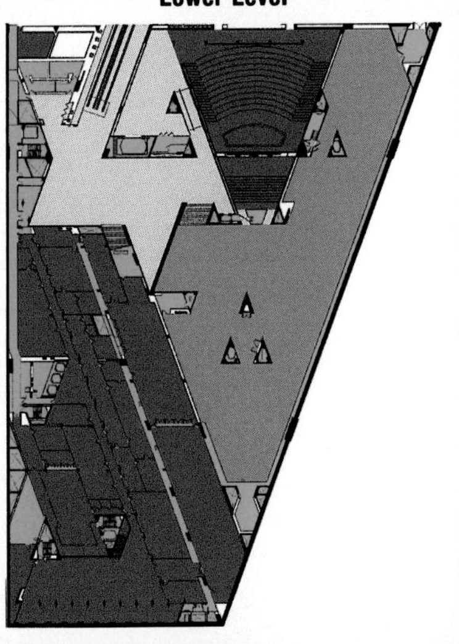

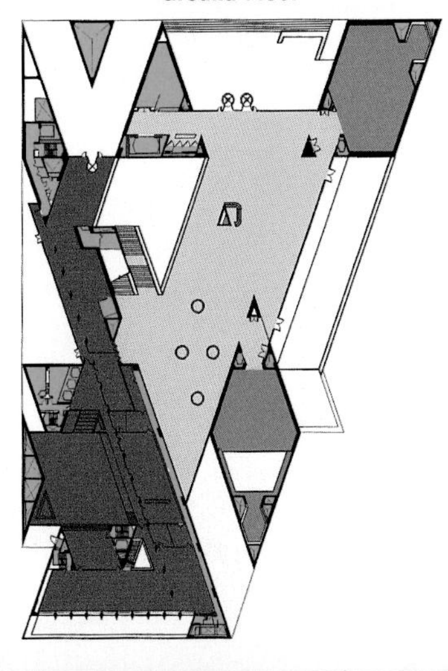

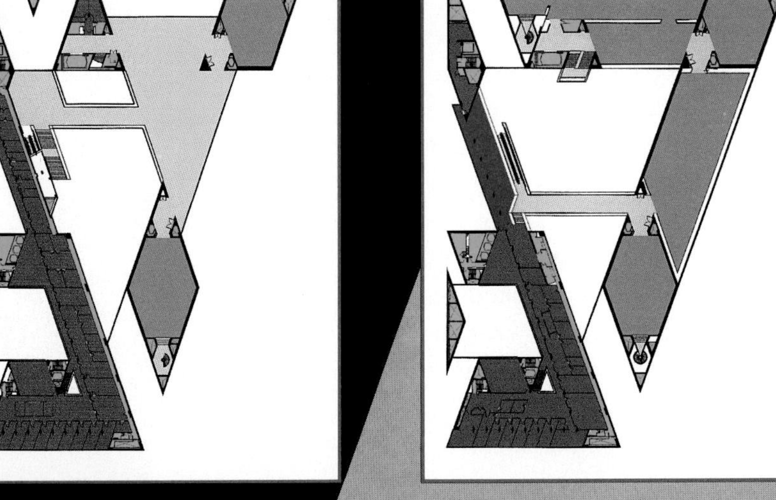

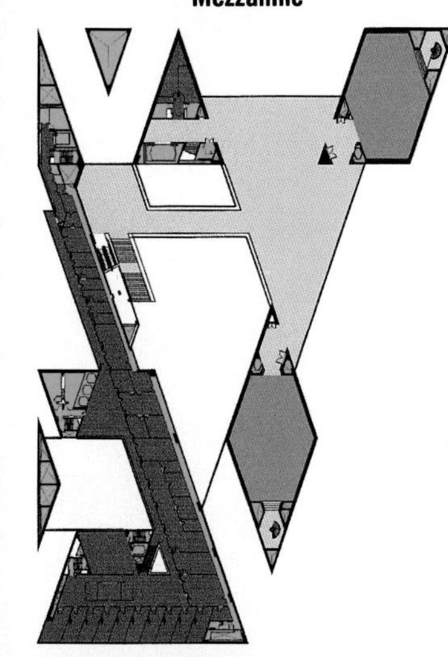

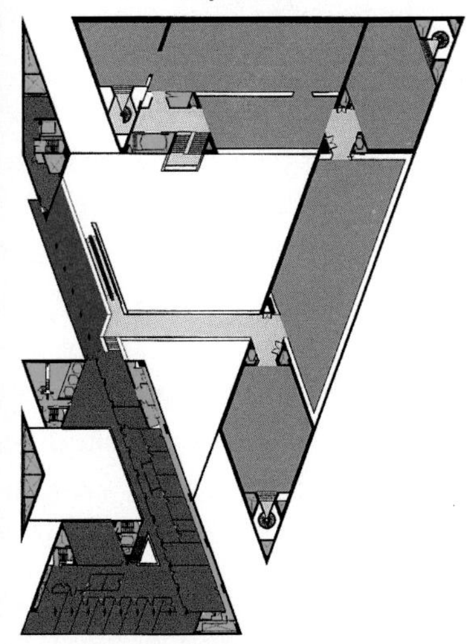

Exhibition Space

Lobbies and Foyers

Study Center

Utility Areas

Public Dining

Color-coded floor plans of each level in the East Building gallery show how space is allocated to various museum functions. Stacked atop each other, they form the structure shown in the transparent model at right, which also includes the eight-level study-center triangle. In designing the gallery, Pei once said that he wished to create "an interesting play of volumes against light." Perhaps the most striking example is the 80-foot-high central court, a triangular atrium rising from below ground level to the glass roof.

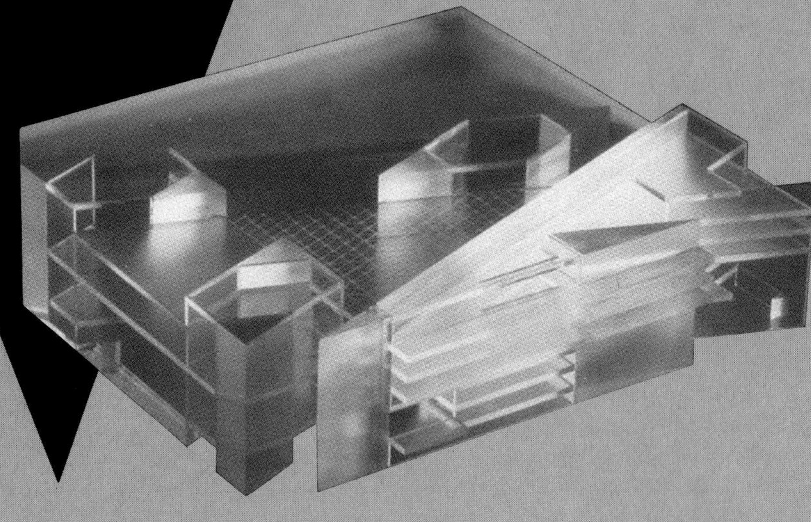

CREATION INCARNATE

Seven years under construction, the East Building opened in 1978 to rave reviews. Connoisseurs of architecture were dazzled. The structure, almost as much a sculpture as a building, turned out to be a marvelous museum.

Intended to allow legions of art enthusiasts to view masterworks in an agreeable setting, the East Building proved "people-friendly" from its first day. More than a million visitors poured through during the first two months. The warmth of the public reaction was evident in a flood of compliments that Pei's office received by mail, even from schoolchildren.

The way the East Building evolved stands as a classic example of the process that underlies a great variety of creative activities, from constructing grand theories in science to finding new ways of solving less profound problems of daily life. Yet, while anyone can put the process to good use, I. M. Pei is one of the relatively few people who have truly mastered it.

Opening-day visitors throng the plaza in front of the East Building *(above)* on June 1, 1978, just part of the 24,000 counted by day's end. A colossal Calder mobile *(right)*, 70 feet wide, turns gently in the air currents of the atrium. The sharpest angle of the East Building is the exterior 19-degree edge of the study center *(far right)*, so fascinating to visitors that their reaching hands have stained its marble surface.

3

Altered States

The Indian yoga master sat quietly, not in a Hindu temple in Calcutta or Varanasi, but in a laboratory at the Menninger Foundation, a temple of Western medicine in Topeka, Kansas. He seemed profoundly relaxed, despite the panoply of wires running from his scalp, chest, and arms to a raft of electronic monitors in the room. He lifted his right hand, palm up. And in the next two minutes, as several scientists watched in astonishment, the left side of the hand turned bright red, while the right side went ashy gray. Instruments measuring his body temperature showed that in the two areas of the hand, a mere two inches apart, there was a difference of 10 degrees Fahrenheit. It seemed that Swami Rama, a middle-aged mystic who had been trained in the psychophysical discipline of yoga since the age of four, had just done what many scientists firmly declared could not be done: He had controlled by his will a body function—blood flow—that was supposed to be strictly involuntary.

Husband-and-wife researchers Elmer and Alyce Green, who in the 1960s and 1970s had helped pioneer Menninger's studies of the links between mind and body, marveled along with their colleagues at the swami's accomplishments. He himself, however, seemed to

find nothing very mysterious in his mastery of his inner mechanics. "All of the body is in the mind," he was wont to explain serenely, "but not all of the mind is in the body."

The swami's lovely, mystifying words, which hint at much and explain little, offered a poetic account of his powers, but not a scientific one. In fact, it has taken Western science many years to become relatively comfortable with the notion that the mind is capable of demonstrating extraordinary powers, or manifesting extraordinary quirks, when it achieves an extraordinary state—an altered state of consciousness.

There are certain characteristics common to virtually all altered states of consciousness, or ASCs, no matter what triggers them. Among these traits are a diminished sense of self, perhaps even a lessening of discrimination between the self and other objects or individuals; a distorted perception of time; and a decrease in inhibitions. But science has no very precise language to define or delineate altered states, except to say that they are something other than ordinary consciousness, the state of mind in which one usually drives a car or chats with a neighbor. In an altered state, by contrast, one might dream or daydream, reach heights of ecstasy, or writhe in madness.

Seated on the banks of the Ganges River in 1973, Indian mystic Swami Rama *(above)* demonstrates his control of supposedly involuntary physiological functions such as heart rate while American psychophysiologists Elmer and Alyce Green monitor readings from electrodes taped to his body. The Greens' research led to the conclusion that almost anyone, with training, could learn to control these functions. A decade later, biofeedback, as the technique is now known, had become a popular medical practice. Today, computers translate measurements of a patient's body temperature, brain waves, heart rate, and other physiological responses into readily understandable visual information *(right)*.

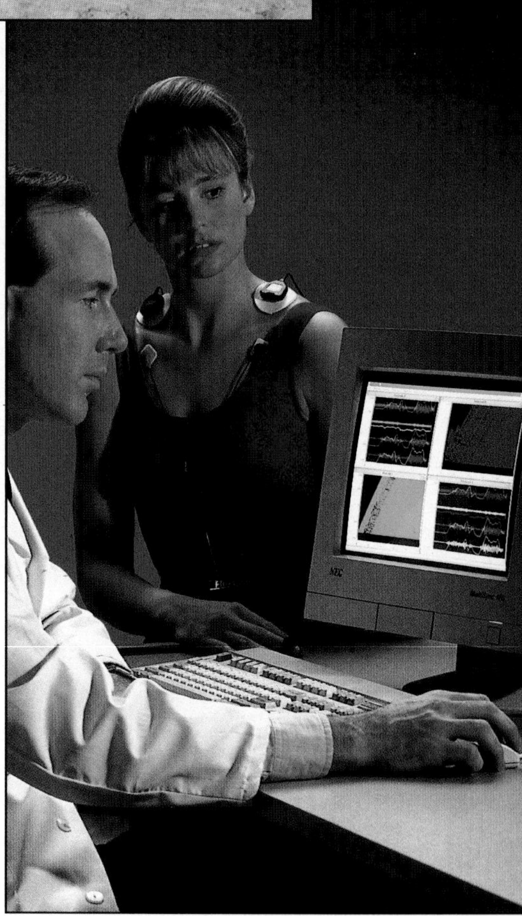

The mysterious realm of altered states is rendered even murkier by the inevitable question of what is "ordinary" and what is not, but even so, science posits two broad types of altered states. One is a quieting of the mind, the "reverie," as the Greens termed Swami Rama's condition. Such powerful mental stillness is produced by the limiting or focusing of sensory stimulation. Meditation is one potential pathway to this profound tranquillity; prayer is another.

The other type of altered state, a virtual opposite of the first sort, is an overexcitation of the mind that is characterized by hallucinations. This hyperexcitement, or sensory overload, can result from a number of stimuli, both internal and external, among them psychoactive drugs, intense fear, sleep or food deprivation, extreme physical pain, or psychosis.

Different as they are, the two ASC categories can interweave and overlap. For example, sensory deprivation, while it can aid mental stillness, can also lead to hallucinations as intense as any induced by hallucinogenic drugs. And meditation can effect not just serenity, but ecstasy, an altered state that more resembles hallucination than reverie. Indeed, the word *ecstasy*, which comes from Greek words that mean "to stand outside oneself," was once synonymous with *madness*, as was the word *rapture*.

Altered states, as such word derivations suggest, are age-old. They manifested themselves in the dreams and trances of shamans in the earliest of human cultures, and they have persisted through many traditions of mysticism. The Islamic mystics known as Sufis, for instance, achieve trances through their whirling dance, and the Hindu practitioners of Tantra seek to achieve union with the Divine through, among other things, sexual ecstasy. In Christianity there are the many reported cases of the stigmata, in which mystics—through fasting or intense meditation and prayer—evince on their bodies the same bloody wounds that Jesus suffered during the Crucifixion.

Exotic as these examples may be, there are far more common forms of altered states. Most people have experienced the mood swings produced by alcohol, drugs, or being in love, or the sense of peace conveyed by the meditative act of watching a beautiful sunset. There are, in fact, so many triggers for producing altered states that any attempt to list them all inevitably turns into a comic enterprise. "Presumably one could flip into an altered state of consciousness by pedaling an Exercycle in a dark room for twelve hours," notes anthropology writer Rob Schultheis, "or smoking six pipes full of strong tobacco on top of a three-day fast, or staring at the test-pattern mandala on the television set from two a.m. until six."

But while altered states are both ancient and ubiquitous, only recently have they become subjects of scientific study. For centuries, rationalism went in one direction, religion in another, and such nebulous matters as trances were considered strictly the province of the latter. Mental states were far too vague and subjective to satisfy the strictures of the scientific method, which depends on objective observation. Poets and mystics and possibly madmen dealt with such things as altered states; scientists did not. But as science progressed to explore more deeply the infinitely large and infinitely small realms of the universe, a sort of revolution took place.

Observation—the mainstay of empirical science—became impossible once the things being studied were too big or too little to see. So, in the 20th century, scientists came to rely more and more on a theory's logical or mathematical elegance to support its validity. In this atmosphere, mysticism and science began to converge.

As scientists got used to the notion that one did not have to see a thing to study it, that elusive and ineffable entity known as consciousness became an ever more respectable subject of inquiry. And in the 1960s, as a social revolution merged with the scientific one, even skewed forms of consciousness—altered states—made their way into scientific laboratories.

During the social upheavals of the 1960s, a hallmark of the counterculture was the intriguing imagery and changes in awareness described by people who were experimenting with psychedelic drugs. The reports aroused the curiosity of several young scientists at the time, among them Charles Tart, a psychologist at the University of California at Davis. In 1970 Tart edited a large book called *Altered States of Consciousness*, which is still considered a landmark volume for students of ASCs. At the time the book came out, Tart was himself rigorously investigating altered states and publishing his results in *Science* and other journals. In 1971, for example, Tart analyzed the responses of 150 marijuana users to a detailed questionnaire, then documented their experiences in *Nature*. Ninety-nine percent of the pot smokers reported an enhanced ability to discern musical notes and other sounds while under the drug's influence; 57 percent responded affirmatively to the statement that, while stoned, "I think I've said something when actually I've only thought about saying it."

Tart, perhaps more than anyone else, brought altered states squarely within the realm of serious science, mostly through his proposals for new investigative methods for exploring them. According to him, the objective observer—that essential figure of classical science—is useless in studying altered states because there may be nothing for him to see: A yogi in deep meditation may appear virtually comatose to the observer, who has no way of seeing or sharing the lush garden that may be flowering inside the yogi's head. The trick, said Tart, is not to apply objectivity, but to join in the subjectivity, to somehow get inside a subject's altered consciousness. This is necessary, he explained, because, in dealing with altered states, reality is relative, depending upon the state of consciousness in which it is perceived.

Tart proposed a new discipline called state-specific science, in which investigators would be trained to undergo certain altered states and report in rigorous, disciplined fashion what they saw. They would, for example, experience the confused and disoriented landscape of sensory deprivation and translate it into a common language, so it could be treated the same way as other scientific data—collected, quantified, replicated, and studied. Today, for the most part, state-specific science exists in theory only. Even so, Tart, in trying to bring some method to ASC investigations, went a long way toward lending legitimacy to such research, thus aiding other young scientists who were entering the field.

One of those was Ronald K. Siegel, a psychopharmacologist who would become one of the world's leading experts on a particular kind of altered state—the hallucinations produced by drugs. Siegel's work in the field began in the 1960s when, as a graduate student in psychology at Dalhousie University in Halifax, Nova Scotia, he had occasion to feed a laboratory homing pigeon a powerful extract of marijuana. As Siegel recalled the experiment years later, the pigeon's normal flight pattern took on bizarre aberrations: "He did this kamikaze nosedive to the ground." A small quantity of the extract remained, and the young scientist decided to take it himself, whereupon, he remembered, "I did a kamikaze nosedive to the ground, where I was laid up for about eight or nine hours, surrounded by these wondrous visions."

Intrigued, Siegel began adapting a

number of standard behavioral experiments he was already doing with laboratory animals. For instance, he gave LSD to pigeons that had been trained to respond to a flashing light on a screen by pecking a button of the same color. If, when confronted by a blank screen, the pigeon nonetheless pecked a blue button, Siegel could surmise that the bird was hallucinating blue. From these beginnings would eventually come years of carefully controlled studies into the effects of LSD, marijuana, cocaine, amphetamines, and various other psychoactive drugs on human volunteers at the University of California Neuropsychiatric Institute in Los Angeles, where the scientist began working in 1970.

One of Siegel's goals in exploring drug-induced ASCs, not unlike Tart's approach to altered states in general, was to develop a standardized vocabulary so that all scientists could understand in the same way a subject's description of the experience. To that end, Siegel schooled his volunteers in precise accounts, using such terms as wavelengths and millimicrons, of the sizes, colors, and forms of their visions. For Siegel, however, the methodology was only the means to an end. While still a graduate student, he had begun collecting the accounts of friends who took drugs, in an effort to find out whether hallucinations—supremely private and subjective experiences—might have some qualities in common, no matter who experienced them. In fact, Siegel found that the stages of his friends' hallucinations followed a pattern: Simple geometric forms came first, then more complex, more personal scenes developed; where some people saw deer heads, for instance, others saw angels, or their mother's face, or little green men.

Struck by the similarities in progression, Siegel was seeking other commonalities when, in 1968, he came across a book that had been written 40 years earlier by Heinrich Klüver, an experimental psychologist at the University of Chicago. Klüver's experiments with mescal showed that everyone who ingested the hallucinogenic peyote cactus saw four basic patterns: tunnel, spiral, cobweb, and lattice, or gridlike, designs. Siegel was stunned; these were the same geometric forms he had found in subjects taking marijuana and LSD.

Siegel wrote to Klüver to let him know of his own findings with drugs other than peyote. The elder scientist expressed no great surprise at the young man's discovery and suggested that the same effects would probably be produced by a number of triggers, including other drugs, the mental disorders paranoia and schizophrenia, as well as vivid dreams, fever deliriums, hunger, thirst, and fatigue. Klüver believed that the study of hallucinations, whatever the stimulus, might open a window to the uncharted territories of the mind, an idea that would guide Siegel's work for years to follow.

In the course of his research, Siegel found that Klüver had been correct. Siegel's psychonauts—"voyagers through the mind," as he called his many volunteers—hallucinated the same four basic geometric forms regardless of the drug they were on. Moreover, Siegel found these same forms in the drug-influenced art of other cultures. The brains of American college students in California and those of Huichol Indians in Mexico (*page* 81) obviously hallucinated in the same way. Even the images of the second, more personal phase of hallucination seemed to follow certain neural rules. The images—whatever they consisted of—pulsated before they revolved, and they multiplied and metamorphosed in common ways. Bright lights clustered in the center of the visual field.

Siegel concluded that hallucinations

express a visual imagery that is common to everyone. That conclusion implied in turn that something in the brain's electrical wiring predetermined the pattern that all hallucinations follow.

Siegel eventually expanded his work to include hallucinations caused by stimuli other than drugs. In one study, for example, he found that people hallucinated when facing a combination of isolation and life-threatening stress. This appeared to be true of prisoners of war as well as victims of rape, kidnapping, terrorism, robbery, and alleged UFO abductions.

Using himself as a guinea pig, as had long been his habit, Siegel submitted to a sensory-isolation test that involved being locked inside a steel cage that was placed in a deserted building. He wanted to see if imprisonment alone, without the threat of death, would be stressful enough to produce hallucinations. Siegel's co-experimenter, a Vietnam veteran who had suffered horrible hallucinations while he was a POW held in a bamboo cage, was supposed to visit and bring rice and water every 24 hours. Then the vet changed the ground rules. "Ever think you would die in a cage, buddy?" he asked Siegel, locking him up and walking away. Faced with the possibility of impending death, Siegel began hallucinating before the first night was over. He saw the expected lattice patterns, heard the sound of his mother's voice, and dreamed about an escape through a maze of dry, dusty passages. Finally, three and a half days later, the veteran returned, rescuing his very angry, if enlightened, colleague.

Hallucinations are often fascinating or troubling, but they can also signal serious underlying problems. Czar Peter the Great and Russian novelist Fyodor Dostoyevsky experienced hallucinations associated with epilepsy; the great German composer Ludwig van Beethoven and the American writer Edgar Allan Poe hallucinated when they drank alcohol. Hallucinations, in fact, have been the hallmark of psychotic disorders for centuries, even though the term *hallucination* was not used in the current sense until 1837, when French psychiatrist Jean-Étienne Esquirol first applied it in a textbook on mental illness. (The term *hallucinate* has Latin roots meaning "to babble," or "to dream," from an earlier Greek word that means "to be disturbed" or "to wander.") Since Esquirol's time, hallucinations have been linked to a variety of mental illnesses, as well as to Parkinson's disease, strokes, infections of the central nervous system, and numerous other neurological disorders.

People who suffer from severe migraine headaches, for example, often hallucinate extraordinary bodily distortions. C. W. Lippman, who in 1952 became the first physician to report this association, told of one patient who felt as if her left ear were "ballooning out six inches or more" when she was afflicted by a migraine. Another sufferer reported feeling so tall as to "be able to look down on the tops of others' heads." And in a third case, a man supposedly felt as if the right side of his body were twice as big as the left. This type of hallucination is known to neurologists as the Alice-in-Wonderland syndrome, because its symptoms resemble the fluctuations in size and shape that plagued the young heroine of Lewis Carroll's 1865 fantastical novel. The novelist himself suffered what he called "bilious headaches" and may have experienced the migraine-induced distortions himself. In fact, it was Lippman's belief that "Alice trod the paths of a wonderland well known to her creator."

However fascinating the triggers and content of hallucinations may be, philosophers and scientists have long pondered other questions concerning these visions: for the philosopher, how do hallucinations operate, and for the scientist, what new information

A Huichol Indian yarn painting, influenced by traditional peyote visions, includes radiating designs that resemble patterns hallucinated by American students high on mescaline, the drug derived from peyote. These and other shapes—spirals, lattices, cobwebs—appear in hallucinations the world over, suggesting that such visions have a neurological basis.

can hallucinations reveal about how the brain works?

Philosopher Daniel C. Dennett of Tufts University in Medford, Massachusetts, explains hallucinations by means of a metaphor involving an elaborate party game. In the game, a person chosen as the dupe is informed that, while he is out of earshot, someone will recall a dream and recount its story line to the others in the room. When the dupe returns, he is to ask questions that can be answered "yes" or "no" so that he may reconstruct the dream and use that information to psychoanalyze, then identify, the dreamer. Once the dupe leaves, however, the host changes the rules. No one is to relate a dream. Rather, the people in the room will answer the dupe's questions according to this rule: "yes," if the last letter of the last word of his question falls in the first half of the alphabet; "no," if the letter falls in the last half of the alphabet. Thus the question "Does the dream take place outdoors?" is answered "no." And "Does it involve food?" is answered "yes." The only other rule is that answers to later questions should not contradict any earlier answers.

The arbitrary responses result in stories so outlandish that the dupe invariably ends up with the impression that the dreamer must be, as Dennett put it, "a very sick and troubled individual." At that point, the assembled party reveals that the dupe—because he asked the questions that evoked the story—is himself the author of the dream. But in another sense, of course, the dream really has no author. In Dennett's opinion, the accumulating details have produced a narrative "with no authorial intentions or plans at all—an illusion with no illusionist."

Like the dupe who expects the game will be played according to the rules he was given, claims Dennett, the brain expects things to function normally. So even though incoming data may be disordered or random—merely arbitrary yeses and nos—the brain will try, according to its lights, to give shape to the nonsense. Or, as Dennett expressed it, the hallucination that unfolds is framed by the "current expectations, concerns, obsessions, and worries" of the person having it. But unlike the game, which requires a noncontradiction rule, hallucinations thrive on contradictions and have no need for any rules to explain why a hand turns into a claw, for example, or why a New Hampshire

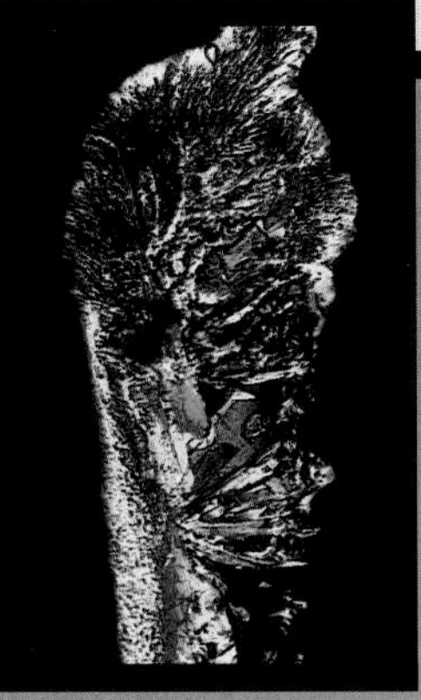

Seeing Things

Intrigued by the fact that virtually all hallucinations feature the same basic geometric shapes—funnels, spirals, lattices, and cobwebs—a prominent mathematician and biologist has formulated a theory that may help explain why. According to the University of Chicago's Jack Cowan, the key lies in the cellular architectures of the eye and the brain.

Each light-gathering cell in the retina of the eye connects to its own small cluster of neurons in the visual cortex, the area at the back of the brain devoted to sight. The position of retinal cells relative to each other is matched in the cortex, with neighboring cells represented by neighboring neuronal clusters, but the precise arrangement of cells and neurons differs. As a result, the particular pattern of retinal cells stimulated by a given object or image causes neurons in the visual cortex to fire in a predictable but different pattern.

Normally, of course, neurons in the visual cortex are activated only when their corresponding retinal cells are stimulated. But Cowan hypothesizes that, under the influence of drugs such as LSD (shown above in crystalline form), the neurons can begin firing on their own, and the brain interprets these signals as if the eyes had indeed seen something. In the early stages of intoxication, according to Cowan's theory, the neurons often fire in regular, striped patterns—a kind of fallback reaction to the drug's overall destabilizing effects on neuronal activity. As illustrated at right, the orientation these striped patterns happen to assume determines which type of geometric shape seems to appear before the eyes.

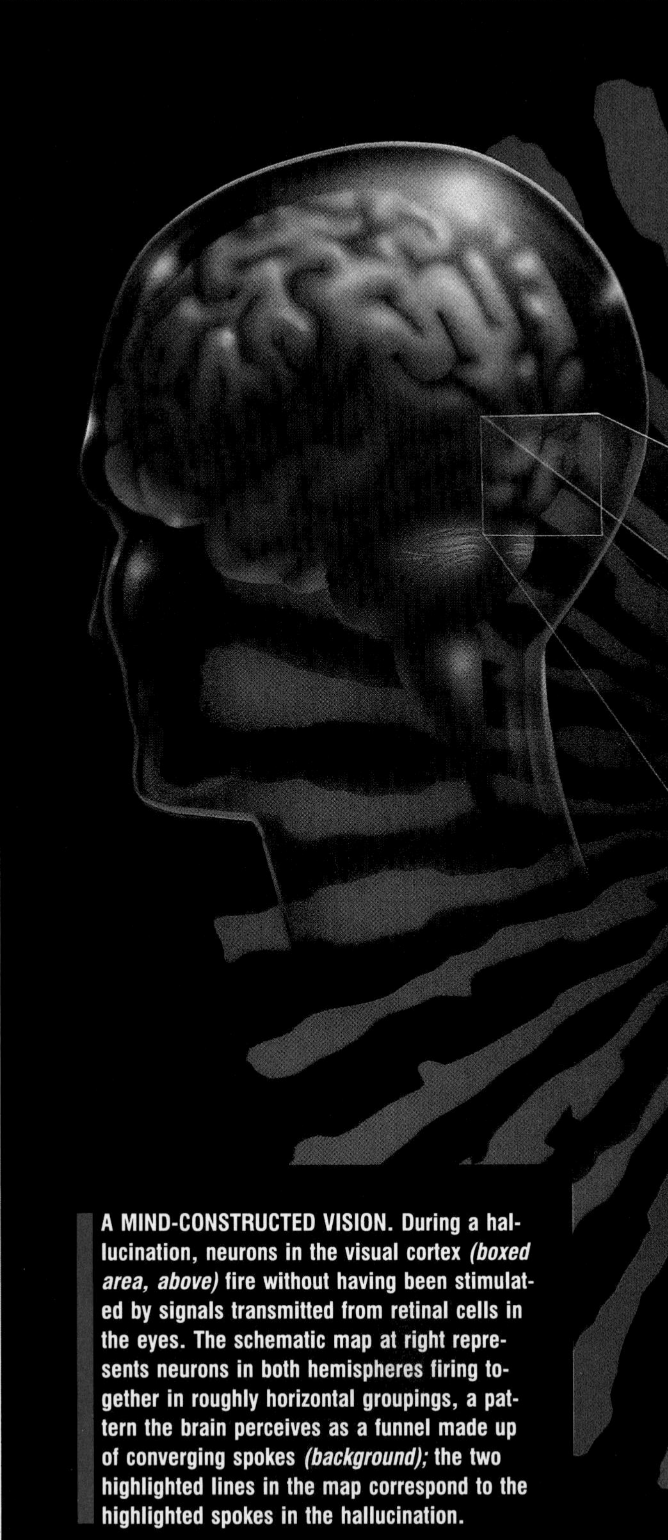

A MIND-CONSTRUCTED VISION. During a hallucination, neurons in the visual cortex *(boxed area, above)* fire without having been stimulated by signals transmitted from retinal cells in the eyes. The schematic map at right represents neurons in both hemispheres firing together in roughly horizontal groupings, a pattern the brain perceives as a funnel made up of converging spokes *(background);* the two highlighted lines in the map correspond to the highlighted spokes in the hallucination.

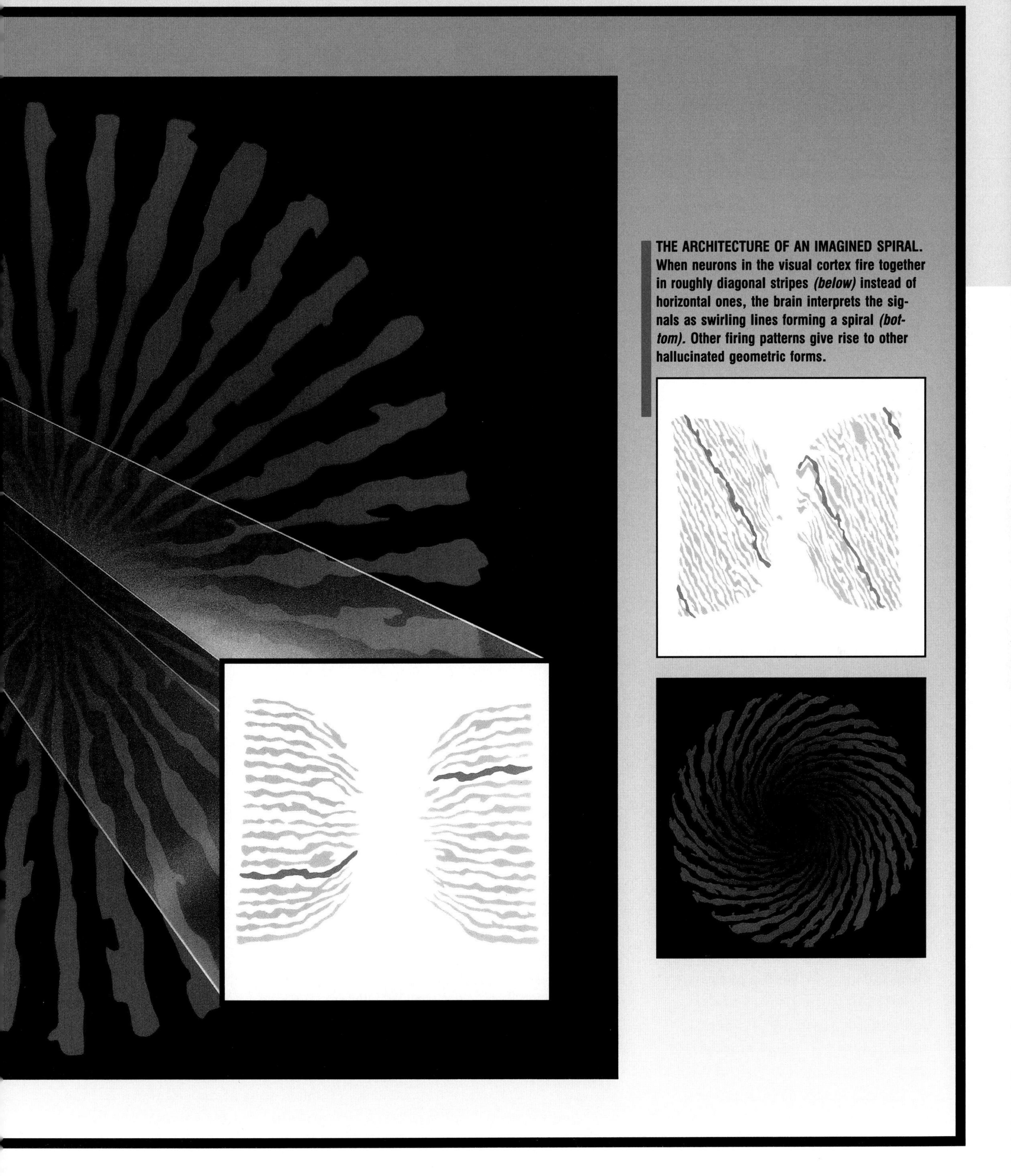

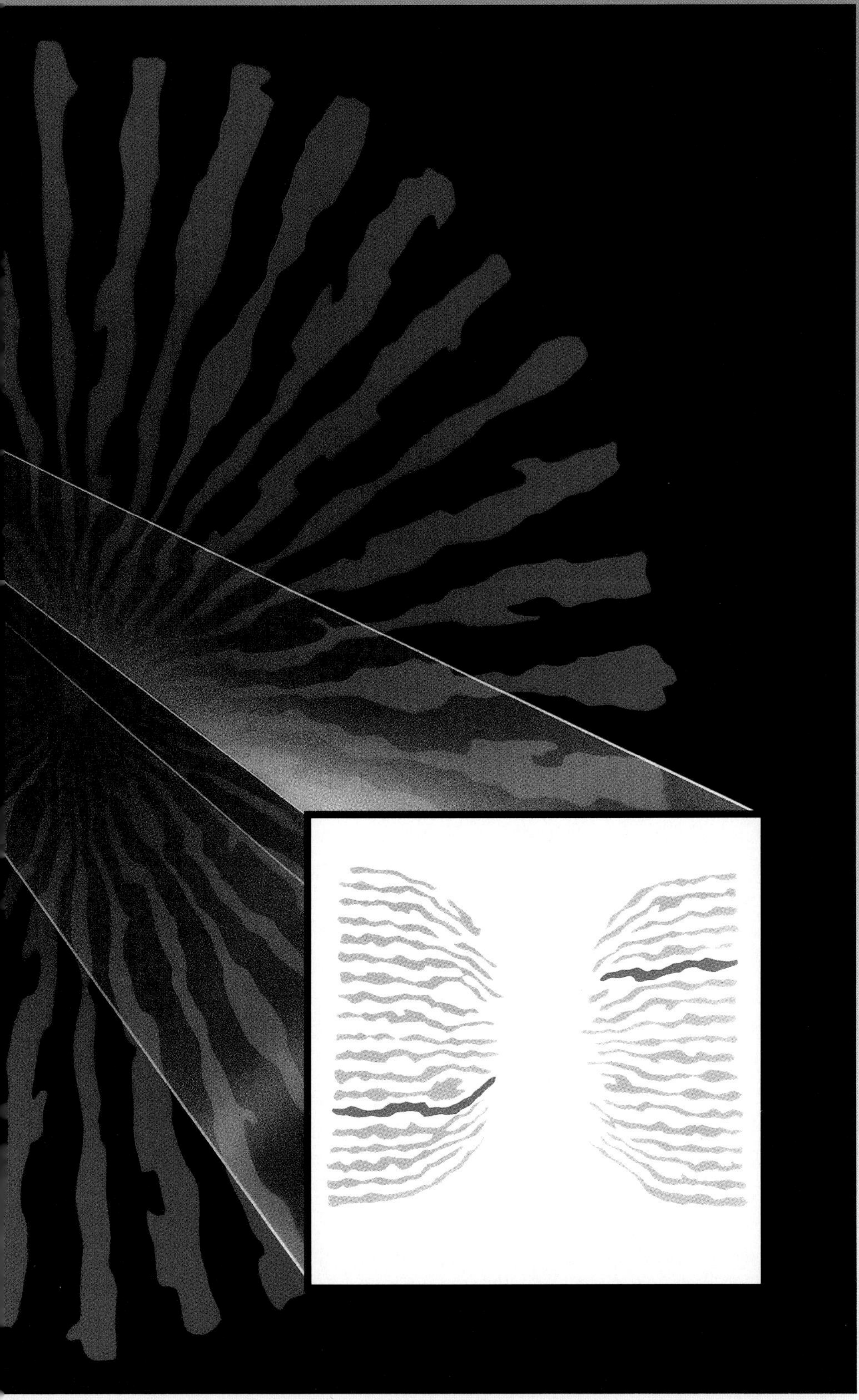

THE ARCHITECTURE OF AN IMAGINED SPIRAL. When neurons in the visual cortex fire together in roughly diagonal stripes *(below)* instead of horizontal ones, the brain interprets the signals as swirling lines forming a spiral *(bottom).* Other firing patterns give rise to other hallucinated geometric forms.

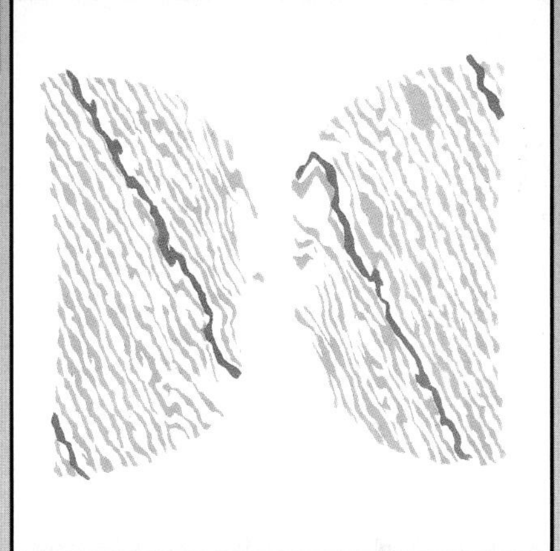

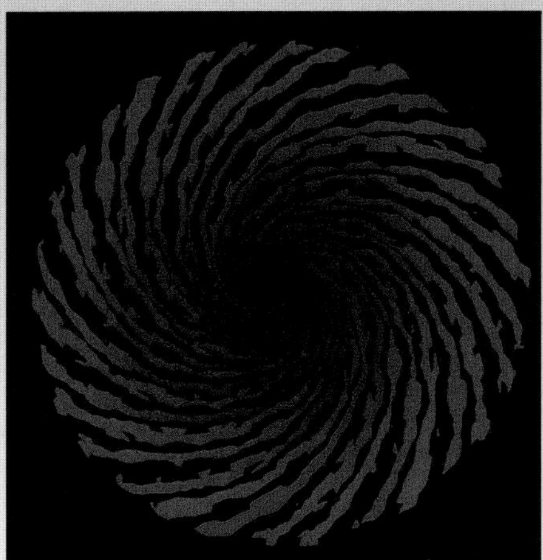

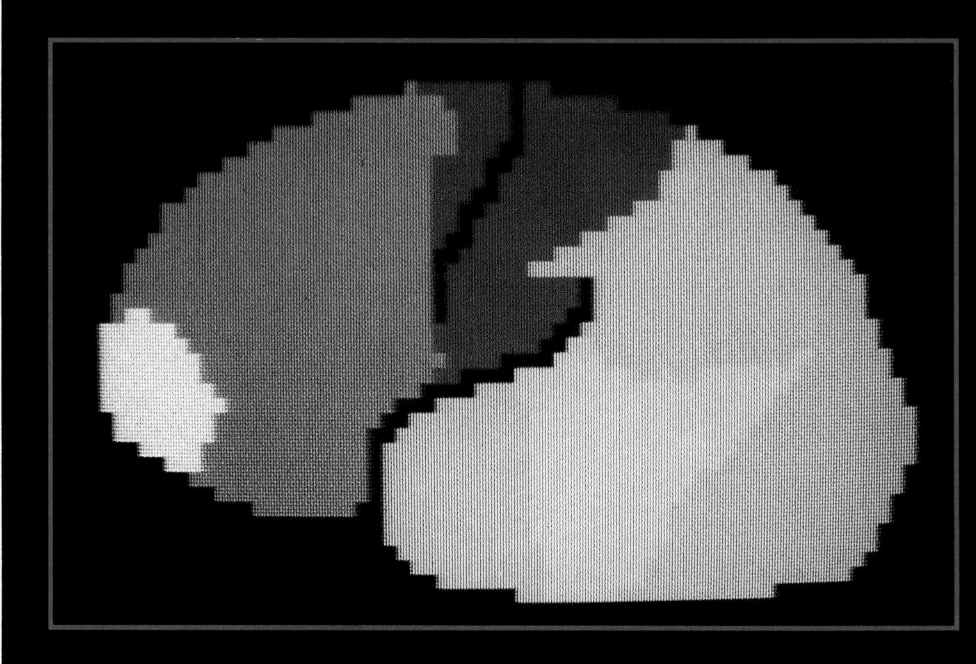

farmhouse becomes, without rhyme or reason, a château in France.

Dennett's model serves to illustrate how prolonged sensory deprivation can produce hallucinations: Because the brain, according to Dennett, is always trying to satisfy its curiosity, always generating hypotheses and testing them, a brain suddenly confronted by a lack of data is forced to lower its threshold for information until some bit of neural noise gets amplified into significance. As the theory has it, the noise is then read as a signal that either confirms or contradicts a hypothesis that the brain is pursuing, until gradually a hallucination develops—born, in Dennett's words, "of nothing more than anxious expectation and chance confirmation." Similarly, a drug that induces a hallucination does not contain the elaborate "story" it produces in the taker. Rather, the drug probably helps to create the illusion of a story by directly raising, lowering, or simply disordering the brain's threshold for significant information.

The sensory-deprived brain, explains Dennett, is like the frustrated hunter who on the last day of the deer-hunting season sees a deer—antlers, white tail, and all—while actually looking at a cow or another hunter. The first hunter so obsessively asks himself "Is it a deer?" and so repeatedly gets a "no," that finally "a bit of noise in the system gets mistakenly amplified into a YES, with catastrophic results."

As philosophers continue to ponder the workings of hallucinations, neurologists search for ways those workings may be grounded in physiology: What can these extreme altered states reveal to advance the ongoing effort to map the brain?

One of the first hints of the neurology underlying hallucinations was provided by the studies of Wilder Penfield at Montreal's McGill University in 1945. The Canadian neurosurgeon and his colleagues discovered that by touching an electrode to the visual cortex or temporal lobe of conscious, locally anesthetized individuals, the investigators could elicit hallucinations of moving colored lights, geometric forms, lines, and stars. By stimulating the amygdala—a component of the limbic system, which apparently plays a role in governing memory and emotions—Penfield could evoke recollections and emotional responses so vivid that it seemed that the subject was actually experiencing what he or she was, in fact, only remembering.

In 1979 researchers in New York and Paris who were experimenting with the powerful hallucinogen PCP, often called angel dust on the street, found further evidence for a connection between the limbic system and the occurrence of hallucinations. By tagging PCP with radioactivity, the researchers found that the drug binds to receptors in the hippocampus, another component of the limbic system, and in the cerebral cortex, the thin covering of the cerebrum and the apparent seat of such higher cognitive functions as thinking, planning, and

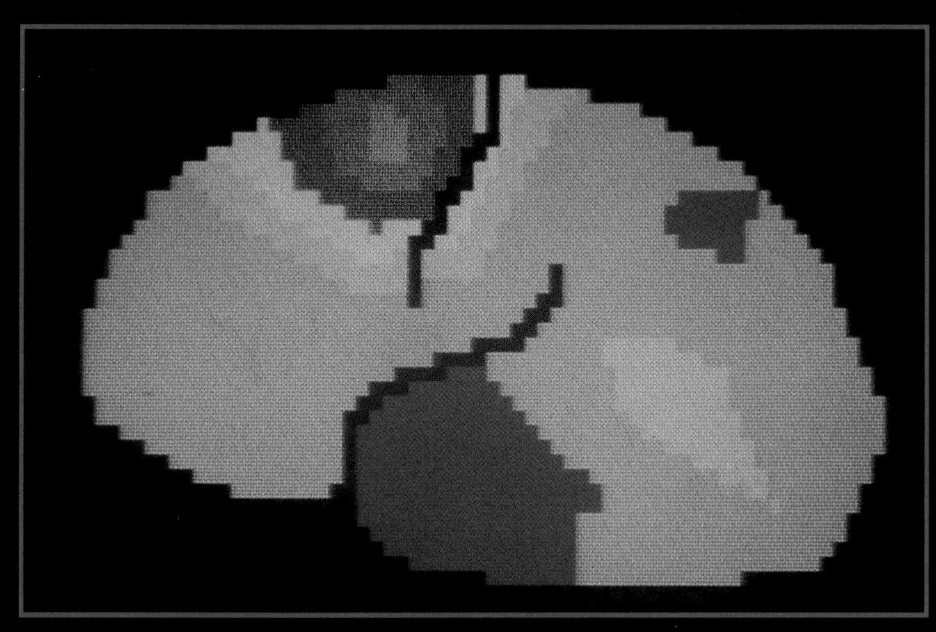

DECEPTIVE ELATION. Words and ideas often seem to flow more easily after the first glass of wine or beer, creating a feeling of pleasant stimulation. Physically, however, the brain actually becomes more sluggish as alcohol reduces blood flow to the brain and interferes with electrochemical messages traveling between cells. The first brain functions to begin shutting down seem to affect anxiety and inhibition, which explains why the mood can lift even while brain activity plummets.

This lowered activity can be seen in heavy drinkers even when unintoxicated. The brain scan of an alcoholic *(near left)* shows very low blood-flow levels, depicted in blue and green; in contrast, the brain scan of a nonalcoholic *(far left)* exhibits normal blood flow, represented by yellow, red, pink, and white.

decision making. Since the cortex exerts control over the limbic system, the investigators wondered if PCP produced its effects by disconnecting these two parts of the brain. In the absence of cortical control, the researchers speculated, the limbic system might operate on its own, producing the kind of uninhibited violence and unpredictable behavior characteristic of angel dust users.

While hallucinations attracted a great deal of attention from researchers in the drug-drenched 1960s, the second broad category of altered states—those entailing an exceptional stillness of the mind—was by no means neglected: The same counterculture that was feverishly pursuing mind expansion through the use of psychedelic chemicals also began to embrace an import to the West from Eastern religions—meditation.

For the Zen Buddhist master or the Hindu yogi, meditation—achieving a profound quietness of the mind—can involve years of single-minded discipline to perfect. The variety of meditation that took root in the West, however, was far less rigorous, much more easily adapted to the smorgasbord mysticism of the Occident during the sixties. It was called transcendental meditation—TM—and it came to the West in the person of India's Maharishi Mahesh Yogi, a rather giggly guru who won considerable fame for instructing the Beatles and other celebrities and for his frequent presence on American talk shows.

The maharishi turned out to be something of a passing fad, but TM took hold. By the mid-1970s, between 400,000 and half a million Americans had taken it up. The technique required only 40 minutes a day—20 in the morning and 20 in the evening—of sitting still and repeating over and over a soothing syllable, one supposedly particular to each individual and supplied to that person, for a fee, by TM instructors. The syllable was called, in Sanskrit, a mantram—for some reason the plural mantra entered the popular language instead—and it was the key to TM. Proponents of TM contended that the practice could bring the mind to a fourth state of consciousness—beyond waking, sleeping, and dreaming—a "cosmic" consciousness that transcended ordinary reality. For 40 minutes a day, the faithful proclaimed, anyone who wanted to could achieve the kind of altered consciousness that Zen monks took 25 years to attain.

At its trendiest, TM was probably somewhat oversold. Nevertheless, when it moved from the talk shows to the science labs, it proved to have a certain substance. The man most responsible for bringing the technique under scientific scrutiny was Robert Keith Wallace. As an undergraduate student at the University of California at Los Angeles in the 1960s, Wallace had become a follower of the maharishi and a practitioner of TM. As a graduate student he decided to do his doctoral thesis in physiology on the technique.

Wallace wired 27 meditators to measure blood pressure, heart rate, rectal temperature, skin resistance, and brain waves during periods of meditation and periods of merely sitting still. His findings were dramatic: His subjects consumed 20 percent less oxygen and released 20 percent less carbon dioxide during meditation than they did while just sitting quietly. Their heart rates slowed by some three beats per minute; their skin response and brain waves suggested extreme relaxation. Their blood pressure dropped just before meditation and remained low during the meditative period. Their blood content of lactic acid, a substance produced by muscle tissue and normally increased under stress, plummeted and stayed down long after the meditation. All the measurements, in other words, suggested that transcendental meditation was a potent stress reliever that produced a highly relaxed, although wakeful, state of mind.

In March 1970 an account of Wallace's study appeared in the journal *Science* and caught the eye of Herbert Benson, a cardiologist and assistant professor of medicine at Harvard Medical School. Benson, who saw the technique as a potential boon to people suffering from high blood pressure, subsequently teamed up with Wallace for a set of experiments showing TM to be distinctly different from taking a nap or sitting quietly with the eyes shut. Their results helped to establish that meditation can assist in reducing blood pressure and thus could be beneficial for the treatment of cardiac arrhythmias, anxiety, and pain.

Benson and Wallace eventually went their separate ways. Wallace became the charter president of Maharishi International University, while Benson continued with his meticulous examination of the physical aspects of meditation. Benson learned, to Wallace's great disappointment no doubt, that although transcendental meditation did produce beneficial physiological responses, so did a number of other meditative techniques, some secular, some religious. Benson came to look at meditation of various kinds as the trigger for an inborn reflex that is physiologically opposite to the fight-or-flight response, in which fear prompts an increase in blood pressure, heart rate, and oxygen consumption. Benson called the physiological changes associated with meditation the "relaxation response."

While meditation was undergoing scrutiny in the West, it was also being studied scientifically closer to its Eastern origins. In Japan, the chief research tool was the electroencephalograph, a device that measures the frequency and amplitude of the tiny electrical currents that travel through the neurons of the brain's cortex. The machine prints out its measurements in the form of electroencephalograms, or EEGs, which show the patterns of electrical activity as oscillating waves. In a wakeful, alert state, the brain usually produces beta waves, which have low amplitude and high frequency. Alpha waves, characteristic of an individual who is awake but very relaxed with eyes closed, have a higher amplitude than beta waves but lower frequency. Theta waves, at an even lower frequency, usually indicate a descent into sleep.

In the 1960s, psychiatrist Akira Kasamatsu and neurophysiologist Tomio Hirai of the University of Tokyo

Déjà Vu: Time out of Mind

Most people have experienced déjà vu—that eerie feeling of having lived through an event before—but the phenomenon remains an abiding mystery. The most commonsensical (but perhaps most unsatisfying) explanation is simply that déjà vu stems from confusing a past experience with a similar situation in the present. Other explanations range from the paranormal to the mechanistic. Some believe déjà vu springs from telepathy or memories from past lives, or from visits undertaken during an out-of-body experience.

At the other extreme, a recurring popular theory proposes that déjà vu results simply from a delay in information transfer from one hemisphere of the brain to the other. Currently, neuroscientists speculate that déjà vu involves some activity, or even a malfunction in the temporal lobe, a region of the brain often linked with memory.

Psychologists, for their part, find the mental and emotional underpinnings of déjà vu a rich mine of unconscious motivations. Indeed, Sigmund Freud himself thought déjà vu would illuminate human psychology. For example, the mind may respond to a disturbing situation by manipulating its sense of time, whether to create a feeling of reassuring familiarity or perhaps to express a wish for a second chance. To complicate matters further, déjà vu experiences may also be related to dreams and waking fantasies, and have been reported to occur while dreaming. The matter seems no nearer resolution than it was in the fifth century, when Saint Augustine first discussed the origins of *falsae memoriae*, initiating the debate on the nature of time, memory, and mind that has intrigued philosophers and scientists ever since.

used EEGs to measure the brain waves of Zen monks meditating with their eyes half-open. Most of the monks produced the alpha waves characteristic of extreme relaxation with closed eyes. In the more experienced meditators, the alpha waves eventually gave way to the very slow theta waves that usually denote drowsiness. But the monks in this state seemed to be, although very relaxed, highly aware.

Kasamatsu and Hirai, in 1966, went on to investigate the relationship between meditation and mental competence, as measured by Zen students' ability to respond to koans, or metaphysical riddles whose solutions often lie beyond the grasp of Western logic. What, for instance, is the sound of one hand clapping? It turned out that Zen masters—who certainly were not measuring brain waves—nonetheless never accepted the solutions offered by trainees whose brains displayed the rapid beta waves typical of a normal, awake, active person. Rather, the researchers discovered, the monks accepted answers only by Zen trainees whose brains showed the alpha and theta waves characteristic of experienced meditators.

In both East and West, the early scientific probes of meditation caused considerable interest. However, much of the Western research that followed the original studies by Wallace and

Benson has proved either inconclusive or contradictory in pinning down exactly what kind of altered state meditation causes. In some studies, meditators produced strong alpha waves, while in others they showed strong beta activity instead.

Some of these apparent contradictions seem to have stemmed from the fact that Western science did not sufficiently take into account that there are many different meditative disciplines, each informed by a different philosophy. It should not be surprising, perhaps, that the brain waves of Kriya yogis, who attempt to control the body through various cleansing techniques and who try to shut out external stimulation, should look quite different from the brain waves of Zen practitioners, for instance, who advocate being open to every aspect of the world.

Science has tended to consider meditation as only passive awareness. But sometimes meditation has other goals. One is ecstasy. The final stage of some forms of Hindu meditation, for example, is known as samadhi, an ultimate bliss in which the material world vanishes and the individual loses the sense of self and finds union with God, or eternity, or some cosmic singularity.

Mystics seeking ecstasy have for centuries used a kind of meditative technique known as contemplation, entailing the intent focus on a soothing object—a tree, perhaps, or running water. The goal of this exercise is to empty the mind and achieve a profound mental quietness in which the barrier between the person and the object of contemplation disappears and a merger of subject and object is achieved. When this happens the state of calm is transformed into ecstasy and the person is overcome with a sense of oneness with the universe or knowledge of the secret of being.

The ecstatic state can also arise spontaneously. Anecdotal evidence suggests that it can happen while having sex or while running a marathon, while giving birth or while reading a poem. Ecstatic experiences are also known to occur in people suffering from schizophrenia and manic-depressive illness. And drugs of various sorts can trigger them as well. One patient under anesthesia for a short operation, for example, told of "a complete revelation about the ultimate truth of everything. I understood the 'entire works.' It was a tremendous illumination. I was filled with unspeakable joy."

Researchers at Yale University investigating the actions of psychedelic drugs on the brain believe they may have pinpointed the source of the ecstatic state and feelings of oneness with the universe. Recent research headed by Yale scientist George Aghajanian concentrated on the locus ceruleus, a part of the brain through which all sights, sounds, smells, tastes, and tactile sensations are funneled and integrated into a "feeling response." The locus ceruleus, in other words, gives emotional coloring to sensory perceptions and by doing so, psychologists believe, probably plays an important role in the individual's awareness of ego, of being a person

In a festival in Mauritius, a Tamil woman carrying two small children strides barefoot and unharmed over a bed of coals, whose temperature can range well over 1,000 degrees Fahrenheit. In debating explanations of the many such firewalks documented each year, some scientists invoke the properties of physics, explaining that coals conduct heat poorly or that moisture on the soles of the feet forms an insulating cushion, protecting the walkers. Other investigators believe that an altered state of body and mind is the key to safe or at least painless passage. Firewalks often occur at night or after fasting, for instance, when the body's metabolism is low, which reduces sensitivity to pain. Studies have also shown that most firewalkers, whether absorbed in religious beliefs or secular "personal empowerment," seem to enter an almost hypnotic state—although how this protects bare feet from burning coals remains a puzzle.

distinct from all other persons and things. The Yale studies suggest that psychedelic drugs overstimulate the locus ceruleus into a breakdown that essentially shatters the normal sense of individuality.

The marriage of Eastern mysticism and Western technology produced at least two offspring. One was the scientific analysis of meditation and other ancient mystical techniques for inducing altered states; the other was a new kind of meditation, a technology-assisted variety known as biofeedback. Biofeedback relies on the fact that many neurophysiological functions can be monitored and amplified by machines, and then revealed to the individual who is experiencing them. This electronic feedback consists of information that gives the individual the opportunity to bring under voluntary control the functions being monitored.

Like most types of meditation, biofeedback involves focusing a subject's attention, in this case on the biofeedback signal, which is usually a tone or a light associated with a particular brain-wave pattern or temperature range. The essence of the technique, however, is not the focusing itself, but the positive reinforcement that the individual gets from the biofeedback signal. By providing instant information on how well certain responses are succeeding, biofeedback continually rewards effective meditative behavior. Thus biofeedback instruments are training devices, constantly apprising users of what their minds and bodies are doing, and rewarding the users for correct technique.

In some cases, biofeedback has enabled perfectly ordinary people to achieve in a short period of time results similar to those of Swami Rama

In an experiment to study the effects of different drugs on arachnids, researchers gave common cross spiders high doses of various psychoactive chemicals, then left the creatures to their own devices. As shown here, the spiders created quite normal-looking webs when operating under the influence of hashish, mescaline, and even LSD—but seemingly spun out of control when dosed with caffeine *(far right)*. Coffee drinkers can take some heart, however: A comparable dosage would be enough to induce seizures in humans.

Normal Spider Web

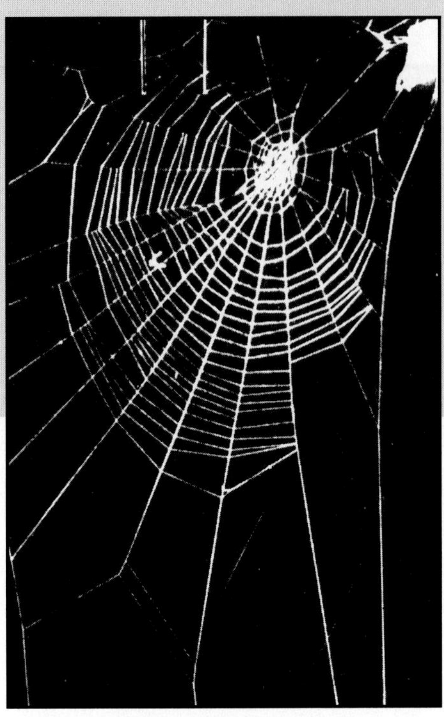

Hashish-Influenced Web

and other mystics who have spent years training their minds to control their bodies. Using biofeedback, subjects have been able to control or alter certain autonomic, or involuntary, physiological functions—cardiovascular, respiratory, and endocrine. Once trained, some biofeedback subjects are able to exercise their mental control without the aid of the biofeedback equipment.

Although the ideas that would lead to biofeedback were first tested in the mid-1940s, the technology did not achieve recognition until two decades later, when a series of experiments by an American psychologist produced some quite sensational results. Neal E. Miller of Rockefeller University in New York and his student Leo DiCara found that, using a reward system involving electrical stimulation of the septum, a structure in the brain believed to generate pleasurable emotions, they could train laboratory rats to increase or decrease their heart rates at will. The rodents also learned to control the rate of urine formation in their kidneys and to dilate the blood vessels of one ear more than the other. At the time of this study, Miller had already spent 40 years studying learning in animals and was widely regarded as one of the world's foremost experimental psychologists.

The results of the experiment appeared to hold important implications for human beings. Since "people are smarter than rats," Miller concluded, "anything rats can do people should be able to do better." Humans, after all, voluntarily control such functions as urination and defecation. Given the proper training, Miller and DiCara reasoned, might not they also learn to control high blood pressure, spastic colons, irregular heartbeats, and other ailments, without the use of drugs or therapy or surgery? The scientists suspected that people were not conscious of most of their bodies' inner workings simply because they had not been trained to observe and label them. Biofeedback could now provide that training.

Miller's rat experiments got the nascent field of biofeedback off the ground, but subsequent attempts by Miller and others to replicate the original experiment proved, to his great puzzlement, unsuccessful. Nevertheless, the original tests with rats had already inspired some highly successful clinical work with humans. In the late 1960s, researchers Bernard Engel and Theodore Weiss at the National Institute on Aging in Baltimore found that some patients with irregular heart rhythms could learn to speed up and slow down their hearts through biofeedback, and eventually could do so even without the help of the biofeedback instruments. Meanwhile, psychologist Barry Sterman at the Veterans Administration Medical Center in Sepulveda, California, began hooking up patients who suffered from epilepsy to electroencephalographs whose output governed lights and bells that helped the patients to alter the physiological changes, such as auras or distinctive smells, that signaled their attacks. The technique succeeded in reducing the frequency of the epileptic seizures.

Other seminal studies on humans were being conducted around the

Mescaline-Influenced Web

LSD-Influenced Web

Caffeine-Influenced Web

same time by pioneer biofeedback researcher Joe Kamiya, a psychologist at the University of Chicago. Working with people who had no special knowledge of mind-training techniques, Kamiya hooked up his subjects to an EEG and had them guess whether their brains were producing the alpha waves indicative of relaxation. Kamiya, who was monitoring their brain activity, would then tell them whether their guess was right or wrong. The accuracy of his subjects' guesses improved rapidly, suggesting that they had learned to recognize the feelings that produced an alpha state. Later, Kamiya had the electroencephalograph emit a constant tone in the presence of alpha activity and asked his subjects to keep the tone going. The subjects, after 12 sessions, learned to turn the alpha rhythm off and on at will. They learned that they could induce it by relaxing and emptying their minds of all thought. On the other hand, any mental effort, such as solving a problem or conjuring a mental image, could shut off the alpha rhythm instantly.

Kamiya's experiments were the first to demonstrate that individuals who monitored their own brain waves were capable of voluntarily enhancing or suppressing alpha activity. The discovery led some researchers to wonder whether alpha activity might actually be the key to the voluntary control of internal states. While this may in fact be the case, researchers have not been able to isolate an alpha link with any one trigger or any single altered state. Alpha is most easily produced by a stimulus-reduced, or relaxed, state of mind—the sort achieved through meditation, for instance. But some experiments have managed to elicit alpha activity in stimulus-enhanced situations—for example, while subjects were trying to solve a problem with their eyes open. This lack of a one-to-one correspondence between brain-wave activity and altered states has disappointed some scientists who had hoped that ASCs would fit into easily quantifiable categories.

In fact, considerable confusion and disagreement persist over what does or does not qualify as an altered state of consciousness. There is, for example, the hypnotic trance—if, indeed, it is a trance. Some proponents of hypnosis have claimed that the controversial technique has powers ranging from the control of pain to the regression of consciousness through previous lifetimes. Critics counter that the hypnotic trance does not even exist or that it is, at best, an altered state no more potent, or interesting, than daydreaming.

Still, hypnosis—whatever it is—appears to induce a kind of imposed

meditative state. Whereas meditation relies on self-imposed mental discipline, hypnosis usually depends on the behest of an exterior source, the hypnotist. Using only his voice, or his voice in combination with some attention-focusing device such as a pendulum or a metronome, the hypnotist suggests that the subject is becoming more and more relaxed and, finally, has entered a trance state—a sleeplike condition of profound absorption and great suggestibility. Deeply hypnotized people usually appear to experience profound relaxation, while their actions and feelings are being controlled by the hypnotist. In response to the hypnotist's suggestions, for example, a subject's arm may float up into the air, seemingly of its own accord. The arm may then be plunged into a container of ice-cold water without its owner's feeling the cold. Or, when asked to smell the perfume under his nose, the hypnotized person may sniff delightedly at

The Hypnotized Mind: A Hidden Observer?

A chance discovery during a classroom demonstration in 1973 led Stanford psychologist Ernest R. Hilgard to a new understanding of the hypnotized mind. To demonstrate hypnotic deafness, Hilgard told a hypnotized subject that he would no longer be able to hear, and, as expected, the man did not react to loud noises or repeated questions. But then, prompted by a query from the student audience, Hilgard instructed the subject to raise a finger if some part of him could still hear. To everyone's surprise, the subject raised his finger. The subject himself immediately asked to have his hearing restored so he could find out what had happened: He had heard nothing, he said, but had felt the finger rise "in a way that was not a spontaneous twitch."

Apparently, the man's conscious self had remained hypnotically deaf, but some part of his awareness continued to register sound. Hilgard called this ability to process information on two levels the "hidden observer" effect, a convenient label not meant to imply the existence of a separate personality. Opponents of his theory contend that the phenomenon arises simply from the subject's desire to fulfill the instructor's expectations, but proponents have found that it sheds light on various topics, from the understanding of consciousness to the origin of multiple personality disorders.

what is actually a bottle of ammonia.

The hypnotic trance has a long history, dating back to the healing trance states, supposedly of divine origin, found among ancient shamans.

Hypnosis flourished in the latter half of the 19th century as a means of relieving pain, and as it gained acceptance among some physicians, it also came to the attention of Sigmund Freud. Supposedly, it was while learning techniques to induce a hypnotic trance and while observing patients enter the trance that Freud began to recognize the existence of the unconscious mind and its role in psychopathology. It seemed to him that hypnosis allowed patients to talk freely about their problems and thus facilitated deep emotional reactions and the subsequent alleviation of a patient's symptoms. But Freud was unable to induce very deep trances in his patients, and he eventually rejected hypnosis in favor of free association and dream interpretation as tools for reaching the unconscious. And then, with the rise of psychoanalysis, came a temporary decline in the popularity of hypnosis.

Midway through the 20th century, however, hypnosis began to enjoy a rebirth: The British Medical Association endorsed its use for controlling pain in 1953, followed by the American Medical Association five years later. Hypnosis was also being extolled by enthusiasts as a cure for asthma, as a behavior modifier that could help dieters and smokers, and even as a treatment for skin disorders. The classic skin-treatment case occurred in the 1950s, when a physician named A. A. Mason reported using hypnosis to clear up 70 percent of the skin of a 16-year-old boy afflicted with "fish-skin disease." The boy's congenital condition, which had left his back, arms, legs, and hands covered with scaly, dark-colored, hardened skin, had been regarded by other doctors as untreatable.

Hypnosis is still used, often with apparent good effect, as a memory aid—a feature useful to therapists and law-enforcement officials. The technique seems to create a relaxed, anxiety-free state of mind that allows people to retrieve painful or upsetting memories that, repressed, have impaired their mental health. Moreover, crime victims under hypnosis have been known to recall a license plate number or another clue to help lead police to criminals.

In spite of the apparent benefits conferred by hypnosis, however, the debate continues as to whether the hypnotic state even exists. In the 1950s, Barry Wyke of the British Royal College of Surgeons described for the first time the neurological changes that appeared to take place during hypnosis. He found that the brain waves of hypnotized subjects could be changed by the evoking of various sensory or emotional experiences. But research conducted later would show no physiological distinction between hypnotic trance and the ordinary waking state, even though numerous investigators have searched for years for physiological correlates of the hypnotic trance.

After three decades of trying to do just that, psychologist Theodore X. Barber at the Medfield Foundation in Medfield, Massachusetts, believes that he has established that hypnotic trance is not a special state. Hypnosis, he says, gives rise to no physiological or biochemical events that cannot be produced without hypnosis. The most convincing aspect of Barber's work has been a series of experiments demonstrating that any human attribute or behavior ascribed to hypnosis—among them analgesia, hallucination, amnesia, enhanced strength, and unusual perceptual effects such as deafness, blindness, and color blindness—could be induced in normal waking subjects without hypnosis, through suggestion alone.

In one experiment, subjects who had not been hypnotized were told to sit quietly with their eyes closed and listen to an imaginary recording of "White Christmas." Questioned afterward, more than half reported hearing the song clearly—though no music had actually been played. Barber and his colleagues found that when people are highly motivated and thinking positively, direct suggestion is more effective than suggestion under hypnosis. The scientist blames the books and movies of popular culture for the widely held misconception, as he sees it, that there is such a thing as hypnotic trance.

Another critic of hypnosis, University of Connecticut psychologist Irving Kirsch, concurs with Barber's finding that hypnotic suggestion is no different from any other kind of suggestion, but he points out that any suggestion can be powerful. Tell people they have received a psychedelic drug, Kirsch says, and half the time they will report having hallucinations, even though in reality they took no drug. Feats of "hypnotic age regression" may also have a rather mundane explanation. Nicholas Spanos, a Canadian psychologist who has worked closely with Barber, believes that patients who are asked to remember incidents from their childhood will, in recalling those events, act not the way children actually behave, but in the way that the patients believe children behave. Suggestions for regression, Spanos asserts, may be little more than invitations to become involved in the make-believe game of being a child again.

In refuting the status of hypnotic trance as an altered state of consciousness, critics of hypnosis revive again a much broader question: What are the criteria that define an altered state? There seems to be no definitive answer. Charles Tart, the West's original ASC guru, does not even like the term "altered states," preferring several other labels, including "discrete state of consciousness." This is because "altered" implies being altered from what is "normal," and normality is merely a matter of consensus. In other words, as Tart would have it, an altered state depends largely on one's cultural context, intelligence, and other factors that create and color one's point of view.

"Western science implicitly assumes that there is a normal state of consciousness and that all others are degenerate forms of it," says Tart. "But that's not true. What one person experiences as an altered state may fall into the sphere of ordinary consciousness for another." Thus the feats of a Swami Rama, for example, may not be extraordinary so much as they are merely unfamiliar to the Western mind; in India, they would seem comparatively "normal."

Even if altered states could be defined to everyone's satisfaction, a final question remains: What is the ultimate point in studying them? Early critics of ASC research carped that science had no business giving serious attention to the foggy blather of drugged-out hippies who claimed that LSD let them see God, or to mind-over-body tricksters who belonged in carnival sideshows.

Over time, however, even the most hardened critics have generally come to concede that ASC research might have contributions to make to even so precise a science as neurobiology in its ongoing effort to map the functional topography of the brain. Ron Siegel's findings on the commonality of hallucinations, for example, indicate that even the most mystical visions are somehow rooted in an electrical vocabulary shared by virtually all human brains. And, neurologists now believe that the pain-control characteristic of some altered states may be the key to accessing the neural seat of such power. Experiments indicate that people who are able to control pain—whether they be yogis sticking acupuncture needles through their skin, women who undergo childbirth with minimal discomfort, or athletes pushed to their physical limits—are somehow accessing brain matter in the periaqueductal gray, an area of the midbrain that is rich in receptors for both natural and pharmaceutical painkillers. Scientists theorize that the periaqueductal gray may be the brain's control center for pain and that it, in turn, can be manipulated by breath control, although no one is sure just how.

But if ASC research had nothing to contribute to any other science, adherents maintain that altered states—mysterious and elusive as they remain—are themselves still essential fodder for study. Research at the University of California at San Diego shows that, for some reason, human beings fall into daydreams about every 90 minutes. Perhaps, some contend, the conscious mind in order to stay in kilter needs these periods of altered reality—occasional relief from the mundane world—just as the unconscious mind needs to dream. If this is so, then humans might do well to keep trying to understand a phenomenon that could be essential to their very nature. "Altered states," says Charles Tart, "remind us that we're more than we think we are."

PERCEPTIONS AWRY

In a hackneyed cartoon, a heat-beat wayfarer struggles across featureless desert sands toward a lush oasis. Of course the beckoning palms turn out to be nothing but a mirage, a cruel trick of the mind. Psychologists call this kind of mental prank a hallucination, a believable sensual experience that arises entirely from within, independent of external stimuli. Hallucinations, which can affect any of our senses, materialize in many different circumstances. Fear, stress, or isolation can induce them, as can mental illness, fever, disease, or drug and alcohol use.

Scientists disagree on how hallucinations originate in the mind. Some favor a psychological explanation: People conjure up things they wish deeply for or revisit memories of past events. Other scientists believe that damage or chemical imbalances in the brain are the cause. A third group argues that probably both psychology and physiology play a role in generating apparitions.

However they may arise, hallucinations vary in persuasiveness. In most cases, they are seen—or felt or heard—as an overlay on reality, readily recognized as what they are. Such figments are called pseudohallucinations. In more extreme cases, especially where mental illness or mind-altering drugs are involved, hallucinations can displace reality for as long as they last.

The following pages explore this bizarre world, beginning with visual hallucinations and continuing through deceptions of the other senses to an unusual variety of mind mischief in which a stimulus to one sense triggers a sensation in another.

HALLUCINATION OR ILLUSION? Psychologists and physiologists who study phantoms of the senses make a distinction between illusions and hallucinations. Illusions have in common that they all spring from something tangible, which the senses misinterpret. To someone afraid, an innocent shadow under streetlights can appear to take on the shape of a lurking assailant. In another type of illusion, called trailing *(right)*, a moving object seems to leave a wake of afterimages.

Hallucinations differ from illusions in that they have no link with reality. For example, at far right is a drawing of a hallucination, based on reports of more than a dozen persons, that combines the lattice and tunnel form constants. The drawing is typical in that none of the subjects were viewing anything upon which the pattern could be based.

SIMPLE HALLUCINATIONS

At one end of the hallucination spectrum lie phenomena that psychologists call simple hallucinations. These tend to have uncomplicated visual content often based on four recurring shapes and commonly perceived as being superimposed on the external world. The shapes—called form constants because they appear in the hallucinations of people across many cultures—are named the tunnel, the cobweb, the spiral, and the lattice. The concentric circles seen here are a variety of tunnel form constant.

In a hallucination, form constants can appear with the eyes open or shut and may change continually in color, size, and number. Although form constants do not occur in every hallucination, their prevalence suggests a physiological basis, a mechanism that is much the same in one brain as in another. Some scientists believe the forms are actually illusions (*box*) that result from light passing through structures inside the eyes, such as red blood cells or folds in the cornea. Others disagree, pointing out that hallucinators can perceive the shapes even with eyes closed. Some of these investigators speculate that form constants result from spontaneous nerve cell firings in the eyes or in the visual centers of the brain (*pages* 82-83). Such a theory also explains why form constants often move independently of any movement of the eyes.

UNWORLDLY VISIONS

Many people have visual hallucinations that elaborate on form constants (*inset*) or transcend them altogether, as in the otherworldly cityscape at right, which was inspired by a schizophrenia patient's descriptions of hallucinations involving "new cities unknown to geography and dazzling in their complexity and size." According to an expert who has studied these phenomena extensively, the composite photograph represents a class of hallucinations taken for reality by those who experience them.

Mental illness is no prerequisite for complex hallucinations, as these enhanced visions are called. Perfectly normal individuals have them and they appear to vary widely both in content and in richness of detail. Nonetheless, researchers have noticed some common features of complex hallucinations. Images tend to multiply as the hallucination evolves. For example, shapes often pulsate and then revolve. And although the most vivid detail usually appears at the edges of the hallucination, people, animals, and landscapes are fully formed. Individual variations include scenes that often mirror a real situation: A person mourning someone's death, for instance, may see the deceased. Finally, complex hallucinations sometimes appear during those moments of waning consciousness just before sleep.

A BASIC SHAPE, EMBELLISHED. The spiral serves as the underlying structure for a painting that combines several hallucinations. Ghostly shapes at lower right represent the artist projecting himself into the spiral to become part of the adventure, which also involved hallucinations of the other senses *(pages 102-103)*. Although the hallucinations were induced by mind-altering drugs (in the course of experiments that were rather common among artists and others during the 1960s), the painting was done after the drugs' effect had passed.

ODORS AND TASTES, TOUCHES AND SOUNDS

No less vivid than visual hallucinations are spurious arousals of the other senses. Such hallucinations, which may occur alone or in conjunction with other sensory hallucinations, happen mostly in people with some kind of disease, either mental or physical.

Auditory hallucinations, which often befall healthy people, are an exception. At their simplest, they sound like popping noises or bells. Disembodied voices are a more complex phenomenon, yet many people report hearing their names called just before crossing the threshold to sleep.

Other voices, the ones that deliver messages or become partners in conversation, usually signal a psychiatric problem. Often the ailment is schizophrenia, a disorder that can also summon tactile hallucinations, in which the hallucinator feels something that does not exist—the rush of the wind in still air, a sensation of falling while on solid ground. Tactile hallucinations also occur in people with a history of drug or alcohol abuse.

Hallucinations affecting the senses of smell and taste usually point to physiological problems in the brain. Olfactory hallucinations, in which individuals report odors no one else can detect, as well as gustatory hallucinations, which involve an imagined taste, can happen in people with brain tumors or epilepsy.

A CACOPHONY OF CRITICS. People with schizophrenia or other psychiatric problems often hear phantom voices criticizing them. Recent studies of such hallucinations indicate that they involve the language center of the brain. PET scans of schizophrenics during periods when they report hearing voices show that language-center activity is similar to that of normal subjects listening to themselves speak. And schizophrenics can often silence their imaginary detractors by beginning to talk or write or, oddly enough, by opening the mouth very wide—actions that appear to reclaim the language center from the demons.

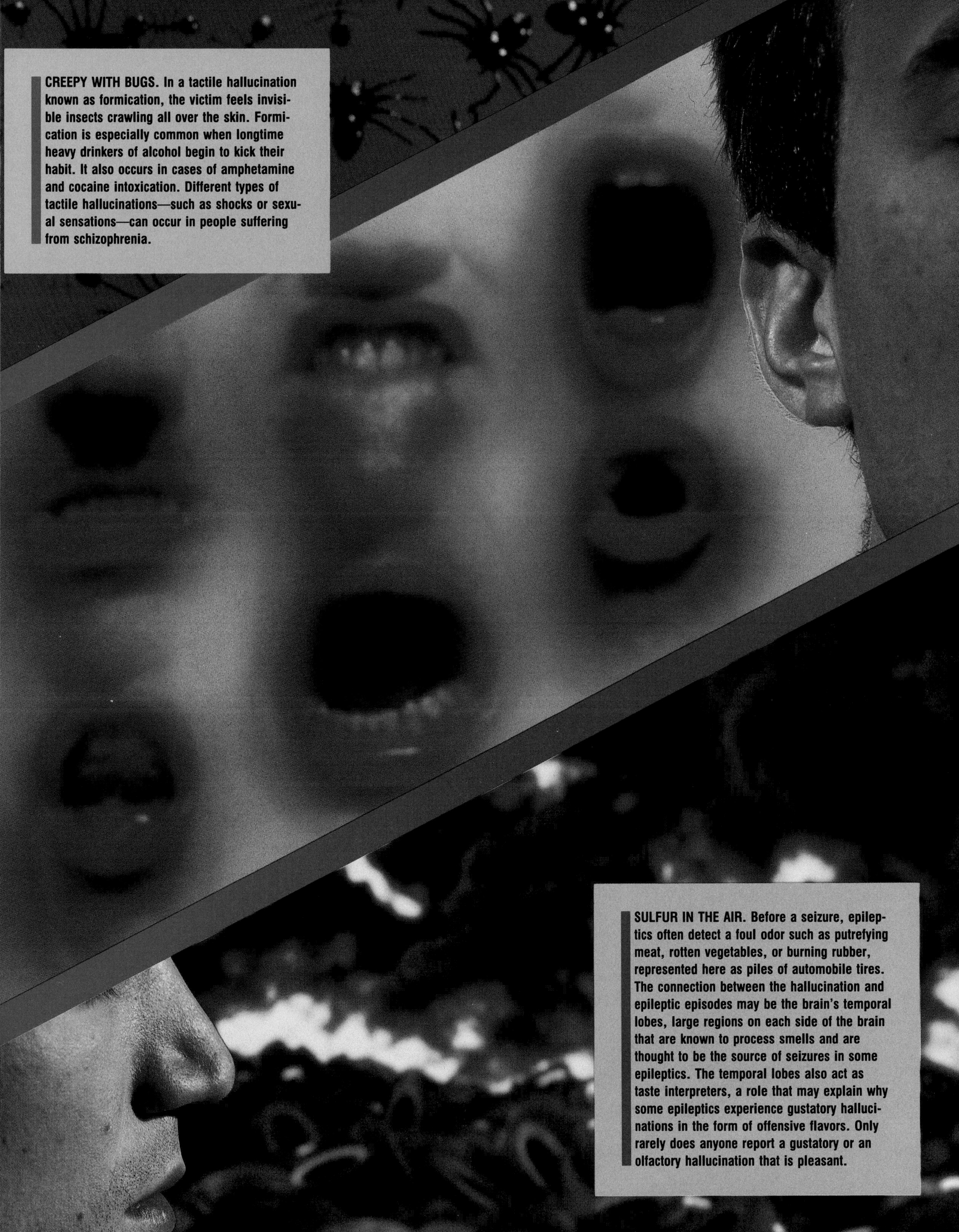

CREEPY WITH BUGS. In a tactile hallucination known as formication, the victim feels invisible insects crawling all over the skin. Formication is especially common when longtime heavy drinkers of alcohol begin to kick their habit. It also occurs in cases of amphetamine and cocaine intoxication. Different types of tactile hallucinations—such as shocks or sexual sensations—can occur in people suffering from schizophrenia.

SULFUR IN THE AIR. Before a seizure, epileptics often detect a foul odor such as putrefying meat, rotten vegetables, or burning rubber, represented here as piles of automobile tires. The connection between the hallucination and epileptic episodes may be the brain's temporal lobes, large regions on each side of the brain that are known to process smells and are thought to be the source of seizures in some epileptics. The temporal lobes also act as taste interpreters, a role that may explain why some epileptics experience gustatory hallucinations in the form of offensive flavors. Only rarely does anyone report a gustatory or an olfactory hallucination that is pleasant.

CROSSED CONNECTIONS

"Colors are very important to me because I have a gift," remarked the late composer Olivier Messiaen. "Whenever I hear music—or even if I read music—I see colors." Messiaen was one of many people with such a gift. So-called colored hearing is a form of hallucination-like experience known as synesthesia, which occurs when a stimulus to one sense causes an additional perception in another.

Colored hearing is only one variety of synesthesia. The Russian author Vladimir Nabokov saw letters as colored. Synesthetes in this mold might experience the pages of a newspaper much differently from a person with the usual perception of black letters on a background of white. "When I taste something with an intense flavor," said a tactile-taste synesthete, "I perceive a shape, weight, and texture as if I'm actually grasping" an object. Other synesthetes experience smells this way as well.

Scientists do not agree on how synesthesia occurs. However, Dr. Richard Cytowic, a neurologist and prominent researcher in the field, suggests that the phenomenon is probably a normal process of the brain—perhaps centered in the limbic system—that is suppressed in most people. Among the relatively few in whom synesthesia surfaces, many value it as a pleasurable, enriching experience and would mourn its loss.

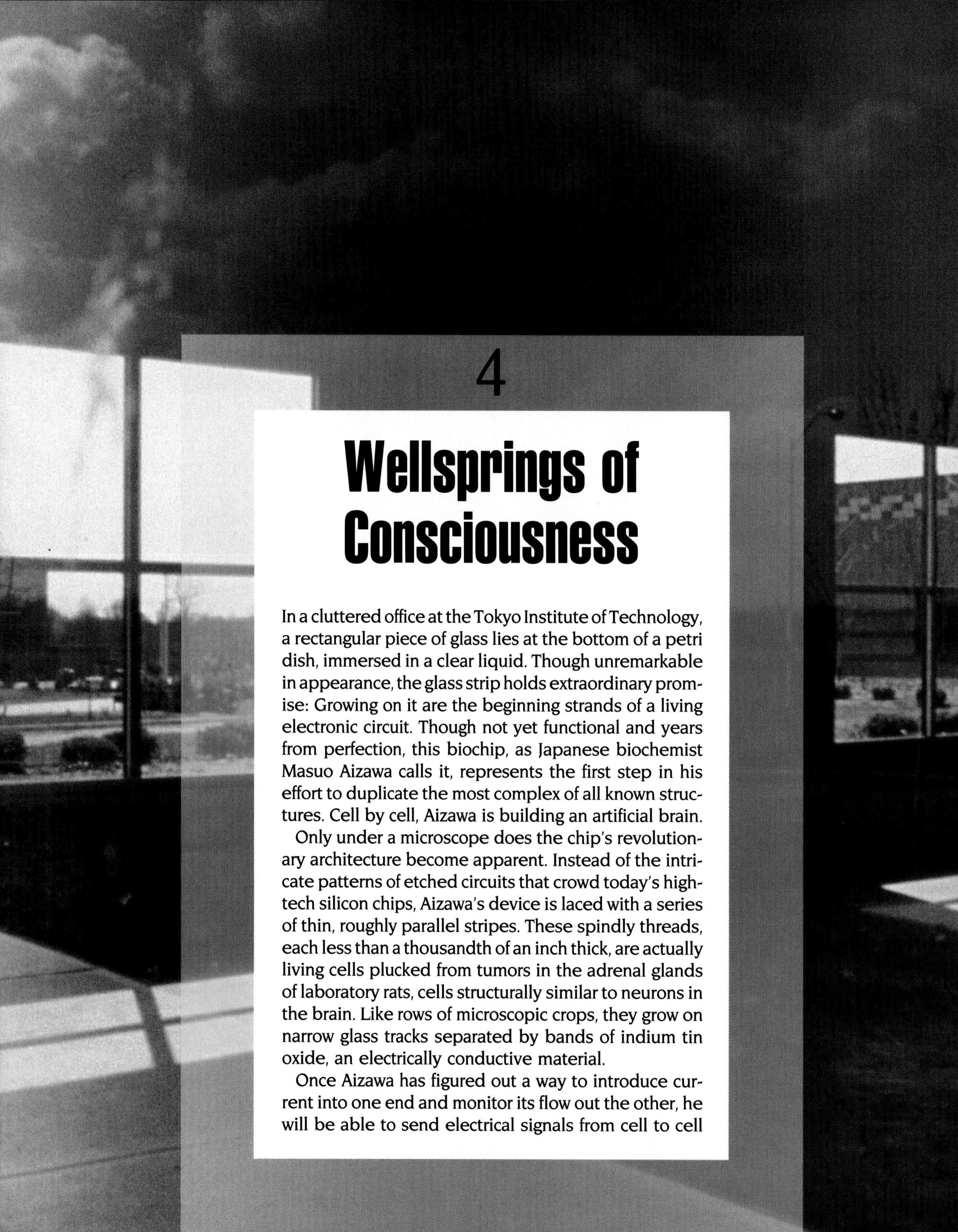

4

Wellsprings of Consciousness

In a cluttered office at the Tokyo Institute of Technology, a rectangular piece of glass lies at the bottom of a petri dish, immersed in a clear liquid. Though unremarkable in appearance, the glass strip holds extraordinary promise: Growing on it are the beginning strands of a living electronic circuit. Though not yet functional and years from perfection, this biochip, as Japanese biochemist Masuo Aizawa calls it, represents the first step in his effort to duplicate the most complex of all known structures. Cell by cell, Aizawa is building an artificial brain.

Only under a microscope does the chip's revolutionary architecture become apparent. Instead of the intricate patterns of etched circuits that crowd today's high-tech silicon chips, Aizawa's device is laced with a series of thin, roughly parallel stripes. These spindly threads, each less than a thousandth of an inch thick, are actually living cells plucked from tumors in the adrenal glands of laboratory rats, cells structurally similar to neurons in the brain. Like rows of microscopic crops, they grow on narrow glass tracks separated by bands of indium tin oxide, an electrically conductive material.

Once Aizawa has figured out a way to introduce current into one end and monitor its flow out the other, he will be able to send electrical signals from cell to cell

Three early steps toward Japanese scientist Masuo Aizawa's dream of a computer chip built of nerve cells appear at right. The nearest photomicrograph shows innumerable connections among rat neurons that are specially cultured for Aizawa's purposes. Such a proliferation would channel electrical signals uncontrollably throughout a chip, however, making it useless as a computer. To limit the connections *(center),* Aizawa applied a small voltage as the cells matured on a glass plate striped with indium tin oxide *(dark bands),* one of a class of substances called semiconductors, which are vital to computers. Besides curbing growth, the voltage repelled the nerve cells from the indium tin oxide stripes onto glass areas between them *(far right).* Aizawa hopes that the resulting strips of neurons, now insulated from one another, could someday become the basis for computer circuits.

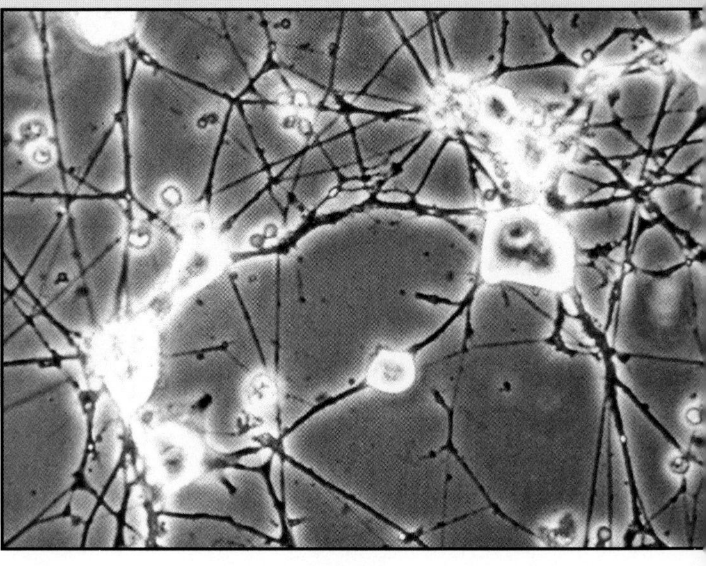

through the entire neuronal string. The circuit will then function much like the brain's own signaling pathways—the interconnected chains of neurons that process sensory impulses and, in humans, constitute the very channels of consciousness itself.

Aizawa is among the scores of scientists and philosophers who are exploring this fundamental but elusive aspect of the human condition, an effort that has occupied thinkers of many cultures and many eras. One widely held view, grounded in the tradition of cause-and-effect materialism that has long formed the basis of Western science, was expressed by British biologist Thomas H. Huxley more than a century ago. "All states of consciousness," Huxley wrote, "are immediately caused by molecular changes of the brain structure."

Proceeding from this assumption, and aided by advanced techniques such as positron emission tomography (PET) and magnetic resonance imaging (MRI), neuroscientists in the latter part of the 20th century have made significant headway in tracing mental activity through the brain's tens of billions of neurons. Yet such expeditions, while yielding plenty of intriguing hints, have so far failed to uncover the hiding place of consciousness. Although most neuroscientists today believe that consciousness somehow resides in the signal traffic among whole populations of neurons, that theory leaves a fundamental question unanswered: If neurons themselves are not sentient—that is, if they do not "know" what the signals they transmit represent—then who, or what, does?

Attacking the problem from a different direction is a small but distinguished cadre of physicists, brain researchers, and philosophers who believe that human consciousness is a kind of transcendent awareness. The stuff of thought and feeling, these investigators maintain, will not be found by teasing apart the brain's gray matter. Instead, some researchers have seized upon notions from the rarefied, more abstract discipline of quantum theory, which is a keystone of modern physics. In this realm of the vanishingly small, the conventional laws of cause and effect are routinely broken, and the observable universe is demonstrated to be a product of interaction with the observer—offering, perhaps, a suitable paradigm for explaining the nuances of consciousness.

This line of thinking has led some scientists to venture even farther afield, to an appreciation of ancient Eastern traditions that view the external world and the internal world simply as different sides of the same elaborate tapestry. The consciousness of the individual, according to some of these philosophies, is but one wave in the great oceanic consciousness of an underlying reality.

However one talks about it—as arising from clusters of firing neurons or as part of some great cosmic sea—individual consciousness is clearly associated with the incredible organ that resides within the human skull. In terms of sheer processing power, the brain has no equal, or at least not yet. Since the 1980s, researchers such as Masuo Aizawa have been working to model a new generation of computers on the structure of the human brain.

Though some of today's computers

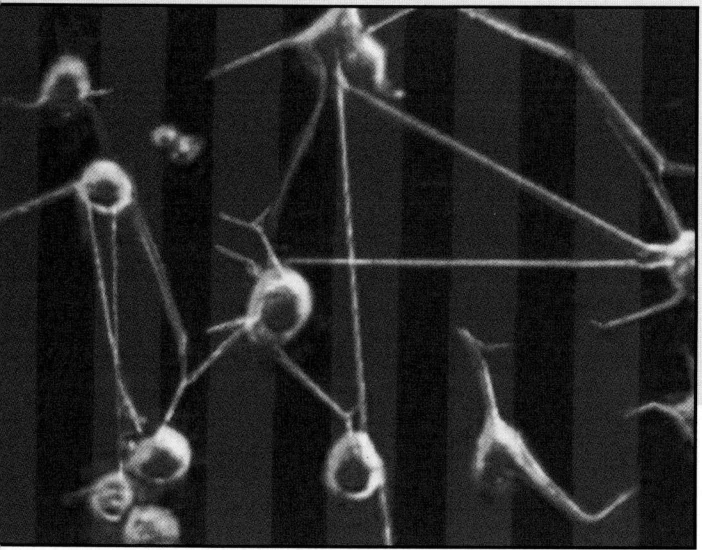

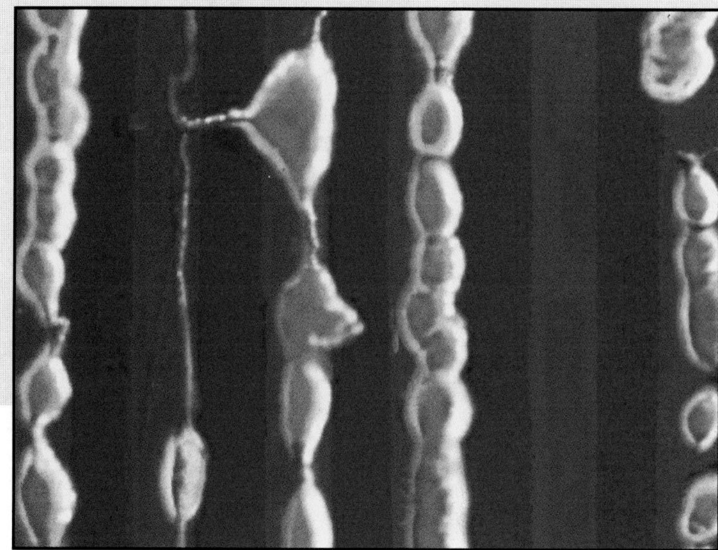

regularly outmaneuver people in chess, and all of them are speedier mathematicians, no machine can so much as recognize a face. The cognitive skills involved in identifying a particular arrangement of eyes, nose, and mouth require a trillion or more computations per second—child's play for the highly evolved circuitry of the human brain but far beyond the capabilities of even the mightiest supercomputer.

The brain manages such feats because it does not process information serially, or one step at a time, as do conventional computers. Instead, its billions of neurons, each capable of accepting and transmitting thousands of signals in an instant, are woven together in a dense, multidirectional communication network. Moreover, the connections among neurons actually improve with use. By growing new links to strengthen frequently used pathways and abandoning those it no longer needs, the brain literally teaches itself. Signals racing back and forth through this complex highway system create patterns of interaction that give rise to perception and, in ways still unexplained, to consciousness.

In their attempt to copy the arrangement of neurons in the brain, computer modelers have replaced the complex central processing unit of conventional computers with thousands of smaller and simpler processors hooked together in clusters called neural nets. Though pale shadows of the living brain, neural nets do mimic some of the brain's more salient features: Just as neurons relay signals streaming in from the eyes and other sense organs, each processor in a neural net can receive and transmit electrical impulses almost simultaneously.

Neural nets have added a new dimension to computer technology, spawning new machines that are actually capable of rudimentary learning. Among the most precocious of them is a system called NETtalk, designed in the late 1980s by Terrence Sejnowski of the Salk Institute in La Jolla, California. NETtalk can scan a page of English text and, through a speaker, transform the written symbols into sounds resembling human speech. At the beginning of a task, according to one researcher, the machine "babbles like a baby." But eventually, coached by programmers who feed in data to correct faulty speech patterns, the computer develops remarkably good pronunciation.

Some scientists believe that even smarter computers are on the horizon, particularly if Aizawa succeeds in his effort to wed biology and high technology. His living circuit, integrated into a neural net where its cells could grow and arrange themselves into a web of sufficient complexity, would boost data-handling power to unimaginable heights, placing future computers at least theoretically on a par with the human brain. A robot fitted with such a device might, if properly programmed, act in ways indistinguishable from human behavior, perhaps musing out loud about the meaning of existence or holing up with a good book—appearing, in short, to be a fully conscious being.

By some definitions, it would be conscious. For example, Marvin Minsky, a pioneer in the field of

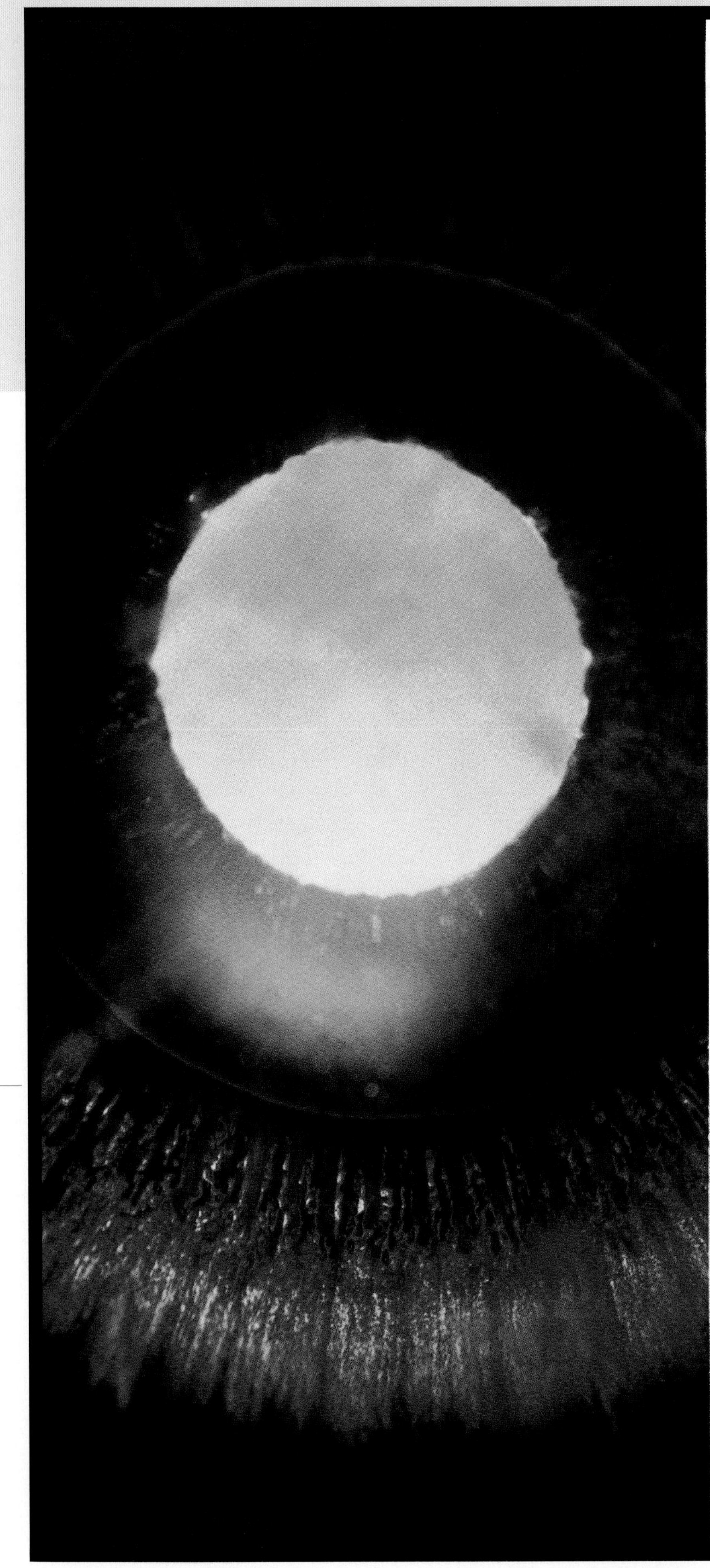

Perception: Gateway to the Mind

In the 17th century, French philosopher René Descartes formulated his famous theory of dualism, pronouncing that the mind—consciousness—existed separately from the physical brain. Hoping to explain how the two could interact, he suggested that mind and brain were linked by a pea-size structure deep in the brain called the pineal gland. For a person to experience something consciously, claimed Descartes, impulses from the senses funneled into this vital kernel, triggering a special alchemy that resulted in the sensation of awareness.

Scientists today have almost universally rejected Descartes's notion of the mind-brain split. Most, in fact, have taken up the opposite view, that the mind somehow arises from activity in the brain.

Presumably, by scrapping dualism modern researchers have also abandoned Descartes's idea of a consciousness "center." But according to Tufts University philosopher Daniel Dennett, residues of Cartesian thinking still contaminate notions about brain function. Dennett cites the example of "filling in," a concept widely used in discussions of how the eyes and brain work together to create one facet of consciousness: visual perception.

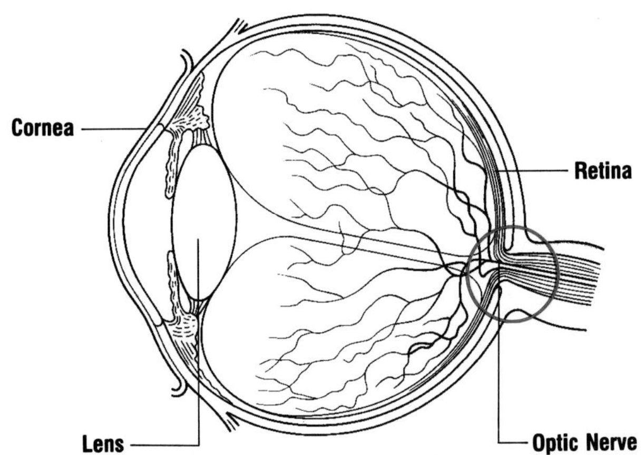

As described below, signals speeding to the brain from the eye contain incomplete information about the visual field because of a gap in the layer of photoreceptors, or light-sensing cells, lining the retina. The viewer, however, is normally unaware that the picture is not complete. Proponents of filling in suggest that the brain compensates for this so-called blind spot in the visual field by constructing material to patch it.

To Dennett, such an argument is fundamentally flawed, for it presupposes the existence of a kind of consciousness headquarters where, as he puts it, everything "comes together." Filling in, he points out, implies that the blind spot is masked for the benefit of some "master discriminator." To escape this Cartesian trap, Dennett argues, "We must stop thinking of the brain as if it had such a single functional summit or central point."

In Dennett's model of consciousness, sensory information pouring in from the eyes and body undergoes constant and simultaneous "editorial revision" by myriad functional networks throughout the brain. Like teams of scribes, these networks toil feverishly to write, edit, revise, and update their versions of the content with every stream of fresh data, churning out countless drafts in less than a second. This swift succession of revisions, the theory goes, produces a sort of narrative stream or sequence—the stuff of consciousness.

Central to Dennett's model is the notion that these networks do not have to pass their drafts along to another level of processing and, therefore, have no need to fill in the blind spot. Why, then, is the hole not apparent? Dennett suggests that because the brain is not accustomed to receiving signals from the gap on the retina, no networks are assigned to keep track of them. So when information fails to arrive from that source, in Dennett's words, "no one complains."

An analogy helps to illustrate his point. If a person enters a room with wallpaper containing, say, hundreds of identical sailboats, the brain need not examine every boat to determine that they are alike. It processes one or two of the images, receives no information to suggest the others are different, then labels the whole region as "more sailboats." Similarly, the brain does not try to accommodate the source of the blind spot, Dennett maintains. "The area is simply neglected."

THE EYE'S BLIND SPOT. Photoreceptors that line the retina at the back of the eye *(left)* convert light into impulses that travel to the brain by way of the optic nerve. At the point where the optic nerve leaves the retina *(circled area)*, an absence of photoreceptors creates a blind spot in the visual field. (The small depression on the retina near the optic nerve, called the fovea, forms the point of sharpest vision.)

To locate your blind spot, hold this page at arm's length and close your right eye. While focusing on the cross with your left eye, bring the page closer. At one point, the red dot will enter the blind spot and seem to disappear. Instead of a hole, however, the eye will see a continuous field of diagonal lines.

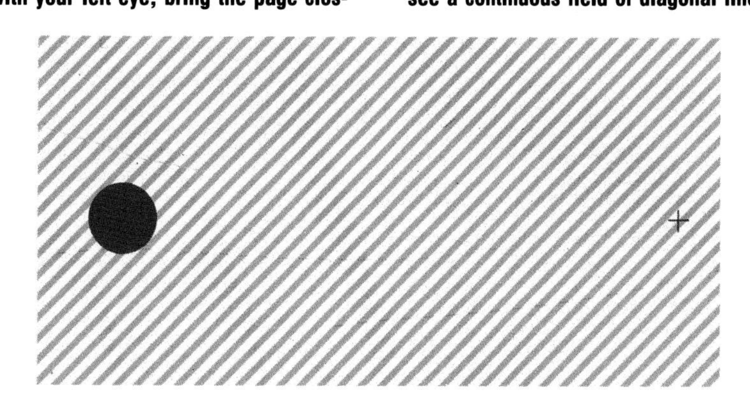

When a photon of light smashes into the nucleus of a hydrogen atom in a bubble chamber *(right)*, the collision transforms energy into matter and matter into energy. For some physicists, the demonstrable interrelatedness of different states in the physical universe suggests aspects of Eastern philosophy regarding states of mind—perhaps providing a link between consciousness and unconsciousness.

artificial intelligence at MIT, suggests that consciousness, or the familiar human sensation of self-awareness, is simply a manifestation of activity buzzing in the physical structure, whether it be the brain of a person or of a sophisticated robot. Specifically, Minsky believes that consciousness is the by-product of billions of data exchanges taking place among "agencies," or groups of neurons in the brain. According to his theory, each agency handles a single aspect of perception—one small piece of the bigger picture. By way of myriad connections, the agencies shuttle signals to and fro, assembling the various fragments and achieving, in effect, a kind of learning.

From Minsky's point of view, mind and brain are inseparable, the one created by the other and contained wholly within it. But to other investigators, swayed by reports of the mind's influence extending to regions beyond the corporeal confines of the skull, consciousness is more than brain. As one researcher cheerfully predicted, the weight of evidence confirming paranormal activity is going to precipitate "a wonderful crisis in the minds of scientists."

Just such a crisis awaited Michael Sabom in 1976 when, as a young cardiologist at the University of Florida in Gainesville, he first grappled with the notion of near-death experience (sometimes referred to as NDE). A friend had given him a copy of Raymond Moody's just-released book *Life after Life*, a popular account of people who had survived a close brush with death. Sabom initially refused to take the phenomenon seriously; to him, the victims' reports of dark tunnels and disembodied souls, of beatific lights and reunions with long-lost relatives seemed absurd. He was also put off by the author's apparent lack of scientific rigor in selecting his subjects and presenting his data: Who were these people? Were they religious fanatics or psychiatric patients? Did they make this stuff up?

His curiosity nonetheless piqued, Sabom decided to conduct his own near-death study. He began by selecting a random sample of 300 or so patients, mostly from northern Florida, whose medical records indicated they had suffered some kind of life-threatening crisis. Without revealing his purpose, Sabom asked whether they recalled anything about their experience. To his amazement, 40 percent of the patients came back with detailed descriptions of otherworldly excursions.

What fascinated Sabom most were the patients' accounts of watching their own bodies being worked over by emergency medical personnel. "Mr. P," a 52-year-old security guard who had suffered a heart attack while in a Florida hospital, told Sabom that he remembered passing out and then looking down at himself sprawled on the black-and-white tile of the emergency room floor. From near the ceiling, Mr. P observed the frantic crew of doctors and nurses load his body onto a gurney. One doctor, Mr. P recalled, "whacked the hell out of me. He came back with his fist from way behind his head and he hit me right in the center of my chest. And then they were pushing on my chest like artificial respiration, not exactly like that but kinda like artificial respiration. They shoved a plastic tube like you put in an oil can, they shoved that in my mouth."

The man also related how medical personnel inserted a needle in his chest—"like one of these Aztec rituals where they take the virgin's heart out"—and attached the body to a "strange machine" (a defibrillator) using two metallic disks with handles to administer bursts of electricity to the heart. "I thought they had given my body too much voltage," he complained. "Man, my body jumped about two feet off the table." Mr. P had no history of heart trouble, had never seen cardiopulmonary resusci-

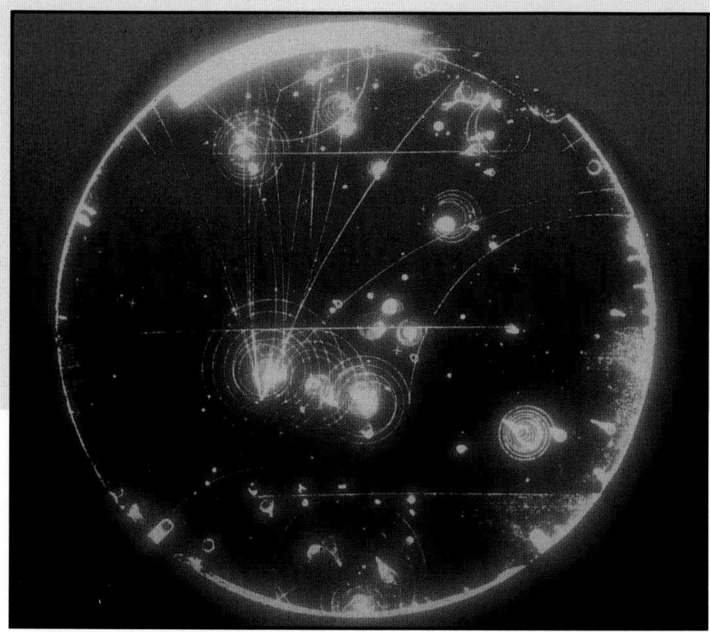

tation (CPR) performed or even simulated, and had only a rudimentary knowledge of medicine. Yet he accurately described every detail of his treatment down to the fuzzy white line on the defibrillator's oscilloscope.

Thirty-one other heart-attack patients in Sabom's study also recalled their ordeal with extraordinary precision. Had they somehow pieced together their uncanny "recollections" from glimpses of cardiac-resuscitation equipment? To determine the likelihood of that possibility, Sabom asked 25 long-term heart patients to describe CPR procedures; 23 of them made major blunders. Next, he guessed that Mr. P and the others had been semiconscious during their treatment. But research has shown that people in a twilight state of awareness remember only what they hear, not what they see.

Like the subjects in Moody's study, many of Sabom's patients said that, while on the brink of death, they found themselves drifting away from their bodies, heading down a fog-shrouded tunnel and toward a dazzling light. At the other end of the tunnel, some reported being greeted by deceased loved ones or figures in flowing robes. Others said they wandered into idyllic valleys where, enveloped by a light that radiated wisdom and love, they watched a three-dimensional, technicolor replay of their lives unfold before them. Many of them experienced feelings of profound bliss coupled with a disjointed sense of time, as if all action were taking place in a twinkling. Even to an avowed skeptic like Sabom, this chorus of bizarre out-of-body accounts seemed to be clear proof that mind was somehow independent of body.

Not everyone, however, has been so willing to suspend disbelief or to abandon materialist convictions. Among the most outspoken critics is Ronald Siegel, a psychologist at the University of California at Los Angeles. According to Siegel, who began studying hallucinations and their causes in the 1960s, near-death experiences are pure fiction, tricks played by the mind on itself. As Siegel has observed, researchers have heard "descriptions of golf courses, even condominiums, in the afterlife." He would argue that what may seem like visits to the other side are actually projections from the patient's own mind: "We can explain it all by the well-known dissociative properties of hallucination."

Siegel would attribute these otherworldly experiences to some as-yet-unidentified mechanism—perhaps the cataclysmic shutdown of the sensory apparatus at the moment of death—that ignites a storm of neuronal discharges in the brain. These crackling nerve cells, as his theory goes, then generate the familiar hallucinations, including out-of-body projections, wind-swept rides down tunnels, wondrous lights—exactly the same sensations often reported by users of psychedelic drugs and by people in the throes of extreme fear or sensory deprivation. Siegel's conclusion: Death-triggered hallucinations are simply the body's way of coping with annihilation.

Believers in near-death experiences contend that such materialist explanations miss the point entirely. In a 1987 essay, Stanislov Grof, a psychia-

Memories from Death's Doorstep

Recent advances in medical technology have inadvertently raised new questions about the nature of consciousness and the relationship of mind and brain. Millions of victims of sudden heart attacks and severe trauma who once would have been given up for dead are now being saved by drugs and electronic devices. And they are returning from the brink of death with remarkable memories. So many of these near-death experiences (NDEs) have been reported that science has ceased asking whether they occur and turned its attention to discovering what is happening.

To one who has gone through it, the near-death experience is a transforming journey down a bright pathway in utter peace, often concluding with a review of the events of life and a glimpse of loved ones who have already died.

Most intriguing—and disturbing—to modern medical researchers are these patients' memories of events that actually happened. Time and again they report watching, from a vantage point outside themselves, as doctors struggle to return life to their pale and moribund bodies. The details they report—about conversations, instruments used, and actions taken—are vivid, rich, and accurate.

A number of explanations have been put forward for NDEs: According to some, they may be hallucinations, reconstructions of conversations heard in a semiconscious state, or reactions to drugs or endorphins, the body's natural opiates. But to a growing number of scientists, near-death experiences may offer new clues to the nature of consciousness, and they may even be evidence that the mind is indeed an entity independent of brain and body.

Some would say that the NDE is an expression of the soul, the self, or a "cosmic consciousness."

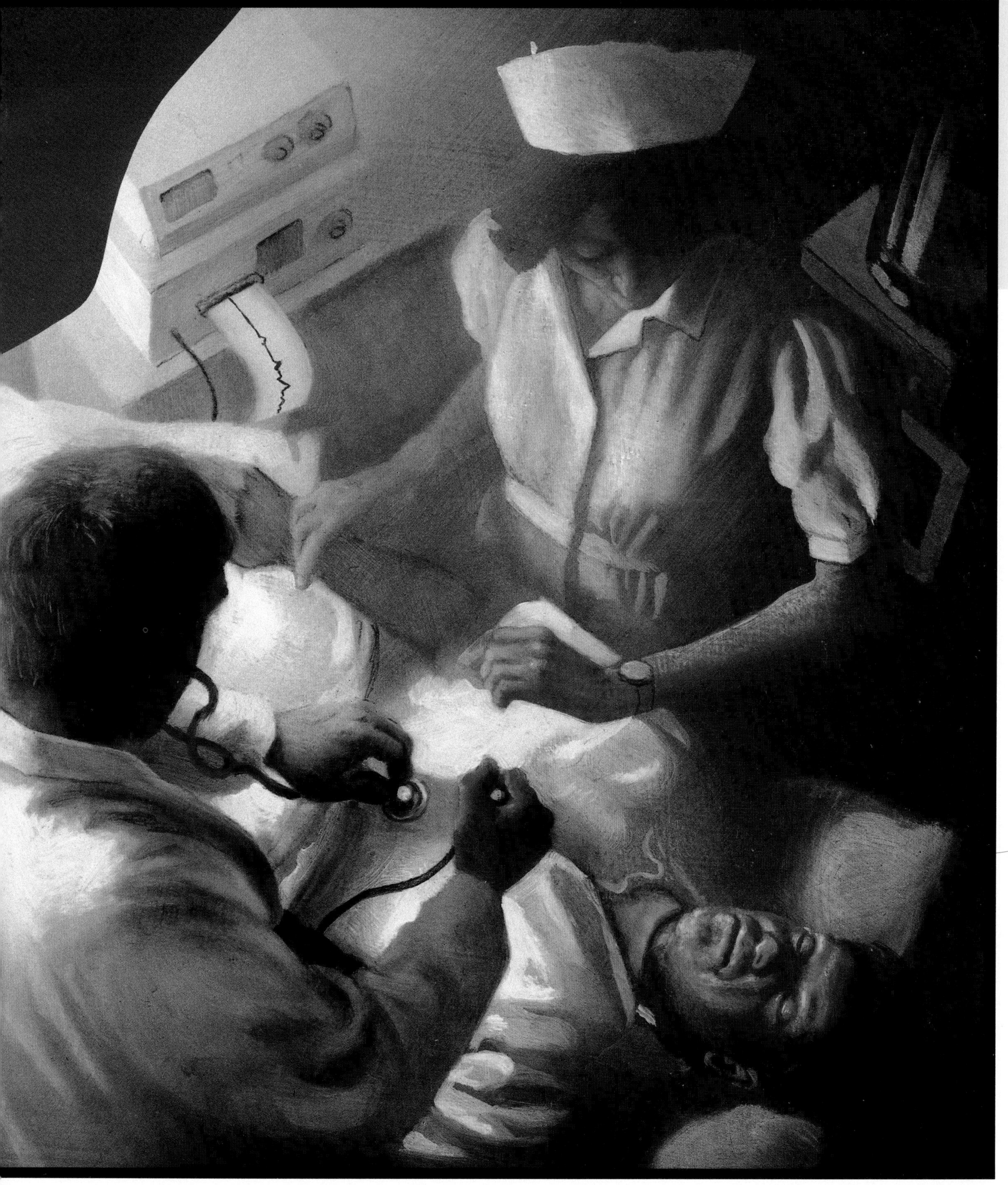

trist at the Maryland Psychiatric Research Center and a 20-year veteran of psychedelic drug research, chided the materialists for "confusing the map with the territory." Close encounters with death do not create the sensation of otherworldly experiences, he argued, nor do psychedelic drugs conjure realms that do not exist. Rather, NDEs and drugs are agents, keys that open doors to hidden, but very real, regions of the mind. By amplifying existing mental processes, Grof wrote, these agents—which also include controlled breathing, evocative music, meditation, dreaming, and hypnosis—"activate the deep unconscious and make its contents available for conscious processing." What we term hallucinations are not merely delusions, according to Grof, but excursions into the so-called transpersonal domain. Here, the individual mind merges with the collective unconscious, that great reservoir of latent consciousness that, according to Carl Jung, unites all beings.

Grof, who spent years as a practicing psychiatrist in Europe, reported that his patients sometimes carried back odd bits of information from their visits to the transpersonal realm. For example, a patient named Richard, while under the influence of LSD, encountered luminous beings who pressed on him the name, street address, and telephone number of a couple in the Moravian city of Kroměříž, insisting that he contact them to let them know that their son Ladislav was all right. Grof decided to follow up on the demand. After dialing the number in Kroměříž, he asked to speak with Ladislav. "To my astonishment," recalled the scientist, "the woman on the other side of the line started to cry. When she calmed down, she told me with a broken voice, 'Our son is not with us anymore; he passed away, we lost him three weeks ago.' "

To Grof and others, the sojourns of Richard and Mr. P in the transpersonal domain not only challenge the materialist model of consciousness, they erode the very foundation on which classical science is built. Such experiences, in Grof's view, "suggest that consciousness is not an accidental product of matter, but an equal partner of matter"—or perhaps consciousness transcends matter entirely, existing apart from the tangible, observable world. He further believes that transpersonal journeys show the "arbitrary nature of all physical boundaries" and the ability of individuals to communicate "through unknown means and channels."

Earlier in the 20th century, long before Grof began attacking the principles of materialism, a similar assault on the conventions of objective reality was mounted in the name of science itself. One of the first shots was fired at the Newtonian precept that matter consisted of minute pellets called atoms. In 1911, British physicist Ernest Rutherford used radioactive particles to probe the interior of atoms. He discovered that the atom's structure was not solid at all, but—like a miniature solar system—a region of nearly empty space in which tiny charged particles called electrons orbited about a central nucleus. So small were these subatomic particles in comparison to their spatial domain that, were the entire atom inflated to the size of the dome of St. Peter's Basilica in Rome, the nucleus would be no bigger than a grain of salt, the electrons motes of dust. Matter, it turned out, was proportionately as vacuous as deep space.

But just as science was reconciling itself to the illusory nature of physical substance, Danish physicist Niels Bohr and other researchers began to notice that the electrons in Rutherford's atom exhibited some rather peculiar behavior. For one thing, the particles did not keep to tidy orbits. Instead, they traced broad, fuzzy swaths in which they seemed to be everywhere at once. Odder still, they jumped from one orbit to another without traversing the space in between. The effect, as one observer expressed it, was no less startling than if "the earth were suddenly transferred into the orbit of Mars without having to travel."

To learn more about the strange conduct of these particles, Bohr attempted in the 1920s to plot the position and momentum of a single electron. What he found, however, was that the more accurately he pinpointed the electron's location, the more uncertain its velocity became. Conversely, the more exactly he clocked its speed, the more indefinite its position became.

This axiom, articulated in 1927 by the German physicist Werner Heisenberg, came to be known as the Heisenberg uncertainty principle. As it turned out, the uncertainty stemmed not from deficiencies in the physicist's methods but from the nature of the particles themselves. For electrons—indeed, for all of an atom's tiny building blocks—position and speed represent distinct states of reality. Thus it is possible to measure one or the other, but not both at the same time. As a result, these minute bits of matter are effectively governed by a randomness and unpredictability that exempts them from normal rules of cause and effect. Scientists can forecast with great accuracy how many atoms in a radioactive sample will decay in a given time, for instance, but they cannot tell which atom will decay next.

In the same way that Rutherford robbed conventional science of its faith in the solidity of matter, Bohr and Heisenberg undermined the long-cherished belief in the inviolability of cause and effect. Meanwhile, Albert Einstein continued chipping away at the Newtonian bedrock of absolute time and space. More than five years before Rutherford first explored the atom's interior, Einstein theorized that, at velocities near the speed of light or in massive gravitational fields, time slows to a crawl, objects shrink, and mass grows infinitely heavy. All measurements (except that of light speed, which is constant) are relative in Einstein's universe, where the three dimensions of space are bound up with the fourth dimension of time.

Such revelations seem to defy common sense because they are not part of our everyday experience: People, after all, do not move about at relativistic speeds. But subatomic particles do. And because they do move at such velocities, they are capable, under certain conditions, of changing instantly from mass to energy; the collision of an electron and a particle called a positron, for example, produces high-energy gamma rays. Feats of this nature call into question the whole definition of matter.

As it turns out, hints that mass and energy are one and the same lie within the very structure of subatomic particles. An electron, for instance, seems to take a different form depending on the circumstances. Colliding with another particle, it behaves like a bullet, a single condensed quantum of energy. But in other situations, physicists have found that its behavior is much more like that of a wave: Changes in an electron's energy level, for example, could best be described as shifts in a wave's frequency.

The particle's schizophrenic nature confounded scientists struggling to squeeze it into a convenient pigeonhole. William Bragg, who shared the Nobel Prize for physics with his son in 1915, drolly observed that electrons seem to be waves on Mondays, Wednesdays, and Fridays, and particles on Tuesdays, Thursdays, and Saturdays. In truth, according to quantum theory, electrons exist in a kind of dualistic limbo until an observer imposes one state or the other upon them by the mere act of looking.

As Princeton University physicist John Wheeler has put it, "Nothing is more important about the quantum principle than this, that it destroys the concept of the world as 'sitting out there.' " A scientist deciding to study electrons, according to Wheeler, must choose whether to measure the electrons' position or their momentum. "To install the equipment to measure the one prevents and excludes installing the equipment to measure the other." The simple act of measuring irrevocably changes the state of the electron and, by extension, all of creation.

An unwatched electron is neither particle nor wave; it becomes one or the other only upon the registering of impressions in the mind. In that sense, consciousness defines reality, literally altering the structure of the physical world. Experiments have shown that, prior to measurement, subatomic particles inhabit a twilight zone where speed, location, and spin are uncertain. Under the weight of such evidence, the classical ideal of reality collapses. "The universe," remarked the late particle physicist James Jeans in 1930, "begins to look more like a great thought than like a great machine."

The parallel between quantum physics and the stuff of consciousness was not lost on Heisenberg, who suggested that the wave-particle duality of electrons accorded neatly with the dualism of mind and matter—the theory, first advanced by 17th-century French philosopher René Descartes, which holds that the mind exists independently of the body. Perhaps Heisenberg thought that the relationship between disembodied consciousness and the physical brain is similar to that mysterious link between the electron's wave function and its role as a particle.

To Paul Davies, however, the distinction between mind and brain is more subtle still. Davies, a professor of mathematical physics at the University of Adelaide in Australia, points out that the double identity of electrons and other subatomic particles does not constitute a true duality. That is, particle and wave are not separate entities but are two manifestations of the same thing. So it is with mind and brain, he claims. The intangible mind, characterized by thoughts, feelings, and emotions, is simply a different conceptual order of the material brain with its billions of buzzing neurons.

Davies borrows a metaphor from the world of computers to illustrate his point. The synaptic connectors in the brain, he suggests, are not unlike the microprocessing circuitry inside a desktop machine. Both are "hardware," as is an electron behaving as a particle. By the same token, mind and electron wave are equivalent to "software," that abstraction of on-off signals that permits the computer to manipulate information. Consciousness, Davies suggests, is thus a form of organization.

This all sounds suspiciously like materialism except for one distinction. "To say a brain is a machine," Davies explains, "need not imply that the mind is nothing but the product of mechanistic processes." In his view, the essential ingredient of mind is information: "It is the pattern inside the brain, not the brain itself, that makes us what we are." As a result, unlike the materialists, Davies postulates that mind survives the death of the physical brain, just as a symphony continues to exist even when it is not being played.

Davies' model of consciousness as ethereal software, however intriguing, leaves unanswered a central question: If the mind consists of information, how is it linked to the world in which it operates?

One possible answer has emerged on the other side of the globe, in the laboratory of American neuropsychologist Karl Pribram. Currently at

The Quest for Consciousness

No mental characteristic is so mysterious and elusive—or so fundamentally human—as consciousness, the self-awareness that attends perceiving, thinking, and feeling. In the famous formula "I think, therefore I am," the 17th-century French philosopher René Descartes identified conscious thought as the very essence of self, belonging to an immaterial sphere and working in ways that are beyond observational reach.

Many scientists today prefer to leave the puzzle of mental awareness to philosophers rather than attempt to pin down so slippery a subject. Even so, the search for the nature of consciousness continues on many fronts. As explained on the following pages, ideas about this aspect of the mind are both very old and very new: They lay at the core of the Buddha's meditations on the cosmos in the sixth century BC, and they glimmer on the frontiers of theoretical physics. Some investigators are looking for the key to self-awareness in the operations of neurons, and others have ventured beyond human bounds, trying to determine if the gift of consciousness extends to animals—or if it may someday be acquired by machines.

Virginia's Radford University, Pribram actually came up with his theory of mind nearly three decades ago, when, as a brain researcher at Stanford University in California, he was seeking a mechanism to explain how the firing of neurons in the brain translates into subjective experience. By chance, he picked up an issue of *Scientific American* featuring a story on the emerging science of holography.

A hologram, unlike a normal two-dimensional photograph, is a three-dimensional image captured on ordinary photographic film. The technique for producing one involves using a mirror to split a laser beam down the middle. One half of the beam is targeted directly at the film. The other is bounced off the object, then directed at the film. When the two beams meet, the interacting waves of radiation create a mosaic of light and dark ripples. Although this seemingly chaotic pattern of wave fronts is recorded on the film, no image is immediately discernible. Instead, it must be reconstituted using another laser called a reconstruction beam. As this third beam passes through the holographic film, it conjures a three-dimensional

From Many Neurons, a Unified Vision

In the 1950s, the eminent scientist Francis Crick helped unravel the mysteries of genetics by working at the basement level: His codiscovery of the structure of DNA, the fundamental vehicle of inheritance, won him the Nobel Prize for medicine and physiology in 1962. Recently, Crick and biophysicist Christof Koch of the California Institute of Technology have pursued a similar strategy in studies of consciousness at the neuronal level. Setting aside such complex mental matters as imagination, they have limited their research to what they call visual attention—the ability of the brain to elevate visual input to the level of awareness—and have sought a neuronal mechanism that might make this power possible.

The phenomenon, metaphorically likened to a spotlight steered through darkness, is familiar to everyone: When a person scans faces in a crowd or reaches for a cup of coffee, only a fraction of the visual information registered by the brain is consciously seen. The rest, like shadowy objects outside the spotlight's glare, is known at some level, but the viewer is not directly aware of it.

Crick and Koch agree with the contention of 19th-century psychologist William James that awareness arises from a combination of attention—the spotlight's concentrated beam—and short-term memory; together they form a sort of temporary adhesive that allows perceptions to be processed for meaning. What makes this mental functioning so mystifying is the way the brain distributes sensory information. In the case of vision, an object's color, motion, edges, and other features are handled by separate, widely distributed sets of neurons in the cortex, yet the brain somehow binds the scattered data into a meaningful whole and briefly retains it for analysis.

Crick and Koch argue that the key to this feat is rooted in coordinated signaling by brain cells. They believe that neurons engaged in conscious seeing fire in unison, perhaps rhythmically, whereas neurons involved in vision below the level of awareness fire randomly. The result is to impose a unity on scattered components, just as bulbs blinking in unison on a Christmas tree stand out from those that display no pattern. Crick and Koch suspect that such timed firing briefly strengthens the links between the neurons, creating short-term memory.

vision of the original object lifelike enough to invite touch but as insubstantial as smoke.

The fact that interacting wave fronts could record information—in this case, visual data—was a revelation to Pribram. Perhaps, he reasoned, the electrical wave fronts generated by activity in the brain create abstract holographic "snapshots" of perceptual experience that are somehow stored in the brain's neural network. What made the hologram model particularly attractive was the fact that, unlike with a photograph, any part of the holographic image, regardless of its size, contains information about the whole. In other words, the entire picture can be reconstituted from the tiniest fragment of film.

To Pribram, this holographic characteristic bore a close resemblance to the workings of human memory. Having spent much of his career probing the brains of monkeys, chimpanzees, and humans in search of clues to how information is stored and retrieved, he knew that memory storage is widely distributed in the brain. Laboratory rats, for example, can still remember their way through mazes even after much of their brain tissue has been removed. Similarly, stroke victims with damage in parts of their brains retain certain memories but lose the

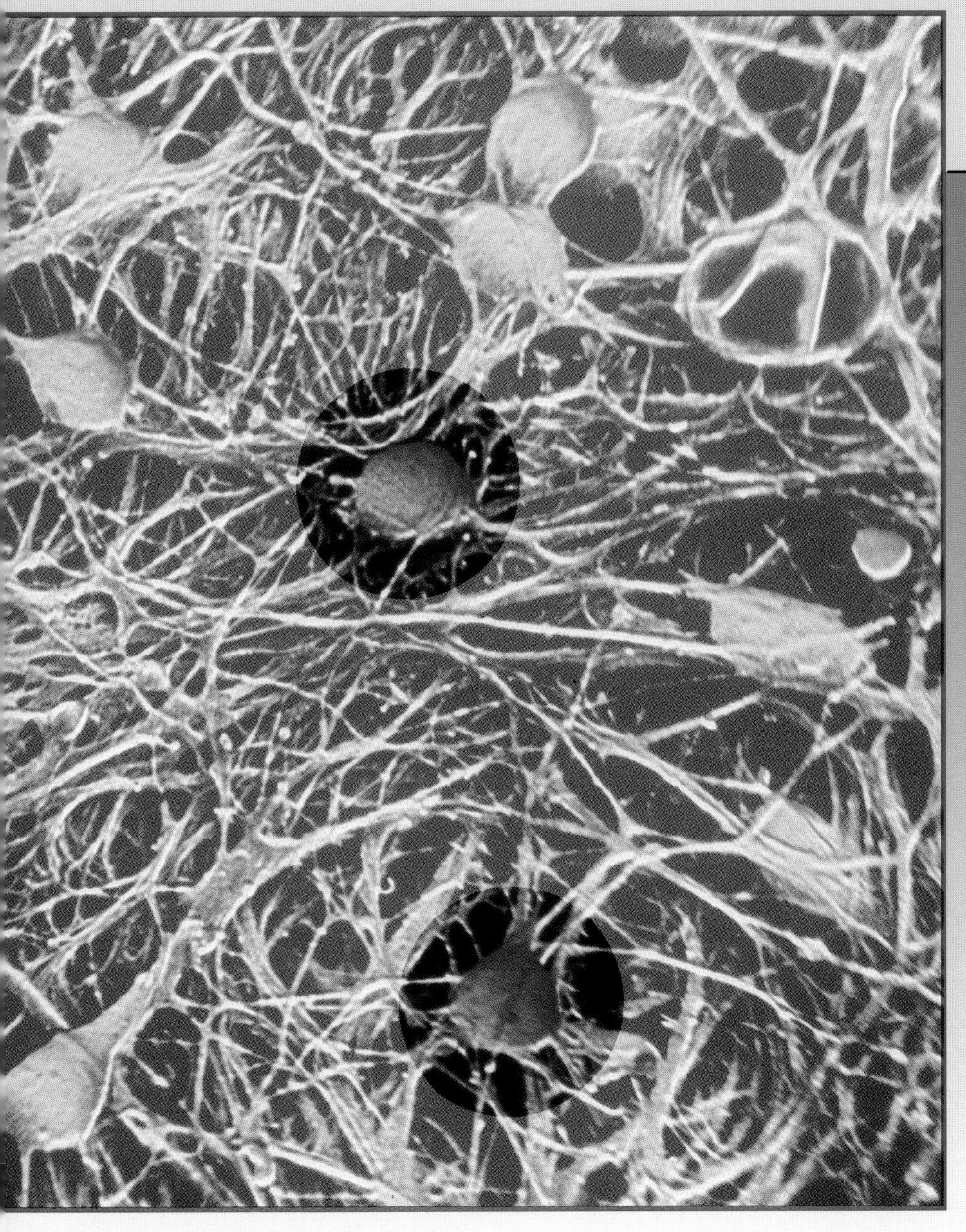

ability to retrieve others; one patient may be able to, say, drive a car but unable to describe how it is done.

Although the mechanisms of storage and retrieval may bear no resemblance to each other, the fact that near-infinite amounts of data could be contained in a speck of holographic film suddenly made it easier for Pribram to comprehend how the human mind could pack a lifetime of memories into an organ the size of a grapefruit. A number of accounts from others attest to the brain's phenomenal storage capacity. In the 1950s, for example, Harold Rosen, a doctor at Johns Hopkins Hospital in Baltimore, reported that one of his patients began writing in a peculiar script while he was under hypnosis. The script was later identified as Oscan, an obscure pre-Latin language used 2,500 years ago only in western Italy. By asking questions of the hypnotized patient, Rosen determined that the man had seen the ancient writing years before—in a book being read by someone next to him in the library.

In view of such evidence, the hologram analogy seems compelling enough, but one component is omitted: There is no laser beam in the brain. How, then, does the mind capture, and later reconstitute, its impressions of the world?

Pribram has suggested that, in lieu of a laser, "the brain performs certain operations, which can be described by the mathematics of holography, to code, decode, and recode sensory input." When we look at a table, for instance, the retinal cells of the eye capture the diffuse light waves, or "scatter," reflected off the surface and convert them into signals, which travel to vision centers in the cortex. Pribram's theory suggests that within the brain's neural network these signals trigger electrical wave fronts that—like a hologram's laser beams—interact to form a pattern that becomes a stored memory. During retrieval, this pattern is decoded to reconstruct the original object. Such a mechanism

Hidden Dimensions of Awareness

Though most researchers believe that consciousness will someday be explained as a neuronal activity, a few suspect that it transcends brain functioning and depends on physical laws not yet fully fathomed. One radical view of this sort has been advanced by British neuroscientist John Smythies. He calls his theory extended materialism, contrasting it to Descartes's notion that consciousness has no material basis and therefore lacks extension in space. Smythies' conception of space, however, is not limited to the familiar three dimensions that, along with time, define the standard physical framework of reality.

Smythies suggests that everyone has a private space in addition to the shared, public version. Each individual's personal framework intersects with the familiar dimensions while remaining distinct from them, and it provides an arena for all conscious sensations that have spatial extension or location—objects discernible by sight or touch. In this private domain, argues Smythies, the information registered by scattered neurons is drawn together and given coherent shape. That reality may include hidden dimensions is not so startling a supposition, he notes; it is a notion common to several leading-edge theories about the structure of the universe.

In simplified form, the diagram at right sums up Smythies' explanation of consciousness, which he defines as "the contents of what we experience." The horizontal plane stands for familiar, public space. The brain, represented by a white shape, is embedded in this space at the "now" of time; the brain is shown lying on a wavy path that indicates its past and future states. The vertical plane is another, distinct space, and the cone-shaped segment represents an individual's private portion of it. Within this private sector, some sort of "causal mechanism" extracts the visual sensory information scattered through the brain and projects it on a perceptual field, indicated by the curved shape at the top of the cone. The causal mechanism, says Smythies, is like the circuitry of a television set. A person is aware only of what is projected on the screen; the apparatus that creates the images—the generator of consciousness—lies invisible behind the glass.

would allow the brain to warehouse a record of sensory input in a coded form similar to the pattern recorded on holographic film. According to Pribram, then, "Perception is not direct. It is a construction."

Karl Pribram has not been the only scientist to seize on the hologram model, nor is his theory the most comprehensive. The late quantum physicist David Bohm, who spent the latter part of his career at London's Birkbeck College, proposed that the universe itself has a holographic aspect. Beneath the world of matter, according to Bohm, lies a vast and unobserved realm of energy governed by the laws of quantum physics. This unseen realm is Bohm's holographic domain, a region that he termed the enfolded order. As he expressed it, "Matter is like a small ripple on this tremendous ocean of energy."

Bohm's theory tries to bridge the gap between the science of holography and the veiled workings of the mind. Just as the complete holographic image resides in each of its parts, he argued, the entire enfolded order is contained within every human being. "Each individual manifests the consciousness of mankind," he told the authors of *The Three-Pound Universe.* The holographic brain, then, is itself a part of the universal hologram.

In reasoning out his theory, Bohm, a follower of Indian philosopher Krishnamurti, drew heavily on Hindu mysticism. Like a number of his scientific colleagues, Bohm had been struck by the similarities between the revelations of modern physics and ancient Eastern philosophies. Both suggest that the observable universe, from subatomic particles to trees and planets and galaxies, is defined only by its interactions with or connections to some form of consciousness.

According to the Hindu philosophy of Vedanta, for example, consciousness is the source of all things and resides in the Supreme Being, or Brahman. Within each individual, Brahman reveals itself as finite consciousness, or mind. Through this mind, people are able to perceive both the world of things (the objective universe) and the inner world of thoughts and feelings (the psychic realm). Yet, according to Vedanta, the self, mind, and universe do not really exist; rather, they are merely illusions, three manifestations of Brahman. Normally, our intellect prevents us from seeing beyond this veil of illusion, in much the same way as ordinary senses hinder our perception of the quantum nature of matter.

At the core of Vedantic thought is the belief that, rather than arising from electrical activity within the skull, consciousness exists prior to and apart from the tangible world, including the brain. If this were not the case, say the adherents of Vedanta, the universe and all that exists within it could not possibly follow such ordered patterns. As Vedantic scholar Swami Satprakashananda wrote in 1965, "That which fashions the material form, develops, animates, and cognizes it, must be something other than the form itself."

The Vedantic notion that the mind exists outside the body and exerts its influence on solid matter would appear to represent one of the widest points in the chasm that exists between Eastern mysticism and traditional Western science. And yet, that

gap has been significantly narrowed by one of science's most esteemed members. According to John Eccles, a 1963 recipient of the Nobel Prize in medicine for his work at the Australian National University in Canberra on signal transmission among neurons, the mind is an entity in its own right, incorporeal and timeless.

Central to Eccles' theory are the results of a series of experiments conducted during the 1970s focusing on the cerebral cortex, the brain's highly developed outer layer, which serves as the seat of higher reasoning and overseer of movement in the body. As that research made clear, milliseconds before a person carries out a willed action, certain neurons in the cortex discharge an electrical "readiness" signal, which in turn cues the appropriate motor neurons to fire. But the experiments, fascinating though they were, failed to resolve the obvious question: What launches the readiness signal?

Eccles, now retired and living in Switzerland, maintains that the answer is human volition: the self-willed mind. As he sees it, something he calls "will influences" somehow gain access to the physical brain via a specialized liaison area in one of the language centers of the cortex. There, Eccles posits, neurons are continuous-

An Ancient Vision of Ultimate Knowledge

Among history's great spiritual seekers, none thought more deeply about the human mind than Siddhartha Gautama, known to his followers as the Buddha—the Awakened One. Born into a noble family in Nepal around 563 BC, he enjoyed riches, honors, and domestic happiness as a young man, yet he gave up everything to look for fundamental truths. Tradition says that, after years of wandering and self-mortification, he finally achieved complete understanding of the meaning of existence as he meditated under a tree not far from the Ganges River.

With enlightenment came perfect inner peace, and the Buddha's demeanor as much as his words helped him win many thousands of followers during the remaining 45 years of his life. Eventually, his teachings took hold throughout eastern Asia, from Tibet to Japan; today, Buddhism in various forms is espoused by more than half a billion people. Its ultimate promise is both subtle and profound: It holds out the possibility of a kind of pure, undefiled consciousness.

One of the central principles of Buddhism is summed up in the term *dukkha*, defined as the feeling of frustration and suffering that arises as the individual attempts to cling to a world that is, by its nature, impermanent. Ordinary consciousness, said the Buddha, contributes to this suffering and dissatisfaction. Acting in association with the different sense organs as well as with the emotions that stir the mind, such consciousness serves to maintain the attachments between the self and a transitory reality—material objects, sensations, perceptions, thought. But the awareness so precious to the self, the Buddha said, is as ephemeral as all that it bears on. Other religions might see consciousness as an eternal soul—transcendent, belonging to some higher sphere. But to Buddhists, it is merely part of the never-stopping flow of life, a river of change impossible to resist.

Buddhism offers no salvation through the mercy of gods, and it does not conceive of a heaven where the self can find fixity. Rather, the Buddha taught that freedom from dukkha can be achieved through meditation. By contemplating the illusory nature of the world, believers may gain a different kind of awareness—a serene acceptance that the self is fleeting and insignificant.

ly poised just below the threshold of firing. Because of the remarkable density of neurons in the cortex—some 40,000 to every 1/700 of a square inch—he believes that the triggering of just one of these specialized nerve cells by will influences would be sufficient to spark the simultaneous discharge of hundreds of thousands of neurons, thus setting off the readiness signal.

Although will influences have yet to show up on any laboratory instrument, Eccles is certain that they exist. He has dubbed them "psychons" and proposes that they work their magic at the quantum level in the brain. If Eccles' theory is correct, every human action is quite literally an act of cerebral psychokinesis—a case of mind over matter.

Such a pronouncement, coming as it has from a renowned brain researcher, has been welcomed with great enthusiasm by the community of scientists around the world who have devoted their lives to investigating the inexplicable in nature—the weird phenomena associated with ESP and other paranormal "powers." As these scientists point out, strange things do in fact happen, bolstering

The Puzzle of Animal Understanding

In the wild, animals often display remarkable ingenuity. A beaver, for example, will cut holes in its dam during the winter, presumably to lower the water level and create breathing space under a pond's frozen surface; a lioness will drive prey toward an ambush; a heron will use twigs to lure minnows. Still more impressive are the mental feats performed by animals that are tutored and tested in laboratories: A pygmy chimpanzee named Kanzi can respond to language at the level of a two-and-a-half-year-old, carrying out such never-before-heard instructions as "Put the melon in the potty." Dolphins in a marine laboratory will report whether a ball is in their pool by touching YES or NO paddles with their snouts. And an African gray parrot named Alex (*right*), trained for 15 years by ethologist Irene Pepperberg of the University of Arizona, has learned the words for more than 70 objects, shapes, colors, and materials. At least 80 percent of the time, Alex can correctly list the attributes of an object such as a red paper triangle even when he has never seen it before. Asked how a green wooden square differs from a red wooden square, he replies "Color!" As for numerical values, he can identify quantities up to six.

Some scientists are wary of ascribing the performances of Kanzi, Alex, and other laboratory stars to conscious thinking. What looks like the intelligent use of language or number, they say, may be no more than rote learning—an extension of animals' natural ability to acquire the tricks of survival. Skeptics often mention Clever Hans, a trained horse around the turn of the century that supposedly could solve mathematical problems, counting out the answers in hoof taps. A psychologist finally showed that Hans's brilliance was based on the horse's detection of cues inadvertently supplied by his handlers. If they did not know the answer, neither did Hans.

Today, studies of Alex and other animal subjects are done under carefully controlled conditions. Given the safeguards and the volume of evidence, many researchers have come to believe that animals should be credited with the power of at least rudimentary thinking. Some, in fact, suspect that the chimpanzee—humankind's closest animal relative—may even be self-aware, able to reflect on its own existence just as humans do.

the notion that the mind is more than a bundle of tissue.

Tales of paranormal events abound in everyday life. In their 1987 book *Intangible Evidence*, authors Bernard Gittelson and Laura Torbet tell the story of a woman who was awakened on her Oregon farm at 3:40 one morning by the sound of people screaming. The cries eventually faded away, but the taste of acrid smoke lingered in the woman's mouth. She woke her husband; together they searched the farm but found nothing unusual. Later that day, while watching the evening news, the couple learned of an explosion at a chemical plant 90 miles away that killed six people. The time of the blast was 3:40 a.m.

Mainstream scientists normally dismiss such mysteries—sometimes called psychic, or psi, events—as coincidence, aberration, or downright fabrication. New York psychologist Lawrence LeShan contends that because psi occurrences "violate laws well established by long and hard scientific endeavor," many scientists conclude that such goings-on "simply cannot have happened."

This kind of reasoning is not good science, argues LeShan, only wishful thinking. After all, he notes, the physics of quantum theory is rife with anomalies that cannot be explained

within the framework of classical science. What is normal on a subatomic level—say, for an electron to leap from one orbit to another without crossing the intervening space—is paranormal teleportation on the level of macroscopic matter.

The perception that psi events defy scientific laws is, according to LeShan, the result of confusion between two distinct spheres of experience. What we observe in the see-and-touch realm is located in geometric space; what we perceive in the realm of consciousness is not. Solving the riddle of how information, such as the agony of explosion victims far away, travels across space from one mind to another is easy: It does not. Just because the bodies of two subjects in an experiment are 300 miles apart, LeShan insists, does not mean their consciousnesses are also 300 miles apart. "We have been fooled," he says, "because we have such a strong impression that our consciousness is located within our body."

Only a new model of consciousness, which transcends conventional notions about the relationship between mind and body, could accommodate these extraordinary happenings. One of those attempting to craft such a model is Charles Tart, a parapsychologist at the University of California at Davis. Like LeShan, Tart maintains that consciousness resides outside the human form, in a domain unbounded by physical rules. With a theory that recalls Eccles' self-willed mind, Tart proposes that the brain serves as a point of exchange between free-floating consciousness and the physical world, and that the mind and brain interact through subtle forms of psychokinesis.

Tart and other believers lament that bona fide paranormal phenomena too often become little more than grist for supermarket tabloids and late-night television, flatly dismissed by orthodox Western psychology. This dismal credibility rating, according to Richard Broughton, director of research at the Institute for Parapsy-

The Merging of Mind and Machine

Back in 1950, a brilliant British mathematician named Alan Turing predicted that, by the end of the 20th century, computers would be able to converse with people so fluently that, if their machine identity was concealed, they would often be mistaken for humans. Although that day remains somewhere out in the science-fiction future, many experts in the field of artificial intelligence—a branch of computer science that aims at endowing machines with aspects of human thinking—are convinced that Turing's prophecy will become a reality. The boldest among them anticipate the emergence of a new species, electronic but sentient.

To measure progress toward humanlike computers, some researchers have been staging an annual contest in Boston since 1991. In a variation on a test proposed by Alan Turing, they set up one-on-one conversations between computer terminals and a group of human judges. A terminal may be controlled either by a computer program or by a human operator in another room; the judges guess which is which by sitting down at the keyboard and engaging in a dialogue. The winner of the contest is the program that the judges score as most humanlike.

Since no present-day program can cover the full range of human knowledge, conversations are limited to a single topic. The first-year winner was a program titled "Whimsical Conversation." In one exchange on the topic of whimsy, a judge asked, "Have you ever gotten yourself in trouble because of your whims?" The terminal replied, "My country is the earth, and I am a citizen of the world, would you agree? You aren't really talking about me, are you?" So convincing were the program's responses that several judges actually thought they were conversing with a person. The program's creator won again the following year with an entry titled "Men vs. Women."

Contest director Robert Epstein notes that the main way humans decide whether another entity is intelligent and conscious is by verbal behavior. In some computer of tomorrow, he says, "we will have a whole new entity that is indistinguishable from a human in the way that it converses. So questions like, 'Is it intelligent?', 'Is it self-aware?', 'Is it conscious?', 'Does it have feelings?' take on a reality that you cannot ignore."

chology in Durham, North Carolina, stems from the fact that most psi occurrences "ultimately boil down to anecdotes—stories about what happened once upon a time."

But the winds may slowly be shifting. Over the past 60 years, parapsychologists in laboratories in the United States and Western Europe have amassed data on thousands of controlled experiments that, in Tart's words, "conclusively demonstrate that there are aspects of the human mind that simply cannot be reduced to materialistic explanations." The first experiments, involving cards that displayed different geometric shapes, were conducted for the most part at Duke University during the 1930s, under the tutelage of pioneer parapsychologist J. B. Rhine.

To test telepathy (literally "distant feeling"), one subject (the sender) in the Duke University study was asked to concentrate on a single card and then attempt to transmit its impression to another person (the receiver) at a distant location. The test for clairvoyance ("clear seeing"), or the ability to perceive unseen objects or events, involved a similar setup. This time, however, the sender removed cards from a preshuffled deck one at a time and, without looking at them, placed them facedown. Meanwhile,

the receiver attempted to guess the order of the cards.

In measuring results, experimenters used a statistical formula to determine the odds against chance. The most impressive performance was that of a shy divinity student named Hubert E. Pearce, Jr., who surmounted odds of 22 billion to one. During a series of tests in 1932, Pearce scored 558 hits out of 1,850 trials, where 370 represented chance. Nevertheless, skeptics complained about the inadequacy of safeguards against fraud or error, noting that no independent researchers had been able to reproduce the Duke results.

By the early 1960s, however, methods for testing hidden mental powers had grown considerably more sophisticated. Among the more inventive were ESP tests employed by Montague Ullman and Stanley Krippner at the Maimonides Community Mental Health Center in Brooklyn, New York. On the belief that sleep promotes telepathic communication, Ullman and Krippner set up a sleep lab in the medical center and devised a series of now-famous experiments. For more than a decade, the Maimonides researchers traveled unknown avenues of the dream world, chalking up an impressive record of "hits" as they worked to determine whether dream content could be controlled through telepathy. In 1973, five years before the Maimonides team ended its dream work, physicists Harold Puthoff and Russell Targ of the Stanford Research Institute in Menlo Park, California, began a battery of tests designed to study clairvoyance. For one subject, the Stanford researchers selected a New York artist and psychic named Ingo Swann. At first, Swann was asked to use powers of clairvoyance to "view" objects that were hidden in another room. This he did with apparent ease; he quickly grew bored with the exercise and requested a more challenging trial.

After giving it some thought, Puthoff came up with an ingenious, and undoubtedly more entertaining, test. Swann was to be supplied with map coordinates for various locations around the world and asked to describe the actual location. To make sure the answers were not based on his knowledge of geography, Swann was required to provide specific details about the target site that did not appear on maps. As an added precaution, researchers working with Swann were told nothing about the area in question.

In one experiment, a set of latitude and longitude figures was mailed to the lab by an East Coast scientist who made no secret of his disdain for all things paranormal. Swann nonetheless zeroed in on the coordinates with characteristic aplomb. "This seems to be some sort of mounds or rolling hills," he pronounced. "There is a city to the north; I can see taller buildings and some smog. This seems to be a strange place, somewhat like the lawns one would find around a military base." He added, "I get the impression of something underground, but I'm not sure."

Swann sketched a picture of what he had seen. The drawing and a transcript of his description were then mailed across the country to the scientist, who phoned in his analysis. Swann's vision, reported the man amid expressions of disbelief, was accurate in every detail, right down to the dimensions and distances on the sketch. The target was a missile site—a small area with controlled access. There was no way the psychic could have visited the location.

The apparent ability to transmit thoughts or to "see" what the eye cannot certainly suggests a complexity and force that would seem to exceed the material brain. Some of the most compelling—and certainly the most controversial—evidence that mind is more than brain comes from research into psychokinesis, or PK. More than any other psi phenomenon, PK has fanned the flames of skepticism among the rationalists. Cynics have run roughshod over a host of PK practitioners, dismissing their demonstrations of mental spoon bending and other stunts as so much sleight of hand or other fakery. It has not been so easy, however, to explain away the abilities of Nina Kulagina.

A Russian woman who served with distinction in the Soviet army during World War II, Kulagina first became aware of her unusual talent while recovering from battle injuries. She remembered feeling very angry one day. Suddenly, she recalled, "a pitcher moved to the edge of the shelf, fell, and smashed to bits." In time she learned to manipulate objects mentally, becoming so adept that she attracted the attention of Soviet authorities, who made her the subject of several controlled experiments in the 1950s and 1960s.

The most dramatic of these tests was conducted by Russian neurophysicist Genady Sergeyev at the A. A. Utomskii Institute in Leningrad. Sergeyev broke an egg into an aquarium filled with saline solution and instructed Kulagina to separate the white from the yolk—using mind power alone. While the movie cameras rolled, Kulagina pinned her concentration on the suspended egg. Slowly, over a 30-minute period, the white collected itself and drifted away. The effort left Kulagina exhausted and temporarily blinded. Monitoring equipment hooked to her body indicated that, during the experiment, her pulse rate soared to an astronomical 240 beats per minute and her body experienced the sudden rise in blood sugar characteristic of a stress reaction. Afterward, researchers confirmed that Kulagina had lost more than two pounds.

While such demonstrations are utterly convincing to those who witness them, they tend to assume the status of tall tales after a few tellings. Making credibility even more elusive, proponents contend, is the fact that truly gifted PK subjects are few and far between. Still the field has begun to enhance its reputation in recent years. Advances in technology have placed psychokinesis at the vanguard of psi-laboratory research, where it has set new records for experimental consistency and control. Perhaps nowhere are scientists finding more clues about the manipulative powers of the mind than at the Princeton Engineering Anomalies Research (PEAR) Laboratory in Princeton, New Jersey.

The PEAR lab got its start in 1979, when Robert Jahn, who was then the dean of Princeton's School of Engineering, began to worry that his human operators—that is, their minds—might start wreaking havoc on sensitive information-processing equipment. Despite taunts from his colleagues, who assailed him as crazy, Jahn managed to get the university's approval for a program designed to look into this possibility. He enlisted the help of Brenda Dunne, a psychologist from the University of Chicago, and together they initiated a series of carefully controlled experiments to test Jahn's hunch.

One key experiment involved a random event generator (REG), essentially a very fast, sophisticated coin flipper. The machine samples a stream of random binary signals—heads and tails, in effect, in the form of pluses and minuses—at the rate of 1,000 per second. For every sequence of 200 electronic "tosses," the REG records how many pluses and minuses were produced, then flashes those numbers on a screen. As with coins, the REG's odds for getting a plus or a minus on any given toss are 50-50.

Jahn and Dunne asked the volunteer operators to try to influence the REG's output by willing the machine to produce either a greater number of heads or a greater number of tails during a given session. As a control, other operators were told merely to observe the REG in action, without trying to influence it. After 12 years and approximately two million trials, the PEAR researchers determined that nearly 100 volunteers did appear to be adept at skewing the outcome, if only slightly: The likelihood of achieving their combined results by chance was only four in 10,000. By comparison, the control operators generated results that conformed to the laws of chance—assuring that the results of the influence tests were not produced by biases inherent in the random event generator.

Admittedly, Jahn and Dunne note, the scale of these effects is tiny. But, as Dunne has pointed out, "They are large enough to exceed the tolerance levels of many modern engineering systems. They are also considerably larger than many of the effects that form the basis of modern physical theories." Furthermore, aside from the practical implications of the results for engineers and physicists, Jahn and Dunne suggest that the experiments offer "scientific evidence that human consciousness plays an active, albeit small, role in the creation of physical reality."

The notion is intriguing, even persuasive. But, at least for now, many questions remain unanswered. Where and how, for example, does the interaction between the inner mind and outer universe take place? (Is that even a valid distinction?) Is consciousness a disembodied cosmic force or a fleeting accompaniment to the activity of the individual, perishable brain? The irony, of course, is that whatever the truth about consciousness may be, it is being pursued by humans, whose chief investigative tool is the quarry itself.

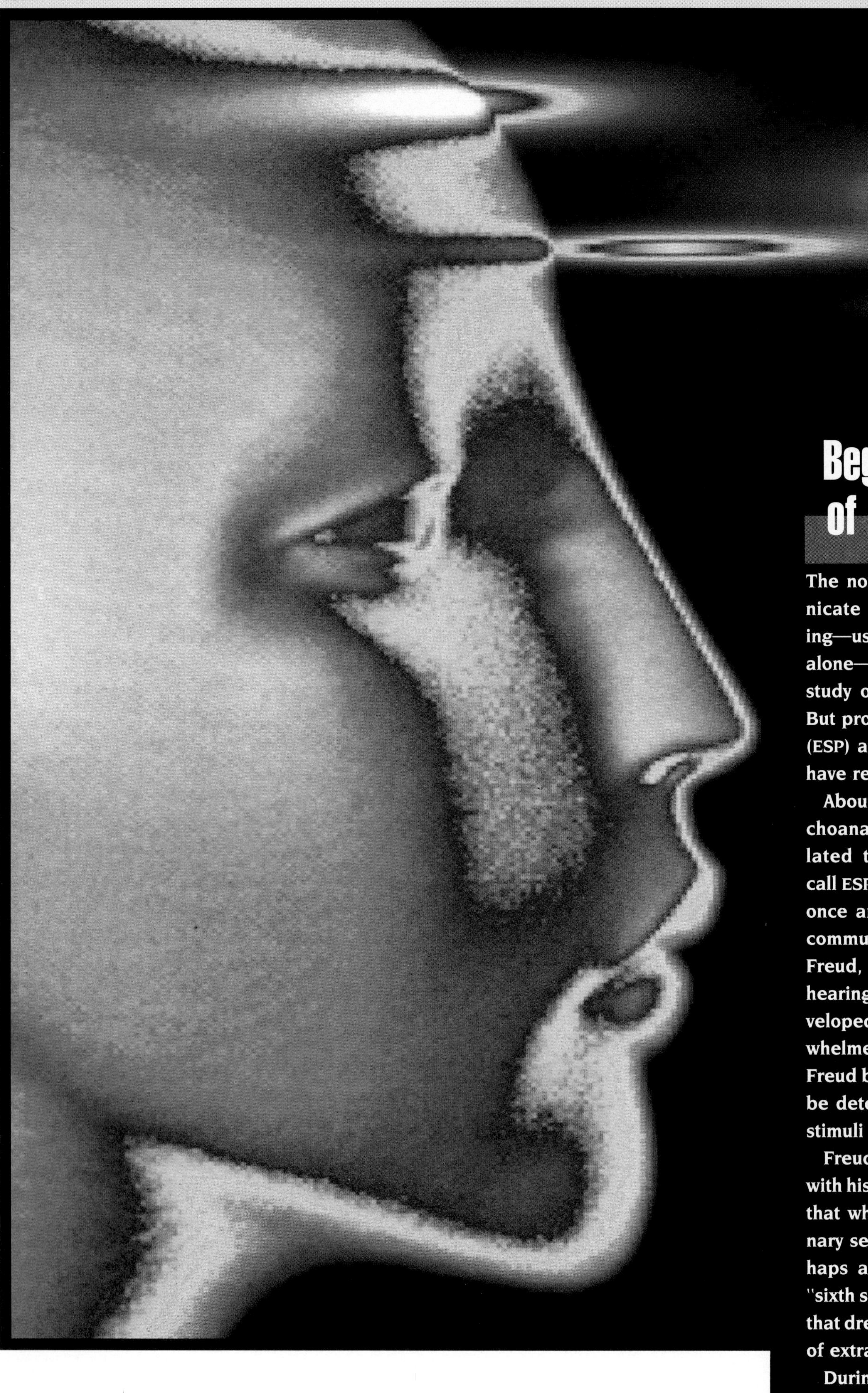

Beguiling Evidence of an Extra Sense

The notion that people can communicate without speaking or signaling—using some power of the mind alone—has lingered at the edge of the study of thought throughout history. But proof of extrasensory perception (ESP) and insight into its mechanism have remained elusive.

About a century ago, father of psychoanalysis Sigmund Freud speculated that what modern scientists call ESP is a true sixth sense, and was once an important means of human communication. Over time, thought Freud, the familiar senses of sight, hearing, touch, taste, and smell developed to the extent that they overwhelmed the delicate voice of ESP. Freud believed that ESP signals might be detected if the clutter of sensory stimuli could be suppressed.

Freud's ideas about ESP converged with his study of dreams. He observed that when people dream, their ordinary senses seem to be dulled—perhaps allowing the operation of the "sixth sense." In fact, Freud theorized that dreams might even be recordings of extrasensory communications.

During the 1970s, this hypothesis

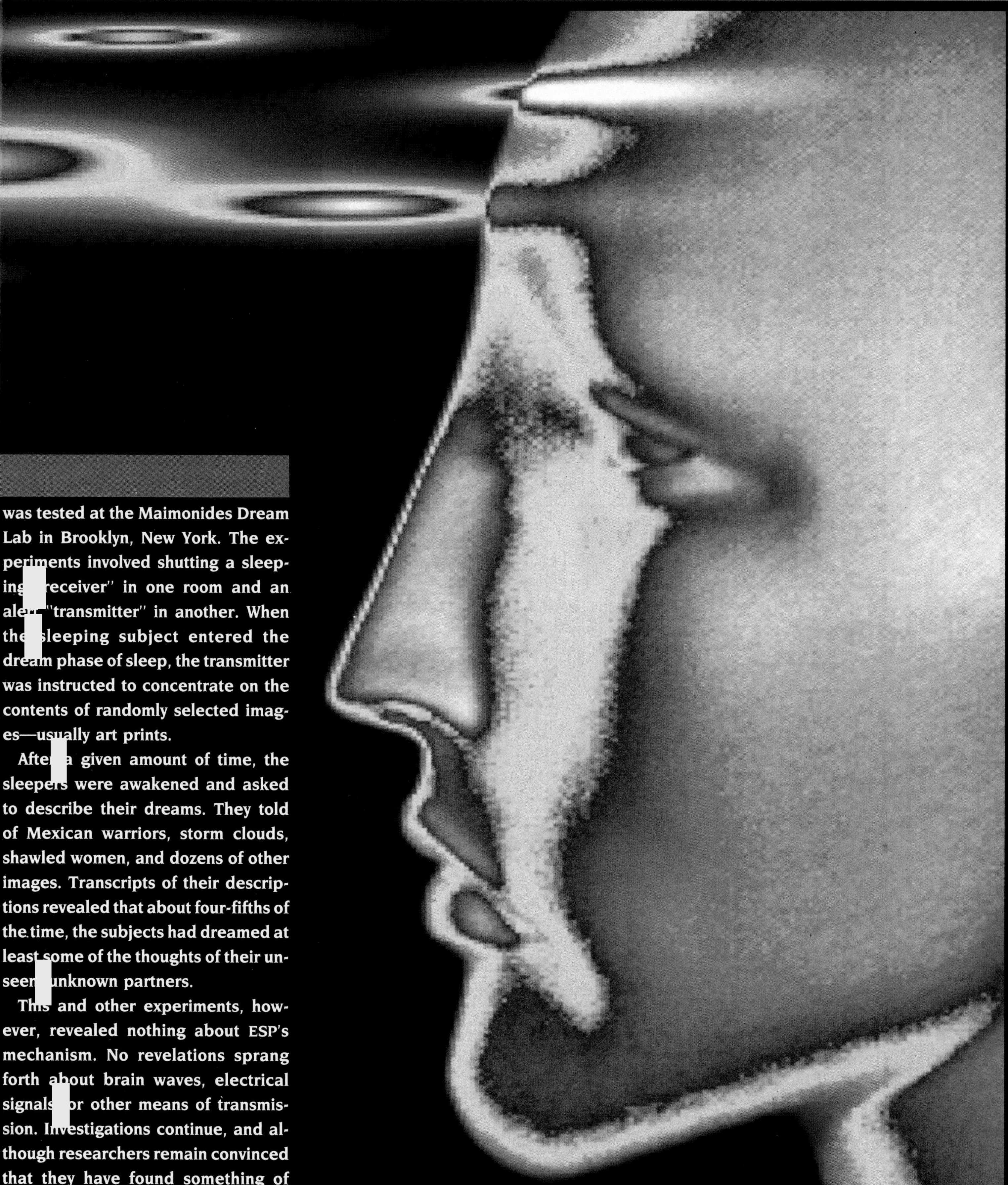

was tested at the Maimonides Dream Lab in Brooklyn, New York. The experiments involved shutting a sleeping "receiver" in one room and an alert "transmitter" in another. When the sleeping subject entered the dream phase of sleep, the transmitter was instructed to concentrate on the contents of randomly selected images—usually art prints.

After a given amount of time, the sleepers were awakened and asked to describe their dreams. They told of Mexican warriors, storm clouds, shawled women, and dozens of other images. Transcripts of their descriptions revealed that about four-fifths of the time, the subjects had dreamed at least some of the thoughts of their unseen unknown partners.

This and other experiments, however, revealed nothing about ESP's mechanism. No revelations sprang forth about brain waves, electrical signals or other means of transmission. Investigations continue, and although researchers remain convinced that they have found something of great significance, they are as puzzled as ever about what, exactly, it is.

GLOSSARY

Alpha waves: electrical activity of the brain during a state of relaxed wakefulness, characterized by frequencies of about eight to 13 hertz, or cycles per second.

Beta waves: electrical activity of the brain during a state of alertness, characterized by frequencies of 13 to 30 hertz or more.

Biofeedback: a technique in which an individual learns to control a normally involuntary function such as brain-wave pattern or blood pressure by responding to information, or feedback, about that function supplied by a monitoring device.

Brainstem: the part of the brain that is continuous with the top of the spinal cord. The brainstem consists of the medulla, the midbrain, and the pons, and is involved in the regulation of such functions as heartbeat, breathing, and sleep.

Brain waves: fluctuations in the electrical activity of many brain cells as recorded on an electroencephalogram (EEG).

Cerebral cortex: the thin outer layer of the cerebrum of the brain in mammals. The cortex is responsible for higher brain functions such as learning, thought, and memory.

Clairvoyance: the alleged supernormal ability to perceive events or objects beyond the range of the physical senses.

Cognition: the processes of knowing and self-awareness.

Collective unconscious: in Jungian psychology, that part of unconscious processes that is common to all humankind; the source of myths and archetypes.

Corpus callosum: a band of nerve fibers connecting the two hemispheres of the brain in mammals.

Creativity: the ability to transcend traditional methods or approaches and bring into existence something new.

Delta waves: electrical activity of the brain usually associated with stage 3 and stage 4 sleep, characterized by frequencies below four hertz.

Electroencephalogram (EEG): a graphic record of the brain's electrical activity, consisting of patterns of fluctuating waves.

Extrasensory perception (ESP): alleged communication or cognition independent of normal sensory processes.

Form constants: basic geometric shapes known as cobweb, spiral, tunnel, and lattice, which appear in many visual hallucinations.

Hallucination: the perception of a visual or other sensory phenomenon that has no physical reality, existing only within the perceiver's mind.

Hippocampus: part of the limbic system of the brain, involved in the storage and retrieval of memories and in the creation of emotions.

Hypnosis: an artificially induced alteration in attentiveness during which an individual is highly susceptible to suggestion.

Illusion: a false or warped perception based on real sensory stimuli, such as seeing cracks in the sidewalk as snakes.

Intelligence quotient (IQ): a score based on the average performance for a given age group on a test designed to measure aspects of intellectual ability.

Limbic system: the collective term for several related structures in the brain that are involved in emotion, memory, and the regulation of certain involuntary functions.

Lucid dream: a dream during which the dreamer is aware that he or she is dreaming and can participate in the development of the action.

Materialism: the philosophy that all phenomena, including mental ones, arise from matter; opposed to dualism, which holds that the mind and the body are separate entities.

Neuron: a nerve cell, consisting of a central body from which extend a number of branches called dendrites for receiving signals, and a single fiber called an axon for transmitting signals; the human brain is made up of somewhere between 10 billion and 100 billion neurons.

Neurotransmitter: any of a number of chemical substances, synthesized by neurons, that are involved in the transmission of electrochemical impulses across the synaptic gap from one neuron to another or from a neuron to a muscle or gland.

Non-REM (NREM) sleep: the four stages of sleep, each characterized by progressively slower brain-wave frequency, during which the bursts of rapid eye movements typically associated with dreaming are absent. Dreams also occur during NREM sleep but tend to be shorter and less vivid than REM dreams.

Pons: a section of the brainstem that links the cerebellum to the cerebral cortex and plays a major role in the regulation of REM sleep.

Positron emission tomography (PET): a brain-scanning technique that traces emissions from a radioactive substance injected into a patient to produce a map of specific receptors in the brain, thereby indicating levels of neuronal activity.

Precognition: alleged supernormal knowledge of future events.

Psychokinesis (PK): the alleged ability to affect matter—moving an object, for example—without physical contact.

Rapid eye movement (REM) sleep: the periods of sleep distinguished by bursts of rapid movements of the eyes, inhibition of the skeletal muscles, and mixed-frequency EEG activity. REM sleep is when the most vivid and longest-lasting dreams occur.

Stage 1 sleep: the period immediately after sleep begins, lasting between one and seven minutes. Brain-wave patterns are similar to those in REM sleep, but without the other accompanying characteristics of rapid eye movement and inhibited muscle activity.

Stage 2 sleep: a frequently recurring period of non-REM sleep with certain characteristic brain-wave patterns, including bursts of high-frequency waves. Sleepers usually spend more time in stage 2 than in any other stage.

Stage 3 sleep: non-REM sleep in which delta waves—indicating relatively low-frequency electrical activity in the brain—begin to dominate.

Stage 4 sleep: non-REM sleep characterized by delta waves and occurring perhaps only once during the night.

Subconscious: see **Unconscious.**

Synesthesia: the condition in which one type of sensory stimulus registers in more than one of the senses, as when a sound also causes an individual to see a color or experience a taste or smell.

Telepathy: the alleged supernormal ability to communicate without using any of the five senses.

Thalamus: a structure in the brain through which all sensory input except smell passes to the cerebral cortex.

Theta waves: electrical activity of the brain typically associated with stage 1 and REM sleep, characterized by frequencies of four to eight hertz.

Transpersonal domain: a theoretical state in which the individual mind merges with the collective unconscious, attainable through altered states of consciousness.

Unconscious: the part of mental processes ordinarily unavailable to conscious awareness.

BIBLIOGRAPHY

BOOKS

ABC's *of the Human Mind.* Pleasantville, N.Y.: Reader's Digest, 1990.

Abrams, Harry N. I. M. *Pei: A Profile in American Architecture.* New York: Carter Wiseman, 1990.

Aronoff, Michael S. *Sleep and Its Secrets.* New York: Plenum Press, 1991.

Asaad, Ghazi. *Hallucinations in Clinical Psychiatry.* New York: Brunner/Mazel, 1990.

Baker, Robert A. *They Call It Hypnosis.* Buffalo: Prometheus Books, 1990.

Beaton, Alan. *Left Side, Right Side.* New Haven, Conn.: Yale University Press, 1985.

Bloom, Floyd E. *Brain, Mind, and Behavior* (2d ed.). New York: W. H. Freeman, 1988.

Boden, Margaret A. *The Creative Mind.* New York: Basic Books, 1991.

Bootzin, Richard R., John F. Kihlstrom, and Daniel L. Schacter (eds.). *Sleep and Cognition.* Washington, D.C.: American Psychological Association, 1990.

Bowers, Kenneth S. *Hypnosis for the Seriously Curious.* New York: W. W. Norton, 1976.

Broughton, Richard S. *Parapsychology: The Controversial Science.* New York: Ballantine Books, 1991.

Capra, Fritjof. *The Tao of Physics* (2d ed.). New York: Bantam Books, 1984.

Cardinal, Roger. *Outsider Art.* London: Studio Vista, 1972.

Carskadon, Mary A., and Allan Rechtschaffen. "Monitoring and Staging Human Sleep." In *Principles and Practice of Sleep Medicine.* Philadelphia: W. B. Saunders, 1989.

Clayman, Charles B., M.D. (ed.). *The American Medical Association Encyclopedia of Medicine.* New York: Random House, 1989.

Coles, Michael G. H., Emanuel Donchin, and Stephen W. Porges (eds.). *Psychophysiology.* New York: The Guilford Press, 1986.

Cranston, Sylvia, and Carey Williams. *Reincarnation: A New Horizon in Science, Religion, and Society.* New York: Julian Press, 1984.

Cytowic, Richard E. *Synesthesia: A Union of the Senses.* New York: Springer-Verlag, 1989.

Dement, William C. *Some Must Watch While Some Must Sleep.* New York: W. W. Norton, 1976.

Dennett, Daniel C. *Consciousness Explained.* Boston: Little, Brown, 1991.

Deutsch, Diana (ed.). *The Psychology of Music.* New York: Academic Press, 1982.

Dienstfrey, Harris. *Where the Mind Meets the Body.* New York: HarperCollins, 1991.

Doore, Gary (ed.). *What Survives? Contemporary Explorations of Life after Death.* Los Angeles: Jeremy P. Tarcher, 1990.

Du Toit, Brian. *Drugs, Rituals and Altered States of Consciousness.* Rotterdam Brookfield, Vt.: Balkema, 1977.

Edge, Hoyt L., et al. *Foundations of Parapsychology.* New York: Routlage, 1986.

Ellman, Steven J., and John S. Antrobus (eds.). *The Mind in Sleep* (2d ed.). New York: John Wiley & Sons, 1991.

Empson, Jacob. *Sleep and Dreaming.* London: Faber and Faber, 1989.

Fisher, Stanley. *Discovering the Power of Self-Hypnosis.* New York: HarperCollins, 1991.

Fromm, Erika, and Ronald E. Shor (eds.). *Hypnosis: Developments in Research and New Perspectives.* New York: Aldine, 1979.

Garfield, Patricia. *Your Child's Dreams.* New

York: Ballantine Books, 1984.

Gazzaniga, Michael S. (ed.). *Handbook of Cognitive Neuroscience*. New York: Plenum Press, 1984.

Glover, John A., Royce R. Ronning, and Cecil R. Reynolds (eds.). *Handbook of Creativity*. New York: Plenum Press, 1989.

Glucksman, Myron L., and Silas L. Warner. *Dreams in New Perspective*. New York: Human Sciences Press, 1987.

Green, C. E. *Lucid Dreams*. Oxford: Institute of Psychophysical Research, 1968.

Green, Judith, and Robert Shellenberger. *The Dynamics of Health and Wellness*. Fort Worth, Tex.: Holt, Rinehart and Winston, 1991.

Griffin, Donald R. *Animal Minds*. Chicago: The University of Chicago Press, 1992.

Hadley, Josie, and Carol Staudacher. *Hypnosis for Change*. New York: Ballantine, 1987.

Hall, Calvin S., and Robert L. Van de Castle. *The Content Analysis of Dreams*. New York: Appleton-Century-Crofts, 1966.

Hartmann, Ernest:

Boundaries in the Mind. New York: Basic Books, 1991.

The Nightmare. New York: Basic Books, 1984.

Hilgard, Ernest R. *Divided Consciousness*. New York: John Wiley & Sons, 1977.

Hilgard, Ernest R., and Josephine R. Hilgard. *Hypnosis in the Relief of Pain* (rev. ed.). Los Altos, Calif.: William Kaufmann, 1983.

Ho, Wai-Ching (ed.). *Yani: The Brush of Innocence*. New York: Hudson Hills Press, 1989.

Hobson, J. Allan:

The Dreaming Brain. New York: Basic Books, 1988.

Sleep. New York: Scientific American Library, 1989.

Hooper, Judith, and Dick Teresi. *The Three-Pound Universe*. New York: Jeremy P. Tarcher/Perigree, 1986.

Hoppe, Klaus D. (ed.). *The Psychiatric Clinics of North America* (Vol. 2, no. 3). Philadelphia: W. B. Saunders, 1988.

Inglis, Brian. *The Power of Dreams*. London: Grafton Books, 1987.

Irwin, H. J. *An Introduction to Parapsychology*. Jefferson, N.C.: McFarland, 1989.

Kalat, James W. *Biological Psychology* (4th ed.). Pacific Grove, Calif.: Brooks/Cole, 1992.

Kaplan, Harold I., and Benjamin J. Sadock:

Comprehensive Textbook of Psychiatry. Baltimore: Williams & Wilkins, 1989.

Synopsis of Psychiatry (6th ed.). Baltimore: Williams & Wilkins, 1991.

Kelly, Dennis D. "Sleep and Dreaming." In *Principles of Neural Science* (3d ed.), ed. by Eric R. Kandel, James H. Schwartz, and Thomas M. Jessell. New York: Elsevier, 1991.

Kirtley, Donald D. *The Psychology of Blindness*. Chicago: Nelson-Hall, 1975.

Koulack, David. *To Catch a Dream*. Albany, N.Y.: State University of New York Press, 1991.

Krippner, Stanley (ed.). *Dreamtime and Dreamwork*. Los Angeles: Jeremy P. Tarcher, 1990.

Krippner, Stanley, and Joseph Dillard. *Dreamworking*. Buffalo: Bearly, Ltd., 1988.

LaBerge, Stephen. *Lucid Dreaming*. New York: Ballantine Books, 1985.

LaBerge, Stephen, and Howard Rheingold. *Exploring the World of Lucid Dreaming*. New York: Ballantine Books, 1990.

LeShan, Lawrence. *The Science of the Paranormal*. Wellingborough, Northhamptonshire: The Aquarian Press, 1987.

Luce, Gay Gaer, and Julius Segal. *Sleep*. New York: Coward-McCann, 1966.

MacGregor, John M. *The Discovery of the Art of the Insane*. Princeton, N.J.: Princeton University Press, 1989.

Marcer, Donald. *Biofeedback and Related Therapies*. London: Croom Helm, 1986.

Martin, John H. "The Collective Electrical Behavior of Cortical Neurons." In *Principles of Neural Science* (3d ed.), ed. by Eric R. Kandel, James H. Schwartz, and Thomas M. Jessell. New York: Elsevier, 1991.

Maybruck, Patricia. *Pregnancy and Dreams*. Los Angeles: Jeremy P. Tarcher, 1989.

The Mind and Beyond (Mysteries of the Unknown series). Alexandria, Va.: Time-Life Books, 1991.

Mind over Matter (Mysteries of the Unknown series). Alexandria, Va.: Time-Life Books, 1988.

Naish, Peter L. N. (ed.). *What Is Hypnosis?* Philadelphia: Open University Press, 1986.

The New Encyclopaedia Britannica (Vol. 9, 15th ed.). Chicago: Encyclopaedia Britannica, 1984.

Ornstein, Robert. *The Psychology of Consciousness*. New York: Penguin Books, 1986.

Pelletier, Kenneth. *Toward a Science of Consciousness*. New York: Delacorte Press, 1978.

Powell, Andrew. *Living Buddhism*. London: British Museum Publications, 1989.

Prinzhorn, Hans. *Artistry of the Mentally Ill*. New York: Springer-Verlag, 1972.

Rahula, Walpola Sri. *What the Buddha Taught* (2d ed.). New York: Grove Press, 1974.

Rao, K. Ramakrishna. *Experimental Parapsychology*. Springfield, Ill.: Charles C. Thomas, 1966.

Reed, Graham. *The Psychology of Anomalous Experience* (rev. ed.). Buffalo: Prometheus Books, 1988.

Restak, Richard. *The Brain*. New York: Bantam Books, 1984.

Rhawn, Joseph. *The Right Brain and the Unconscious*. New York: Plenum Press, 1992.

Schreiner, Gérard A. (ed.). *European Outsiders*. Vienna, Austria: The Schreiner-Notter Collection, 1986.

Schultheis, Rob. *Bone Games*. New York: Fromm International, 1986.

Sethi, Amarji. *Meditation as an Intervention in*

Stress Reactivity. New York: AMS Press, 1989.

Shreeve, Caroline, and David Shreeve. *The Healing Power of Hypnotism*. U.K.: Thorsons, 1984.

Siegel, Alan B. *Dreams that Can Change Your Life*. Los Angeles: Jeremy P. Tarcher, 1990.

Siegel, Ronald K. *Fire in the Brain*. New York: Dutton Books, 1992.

Siegel, Ronald K., and L. J. West. *Hallucinations*. New York: John Wiley & Sons, 1975.

Simonton, O. Carl, Stephanie Matthews-Simonton, and James Creighton. *Getting Well Again*. Los Angeles: J. P. Tarcher, 1978.

Smith, Adam. *Powers of the Mind*. New York: Random House, 1975.

Snyder, Frederick. "The Phenomenology of Dreaming." In *The Psychodynamic Implications of the Physiological Studies on Dreams*, ed. by Leo Madow and Laurence H. Snow. Springfield, Ill.: Charles C. Thomas, 1970.

Snyder, Solomon H. *Drugs and the Brain*. New York: Scientific American Books, 1986.

Spong, John S. (ed.). *Consciousness and Survival*. Sausalito, Calif.: Institute of Noetic Sciences, 1987.

Stevenson, Ian. *Twenty Cases Suggestive of Reincarnation*. New York: American Society for Psychical Research, 1966.

Stukane, Eileen. *The Dream Worlds of Pregnancy*. New York: William Morrow, 1985.

Tinbergen, Niko. *Animal Behavior* (rev. ed.) (Life Nature Library). Alexandria, Va.: Time-Life Books, 1980.

Tortora, Gerard J., and Nicholas P. Anagnostakos. *Principles of Anatomy and Physiology* (6th ed.). New York: HarperCollins, 1990.

Tuchman, Maurice, and Carol S. Eliel. *Parallel Visions: Modern Artists and Outsider Art*. Princeton, N.J.: Princeton University Press, no date.

Udolf, Roy. *Handbook of Hypnosis for Professionals* (2d ed.). New York: Van Nostrand Reinhold, 1987.

Vale, Ronald S., and Rolf von Eckartsberg (eds.). *Metaphors of Consciousness*. New York: Plenum Press, 1981.

Van de Castle, Robert L. *Our Dreaming Mind* (in press). New York: Ballantine, 1994.

Vance, Bruce A. *Dreamscape: Voyage in an Alternate Reality*. Wheaton, Ill.: Theosophical Publishing House, 1989.

Vander, Arthur J., James H. Sherman, and Dorothy S. Luciano. *Human Physiology*. New York: McGraw-Hill, 1990.

Vilenskaya, Larissa, and Joan Steffy. *Firewalking: A New Look at an Old Enigma*. Falls Village, Conn.: Bramble Co., 1991.

Vogel, Susan. *Africa Explorers: 20th Century African Art*. New York: The Center for African Art, 1991.

Weil, Andrew. *The Natural Mind* (rev. ed.). Boston: Houghton Mifflin, 1986.

Weil, Andrew, and Winifred Rosen. *From Chocolate to Morphine*. Boston: Houghton Mifflin, 1993.

Winget, Carolyn, and Milton Kramer. *Dimensions of Dreams*. Gainesville, Fla.: University Presses of Florida, 1979.

Winson, Jonathan. *Brain and Psyche*. Garden City, N.Y.: Anchor Press/Doubleday, 1985.

Wolman, Benjamin B. (ed.). *Handbook of Dreams*. New York: Van Nostrand Reinhold, 1979.

Wolman, Benjamin B., and Montague Ullman (eds.). *Handbook of States of Consciousness*. New York: Van Nostrand Reinhold, 1986.

Wright, E. (ed.). *The New Representationalisms* (in press). Oldershot, U.K.: Avebury, 1993.

Zhensun, Zheng, and Alice Low. *A Young Painter: The Life and Paintings of Wang Yani*. New York: Scholastic, 1991.

PERIODICALS

Abercrombie, Stanley. "A Gentle Master Builder." *Horizon*, Apr. 1978.

Allison, Truett, and Henry Van Twyver. "The Evolution of Sleep." *Natural History*, Nov. 1970.

Altshuler, K. Z., M. Barad, and A. I. Goldfarb. "A Survey of Dreams in the Aged." *Archives of General Psychiatry*, Jan. 1963.

Amadeo, Marco, and Evaristo Gomez. "Eye Movements, Attention and Dreaming in Subjects with Lifelong Blindness." *Canadian Psychiatric Association Journal*, Dec. 1966.

Barad, M., K. Z. Altshuler, and A. I. Goldfarb. "A Survey of Dreams in Aged Persons." *Archives of General Psychiatry*, Apr. 1961.

Berger, R. J., P. Olley, and I. Oswald. "The EEG, Eye Movements and Dreams of the Blind." *The Quarterly Journal of Experimental Psychology*, 1962, Vol. 14, Part 3.

Birchwood, Max. "Control of Auditory Hallucinations through Occlusion of Monaural Auditory Input." *British Journal of Psychiatry*, 1986, Vol. 149, pages 104-107.

Bond, Constance A. "A Child Prodigy from China Wields a Magical Brush." *Smithsonian*, Sept. 1989.

Bower, Bruce:

"Consciousness Raising." *Science News*, Oct. 10, 1992.

"Rethinking the Mind." *Science News*, Oct. 17, 1992.

Brenneis, C. B. "Developmental Aspects of Aging in Women." *Archives of General Psychiatry*, Apr. 1975.

Carter, Jerry. "Visual, Somatosensory, and Olfactory Hallucinations." *Psychiatric Clinic of North America*, June 1992.

Cartwright, Rosalind D., et al. "Broken Dreams: A Study of the Effects of Divorce and Depression on Dream Content." *Psychiatry*, Aug. 1984.

Cleghorn, John M., et al. "Toward a Brain

Map of Auditory Hallucinations." *American Psychiatry*, Aug. 1992.

Cowan, Jack D. "Spontaneous Symmetry Breaking In Large Scale Nervous Activity." *International Journal of Quantum Chemistry*, 1982, Vol. 22, pages 1059-1082.

Crick, Francis, and Christof Koch. "The Problem of Consciousness." *Scientific American*, Sept. 1992.

Crick, Francis, and Graeme Mitchison. "The Function of Dream Sleep." *Nature*, July 14, 1983.

Cytowic, Richard E. "Synesthesia and Mapping of Subjective Sensory Dimensions." *Neurology*, June 1989.

Dement, William C. "The Effect of Dream Deprivation." *Science*, June 10, 1960.

Dement, William C., and Edward A. Wolpert. "The Relation of Eye Movements, Body Motility, and External Stimuli to Dream Content." *Journal of Experimental Psychology*, May 1957.

Diamonstein, Barbaralee. "I. M. Pei: The Modern Movement Is Now Wide Open." *Art News*, Summer 1978.

DiCara, Leo V. "Learning in the Autonomic Nervous System." *Scientific American*, Jan. 1970.

Doherty, Jim. "Hot Feat: Firewalkers of the World." *Science Digest*, Aug. 1982.

Dolnick, Edward. "What Dreams Are (Really) Made Of." *The Atlantic*, July 1990.

Epstein, Robert. "The Quest for the Thinking Computer." *AI Magazine*, Summer 1992.

Fischbach, Gerald D. "Mind and Brain." *Scientific American*, Sept. 1992.

Foulkes, David. "Understanding Our Dreams." *The World and I*, Dec. 1989.

Gross, Joseph, Joseph Byrne, and Charles Fisher. "Eye Movements during Emergent Stage 1 EEG in Subjects with Lifelong Blindness." *Journal of Nervous and Mental Disease* (Baltimore), 1965, Vol. 141, no. 3.

Hachinski, Vladimir C. "Effect of Strokes on Musical Ability and Performance." *Seminars in Neurology*, June 1989.

Hemmingsen, Ralf, et al. "Cerebral Blood Flow During Delirium Tremens and Related Clinical States Studied with Xenon-133 Inhalation Tomography." *American Journal of Psychiatry*, Nov. 1988.

Hilgard, Ernest R. "Research Advances in Hypnosis." *International Journal of Clinical and Experimental Hypnosis*, Oct. 1987.

Howe, Joan B., and Kenneth A. Blick. "Emotional Content of Dreams Recalled by Elderly Women." *Perceptual and Motor Skills*, 1983, Vol. 56, pages 31-34.

Kerr, Nancy H., David Foulkes, and Marcella Schmidt. "The Structure of Laboratory Dream Reports in Blind and Sighted Subjects." *Journal of Nervous and Mental Disease* (Baltimore), 1982, Vol. 170, no. 5.

Koch, Christof. "What Is Consciousness?" *Discover*, Nov. 1992.

Leikind, Bernard J., and William J. McCarthy. "An Investigation of Firewalking." *Skeptical Inquirer*, Fall 1985.

Linden, Eugene. "Can Animals Think?" *Time*, Mar. 22, 1993.

Long, Michael E. "What Is This Thing Called Sleep?" *National Geographic*, Dec. 1987.

Lotfi, Jamshid, and John Stirling Meyer. "Cerebral Hemodynamic and Metabolic Effects of Chronic Alcoholism." *Cerebrovascular and Brain Metabolism Reviews*, Spring 1989.

Lynes, Russell. "National Gallery's New Building Is Triangular Triumph." *Smithsonian*, June 1978.

"Machines Who Think." *Science*, Nov. 29, 1991.

"The Mathematics of Hallucination." *New Scientist*, Feb. 10, 1983.

Mazziotta, John C., et al. "Tomographic Mapping of Human Cerebral Metabolism: Auditory Stimulation." *Neurology*, Sept. 1982.

Morrison, Adrian. "A Window on the Sleeping Brain." *Scientific American*, Apr. 1983.

Offenkrantz, William, and Allan Rechtschaffen. "Clinical Studies of Sequential Dreams." *Archives of General Psychiatry*, May 1963.

Pert, Candice. "Neuropeptides and Their Receptors." *Journal of Immunology*, Aug. 1985.

Ramachandran, Vilayanur S. "Blind Spots." *Scientific American*, May 1992.

Rismiller, Peggy D., and Roger S. Seymour. "The Echidna." *Scientific American*, Feb. 1991.

Rizzo, Matthew, and P. J. Eslinger. "Colored Hearing Synesthesia." *Neurobiology*, June 1989.

Rolak, Loren A. "Alice in Wonderland." *Archives of Neurology*, June 1991.

Sacks, Oliver. "To See and Not See." *New Yorker*, May 10, 1993.

Schulze, Franz. "The East Building: Trapezoid Triumphant." *Art in America*, July/Aug. 1978.

Siegel, Ronald K. "Hallucinations." *Scientific American*, Aug. 1977.

Smith, Mark Scott, and William M. Womack. "Stress Management Techniques in Childhood and Adolescence." *Clinical Pediatrics*, Nov. 1987.

Smith, Robert C. "Do Dreams Reflect a Biological State?" *Journal of Nervous and Mental Disease* (Baltimore), 1987, Vol. 175, no. 4.

Spanos, Nicholas P., and Erin C. Hewitt. "The Hidden Observer in Hypnotic Analgesia." *Journal of Personality and Social Psychology*, 1980, Vol. 39, no. 3, pages 1201-1214.

Starr, Douglas. "This Bird Has a Way with Words." *National Wildlife*, Feb./Mar. 1988.

Stoyva, Johann Martin. "Finger Electromyographic Activity during Sleep." *Journal of Abnormal Psychology*, Oct. 1965.

Tart, Charles T. "Marijuana Intoxication." *Nature*, May 23, 1970.

Van de Castle, Robert L. "Dreams and the Aging Process." *Dream Network Bulletin*, Sept./Oct. 1985.

Van de Castle, Robert L., and Peggy Kinder. "Dream Content during Pregnancy." *Psychophysiology*, Jan. 1968.

Walker, Jearl. "The Amateur Scientist: Drops of Water Dance on a Hot Skillet and the Experimenter Walks on Hot Coals." *Scientific American*, Aug. 1977.

Winson, Jonathan. "The Biology and Function of Rapid Eye Movement Sleep." *Current Opinion in Neurobiology*, 1993, Vol. 3, pages 243-248.

OTHER SOURCES

Cowan, Jack D. "Brain Mechanisms Underlying Visual Hallucinations." Santa Fe Institute Founding Workshop, 1986.

1992 Loebner Prize Competition. Cambridge, Mass.: Cambridge Center for Behavioral Studies, 1992.

Rechtschaffen, Allan, and Anthony Kales (eds.). *A Manual of Standardized Terminology, Techniques and Scoring System for Sleep Stages of Human Subjects.* Washington, D.C.: Public Health Service, U.S. Government Printing Office, 1968.

INDEX

Page numbers in boldface refer to illustrations or illustrated text.

A

B

ACKNOWLEDGMENTS

The editors of *Secrets of the Inner Mind* wish to thank these individuals for their valuable contributions:

Isaac Abrams, Woodstock, N.Y.; Masuo Aizawa, Tokyo Institute of Technology, Tokyo; Francisca Bantly, Georgetown University, Washington, D.C.; Joseph E. Bogen, Pasadena, Calif.; Jack Cowan, University of Chicago, Chicago; Richard E. Cytowic, Washington, D.C.; Daniel Dennett, Tufts University, Medford, Mass.; Bill Domhoff, University of California, Santa Cruz; Robert Epstein, Cardiff by the Sea, Calif.; Pierre Etévenon, D.Sc., Directeur de Recherche, INSERM, Caen; Donald Griffin, Barnstable, Mass.; Jim Groupie, National Gallery of Art, Washington, D.C.; Elda Hartley, Hartley Film Foundation, Cos Cob, Conn.; Ernest Hartmann, Boston; Lawrence Klein, Thought Technology, Ltd., Montreal; Christof Koch, California Institute of Technology, Pasadena; Stanley Krippner, Saybrook Institute, San Francisco; Stephen

LaBerge, Lucidity Institute, Palo Alto, Calif.; David Malvin, J. P. Tarcher, Inc., Los Angeles; Patricia Maybruck, St. Helena, Calif.; Marvin Miles, Stanford Sleep Disorder Clinic and Research Center, Stanford University, Palo Alto, Calif.; Neal Miller, Yale University, New Haven, Conn.; Beverly Olatter, Ronin Publishing, Berkeley, Calif.; B. J. Purdum, Alexandria, Va.; Allan Rechtschaffen, University of Chicago Sleep Laboratory, Chicago; Sabine Schiebler, Hamburg; Martha Shears, National Gallery of Art, Washington, D.C.; Jerry Siegel, Sepulveda Veteran's Administration Medical Center, Sepulveda, Calif.; Ronald Siegel, Veteran's Administration Hospital, Los Angeles; John Smythies, York, England; Janet Adams Strong, Pei Cobb Freed & Partners, New York; Trattoria da Franco, Alexandria, Va.; D. W. Zaidel, University of California, Los Angeles.

PICTURE CREDITS

The sources for the illustrations in this volume are listed below. Credits from left to right are separated by semicolons, from top to bottom by dashes.

Cover: Time-Life Books Photo, photo retouching by Harriet Standish, photo illustration by Fred Holz. **7:** © Keijiro Komine/Photonica—courtesy Dolphin Books—Howard Ehrenfeld (2). **8, 9:** Mel Curtis. **12, 13:** Howard Ehrenfeld. **15:** James Holmes/Janssen Pharmaceutical Ltd./Science Photo Library/Custom Medical Stock. **17:** Art by Fatima Taylor. **19:** Alan Hobson/Science Source/Photo Researchers. **20, 21:** Art by Stephen R. Wagner—*A Manual of Standardized Terminology, Techniques and Scoring System for Sleep Stages of Human Subjects*, ed. by Allan Rechtschaffen and Anthony Kales, U.S. Department of Health, Education, and Welfare Public Health Service, 1968. **22:** Alan Hobson/Science Source/Photo Researchers. **24:** © Louis Psihoyos/Matrix. **27:** © Keijiro Komine/Photonica. **29:** Tom McHugh/Photo Researchers. **33:** © Yu Amano/Photonica. **34, 35:** Peter Angelo Simon/PhotoTake; Arthur Swoger. **36, 37:** © 1992 Comstock, Inc.; © Peter A. Simons/The Stock Market, 1993. **38, 39:** Arthur Swoger; photo illustration for *Time* magazine by Chip Simons. **40, 41:** Eiichi Anzai/Photonica. **42, 43:** Brown Brothers, background Kory Addis, image manipulation by Time-Life Books. **47:** CEA-Orsay/CNRI/Science Photo Library/Photo Researchers. **48:** Collection Gimpel Fils, London—Detroit Institute of Arts Founders Society. **49:** © Adolf-Wölfli-Stiftung Kunstmuseum Bern; courtesy Los Angeles County Museum of Art—painting by Aloïse Corbaz, courtesy Musée des Beaux Art, Lausanne. **51:** Collection Deutsche BP Holding AG Foto: CKS. **53:** Courtesy Dolphin Books. **54, 55:** Courtesy New China Picture Co.; collection of Dr. Sylvia Feinburg (2); courtesy Nelson-Atkins Museum of Arts, Kansas City, Mo. (2). **57:** Museum voor Voltenkunde, Rotterdam, photo by Erik Hesmerg-Sneek (2)—Kansas State Historical Society. **59:** John C. Mazziotta/University of California, Los Angeles. **60:** GJLP/CNRI (inset)—art by Stephen R. Wagner. **61:** From *The Psychiatric Clinics of North America*, ed. by Klaus D. Hoppe, Vol. 2, no. 3, 1988. **65:** Evelyn Hofer. **66, 67:** National Gallery of Art, Gallery Archives, photos by Dennis Brack. **68, 69:** Private Collection; courtesy Pei Cobb Freed & Partners (2). **70:** National Gallery of Art, Gallery Archives, photo by Dennis Brack. **71:** National Gallery of Art photos by Dennis Brack (4)—courtesy Pei Cobb Freed & Partners. **72, 73:** Christopher Little; National Gallery of Art, Gallery Archives, photo by Dennis Brack (2), bottom middle courtesy Pei Cobb Freed & Partners. **74, 75:** Howard Ehrenfeld. **76:** Elda Hartley/Hartley Film Foundation—Thought Technology, Ltd. **81:** KHL Muller/Woodfin Camp & Associates. **82, 83:** CNRI; art by Alfred T. Kamajian, boxes redrawn from work by Gerald Öster. **84, 85:** Dr. Luft/CNRI. **89:** Hans J. Burkard/Bilderberg/The Stock Market. **90, 91:** Reprinted from *Psychedelic Encyclopedia*, 3d ed., by Peter Stafford, by permission of Ronin Publishing, Berkeley, Calif., photos by Peter Witt. All rights reserved. **92, 93:** Neal Lavey/PhotoTake. **96, 97:** Marco Monti/Photonica. **98, 99:** Howard Ehrenfeld, except upper right from *Hallucinations: Behavior, Experience and Theory*, ed. by R. K. Siegel and L. J. West, University of California, Los Angeles, John Wiley & Sons, 1975. Drawing by Sheridan. Used with permission of R. K. Siegel. **100:** Howard Ehrenfeld—inset Isaac Abrams. **102-107:** Howard Ehrenfeld. **108:** Erik Scheitzer, © 1993 *Discover* magazine. **109:** Masuo Aizawa, © 1992 *Discover* magazine. **110:** Photo Lennart Nilsson, *Behold Man*, Little, Brown; art by Fred Holz. **111:** Mark Holmes, © National Geographic Society. **113:** © Omikron/Photo Researchers. **114, 115:** David York/Stock Shop, Inc./Medi-Chrome; art by Bryan Leister. **119:** Graham Harrison, London; © Yoav Levy/PhotoTake. **121:** A. Pol/CNRI. **122, 123:** Art by Alfred T. Kamajian. **124:** Graham Harrison, London. **127:** Michael Goldman. **129:** Comstock, Inc. **132, 133:** © Digital Art/Westlight.